AN UNORTHODOX SOLDIER

AN UNORTHODOX
SOLDIER

Peace and War and the Sandline Affair

AN AUTOBIOGRAPHY
LIEUTENANT-COLONEL TIM SPICER OBE

MAINSTREAM
PUBLISHING

EDINBURGH AND LONDON

First published in Great Britain in 1999 by
MAINSTREAM PUBLISHING COMPANY (EDINBURGH) LTD
7 Albany Street
Edinburgh EH1 3UG

ISBN 1 84018 180 X

A catalogue record for this book is available from the British Library

Typeset in Copperplate and Garamond
Printed and bound in Great Britain by Butler and Tanner

CONTENTS

ACKNOWLEDGEMENTS

Writing a book goes against the grain – but I was eventually persuaded that the story was worth telling. It's a long story that covers thirty-odd years of my life and there are people with whom I've crossed paths (and swords!) who deserve acknowledgement. Unfortunately they are too numerous to mention – some of them appear in the text; others don't. I hope they know who they are.

Those who deserve special mention include, first of all, the Sandline team who believed in the idea – Simon, for creating the opportunity; Tony, for picking up the ball and running with it; Michael, for helping run the show with me through thick and very thin. Thanks also go to our friends and supporters in the business: AM, JP, RB, GMS, etc. To the office team, Trevor, Sue, Nanette and Paul. To the operators, JO, JF, PW, NB and, above all, my great friend and great field operator, BM. Also, someone who could have been the enemy but turned out to be a good friend.

Next, Richard Slowe, his legal team and his family, for providing the common sense, judgement and support when we had serious problems. To Sara Pearson and her team for educating us in the ways of the 'street of shame' and for driving this project through in the face of some difficulty.

To Robin, without whom this wouldn't have happened – he did a damn fine job.

To all the officers and soldiers who served in the 2nd Battalion, Scots Guards, in the Falklands, those who served with me in Crossmaglen and all those who served in the 1st Battalion when I was commanding. The high spot of anyone's career is commanding their own regiment. I was lucky – I commanded on operations and I had total support of every man, and that is why we did so well. If I had to single anyone out it would be Phil Jackson, but also Guardsmen Fisher and Wright, who were disgracefully treated.

Finally, to my family, for putting up with a lot, for being there and for providing fun, security and the refuge between storms – Caroline, Sam, Ben, Jessy and Fan.

Those who don't deserve any acknowledgement at all, ever – not just from me but from anyone – are the gutless, the boring and the useless who pontificate and cower, some of whom supposedly represent Britain. I feel sorry for them – they've never been to the edge and looked over. They'd be better off if they did.

Tim Spicer, Mougins, September 1999

INTRODUCTION

Expecting the Unexpected

One of the lessons I have learned in a lifetime of unorthodox soldiering is that you must always expect the unexpected. Try as you will, things creep up on you, and what might appear at first sight to be a perfectly normal process can rapidly turn into a very dicey situation or become completely surreal. This book is full of such events, but I shall give two examples of what I mean, illustrating both eventualities. The first incident took place during our time in Papua New Guinea, the second during a visit to an African country which will remain nameless.

When the Sandline operation was in its final stages, it was thought necessary to visit the PNGDF Special Force unit which was then in training at Wewak, on the northern side of the main island. Wewak lies about two hours by air from the capital, Port Moresby, and since many people were interested in the training we were giving to the PNGDF units, we filled our CASA 212 aircraft with representatives from the government and the PNG military, including the Deputy Prime Minister and the Defence Minister. The visit went well, the standard of training – mortar training, range work, battle drills and some physical training – reached by the PNGDF was found to be impressive, and the day concluded with lunch in the officers' mess of the 2nd Battalion, The Pacific Islands Regiment, one of the elements of the PNG Defence Force. We returned to the aircraft in the early afternoon, ready to fly back to Port Moresby. At that point a rather agreeable day turned very nasty indeed.

The weather was already beginning to break when we got back to the airfield at Wewak. Heavy storm clouds were building up, lightning was flickering about and there was the constant rumble of thunder. To this can be added periodic tropical downpours and winds rising to gale force. All in all, it was not the sort of day to go flying about the mountains in a light aircraft – but we had to get back to Port Moresby.

Papua New Guinea – mountainous, tropical, sparsely populated – is difficult flying country at any time and our pilots, both Americans, were anxious to get away before the impending storm broke or we ran out of daylight. The CASA 212 is a great little aircraft with a few passenger seats and good freight-carrying capacity, and we took off and battered our way back towards Port Moresby against a driving headwind and torrential rain, stopping midway at another airfield to drop off some of our passengers. Then we took off again.

This was not entirely wise. Visibility was practically zero and the aircraft was constantly being buffeted and thrown all over the place. It got incredibly dark, with lots of lightning and driving rain. I am never very happy just sitting about, strapped in on an aircraft; I like to stand in the space behind the pilots, so I can talk to them and see what is going on. In this case the pilots were clearly struggling to control the aircraft and were very worried about either being struck by lightning, which could knock out our electronics, or flying into a mountain.

Eventually, after about an hour, when we were nearing Port Moresby and it was getting rougher and rougher, I had a conversation with the pilots, who told me that because of the visibility and the lightning they could not pick up the usual landmarks and radio beacons. Therefore they could not land – and because of the headwinds we had been battling we were getting low on fuel. In fact we were very short on fuel, and unless we found Jackson Airport soon we would have to fly out to sea and ditch. I did not find this news particularly comforting; thoughts of swimming about in dark, gale-tossed, shark-infested seas began to drift into my mind.

We circled around as long as we could, trying to pick up the red marker beacons leading to the runway. We were all concerned because the airport is surrounded by hills, each with a marker beacon, and we did not want to fly into a hill while attempting to pick up a beacon. This went on for some time. Then there was more discussion about ditching and I said that, on balance, I would rather ditch in the sea than attempt a landing in the mountains or the jungle, but before it got to that would it not be sensible to fly out to sea and try and fix our position along the coast, before coming back in on a compass bearing for another go? If we ran out of fuel in the interim, we could ditch in the sea. It was not a very enticing prospect – an encounter with a salt-water crocodile now joined the one with a shark at the back of my mind – but what choice had we?

Just at the point when it was getting critical, we saw, just ahead and slightly to our right, one of the red beacons. We were too low and climbed immediately, circled to the left and, through a brief gap in the cloud, picked up the landing lights of Jackson. This was a great relief, but we were still being hurled about the sky and the pilots braced themselves for landing in just about all the conditions you don't want for landing a light aircraft: terrible crosswinds, zero visibility. It looked distinctly hairy, and they advised me to go back, strap in and cross my fingers.

As we came in I could see that we were crabbing about, veering from left to right of the centre line of the runway. We eventually landed, almost sideways, and out of the windows we saw scenes of incredible devastation around us. A DC3 Dakota had been blown from its position and was standing completely up on its nose and resting on the side of the hangar, while other light aircraft had been picked up by the gale and tossed into heaps, like piles of leaves. It was a total shambles.

We taxied steadily towards our hangar but were met on the way by one of our ground staff, who banged on the door and then scrambled in to tell us that if we were unwise enough to switch off our engine we would probably blow away. Since we were due to run out of fuel at any moment, this prospect was pending, the alternative being to try and taxi into one of the hangars for shelter before this happened. To drive into the hangar involved turning the aircraft into the wind and this we were eventually able to do, stopping at last in shelter and in safety. The relief was considerable. Before I left the hangar I went to congratulate the pilots, who were still in the cockpit, looking thoroughly drained. I asked them if there was anything I could do and one said, 'Yes, Boss, you can help pull this cushion out of my ass. It's so far up there that I hope never to fly like this again!'

So much for how the best days can turn into nightmares; now for an example of the surreal. This event took place shortly after I returned from Papua New Guinea, when we received a request for assistance from that aforementioned unnamed African country, which was then in the middle of a civil war. The first step is always to take a look at the situation and to do this I flew to the capital, accompanied by an American lawyer who had business interests in the country.

We arrived in a small, privately chartered jet, and even before the pilots switched off the engines it was apparent that all was not well. Gunfire, both machine-gun and rifle, could be clearly heard, shells were crumping in nearby and the airport was swarming with troops and tanks, with many of the troops in a highly excited state but hopefully friendly. This was one of those moments when you think that some other career, like bullfighting, might be safer, but here we were and we had to get out and go and see the President.

We were hustled into an armoured motorcade which left the airport at a rate of knots and drove into the city. The capital was a ghost town; Saigon as it fell must have been like this. There was hardly anyone on the streets, many of the buildings had been wrecked or looted and, apart from plenty of soldiers, there was no one about. When we arrived at the palatial presidential palace, that too was in a dreadful state. At some recent time it must have been beautiful, elegant and surrounded by well-tended gardens. Now a tank or two stood on the lawn, artillery pieces were dotted about in the shrubberies and a host of troops, rather anxious ones, watched us sweep up to the steps and go inside. As background, the sound of gunfire was somewhat louder.

Once we were inside, it got really surreal, for a butler, immaculate in tailcoat and white gloves, came to ask us if we would care for some refreshment and brought us a pitcher of delicious iced lemonade. We were then ushered in to see the President for a brief, constantly interrupted meeting. Those doing the interrupting were either military people or his diplomatic staff, but their common intention was to demonstrate to us that they were allowed to burst into the presidential office and interrupt whatever was going on.

The talks were somewhat inconclusive. At one point one of the officers showed me an RPG rocket tube that appeared to be stuffed with marijuana and black magic charms, which, he said, was an example of what the rebels were using. I would have been far more interested in a proper military assessment of what the rebels were doing, how far into the capital they had advanced and what they amounted to in terms of arms and equipment. However, before we could get that point across, the President got to his feet and announced that we were leaving. The lawyer and I looked at each other, wondering what was going on, and were somewhat dumbfounded when it became apparent that not only were we leaving but the President intended to leave with us.

We had intended to fly out after the meeting and stay in one of the calmer and more secure provincial cities of this benighted country, but this new development was a surprise. The President declared that he had decided to come with us in order to make a brief visit to his supporters elsewhere, but when we got out to the palace foyer it appeared that something rather more permanent was in his mind. A number of his entourage were waiting to leave, all standing by a large pile of suitcases including a number of Vuitton trunks; the contents of these trunks seemed to be of particular concern to the President, and the lawyer and I speculated on what they might contain. Probably the contents of the national treasury.

This presented us with a problem, not least that our jet was small and could not possibly take all these people and a great heap of luggage. We also began to suspect that the only reason we had been asked to visit was to provide the President with an escape route. However, there was no time to debate that point, for we were rushed outside and the lawyer and I found ourselves pushed in to the front car of the waiting motorcade – not the place to be if the motorcade was ambushed on the way to the airport. A large crowd of curious soldiers drifted over to see what was going on and the President got up on a four-by-four to tell them that he thought they were doing a magnificent job and that he wanted them to go on doing that while he went off to visit his army elsewhere but that he would be back shortly. That done, the motorcade departed the Palace at great speed and raced back to the airport, with tracer zipping to and fro across the streets as we sped by.

At the airport, matters had deteriorated somewhat in the last few hours. The machine-gun and rifle fire had drawn closer and shells were now dropping with some accuracy and regularity. We found our pilots very anxious to leave and, having piled the President's luggage on board, the lawyer, myself, the President and a few of his chosen followers clambered in and shut the door. Those left behind on the airport ramp looked most unhappy as they watched us taxi away for a 'hot' take-off.

I was in a seat looking forward, facing one of the President's acolytes who was sitting opposite me and looking backwards. As we began to race down the runway, I saw his face change and his eyes widen. Straining against my seat belt, I turned round and saw a line of mortar explosions following the aircraft up the runway, falling neatly behind us as we lifted off the runway and climbed away into the sky. Believe me, we were very glad to be going.

There is a saying in soldiering circles that 'If you can't take a joke, you shouldn't have joined', and that works for some of my Sandline experiences as well as for the other part of my life as an unorthodox soldier. This is the story of those times, and I hope you enjoy it and see the jokes.

ONE

SANDLINE

'Everything changed with the end of the Cold War. Up to then we knew what we had to do and who the potential enemy was and we could train and prepare accordingly. Now it's all guesswork.'

GENERAL SIR PETER INGE,
CHIEF OF THE DEFENCE STAFF, 1996

This is a story in three parts. Part of this book concerns the events leading up to what became known as 'The Sandline Affair', in which, during 1998, the British government tied itself into an almighty knot over the work of my company, Sandline International, in Sierra Leone. That may seem a small, transient incident, worth a few feature articles in the national press or an in-depth analysis on television, but the issues raised by the Sandline Affair are not going to go away.

However, I did not create Sandline International on my own, nor start it without a great deal of previous experience in the military arena. Over the years, in different places and at different times, the need for something like Sandline began to grow in my mind. Therefore a major part of this book is autobiographical, tracing my military career over two decades, from my time at Sandhurst to the time I commanded the 1st Battalion, Scots Guards, on operations in Northern Ireland. Sandline came later, after I had served in Bosnia and seen what level of chaos the world is heading for unless some practical steps are taken to tackle the growing list of problems in a pragmatic way. The last part of the book offers my views on those issues that are likely to trouble the world in the next century, issues where private military companies like Sandline may have a useful role to play.

Private military companies – or PMCs – are corporate bodies specialising in the provision of military skills to legitimate governments: training, planning, intelligence, risk assessment, operational support and technical skills. Sandline International is just such a company and was created to tackle a growing number of situations which the world's major nations are unwilling or unable to tackle themselves, or to assist smaller nations where these military skills were found necessary – and lacking. This raises the 'Sandline Affair' from an issue that affected only a small number of people in a couple of countries – in this case Britain and Sierra Leone – to something that will affect many governments and many people in many parts of the world for decades to come.

The hard fact is that the world, having come out of the Cold War into the 'New World Order', is not actually getting any safer. One of the greatest of the Cold War warriors, Henry Kissinger, said as much in an interview in January 1999. Asked if the world seemed a safer place now than when he was in government, he replied:

> From the point of view of nuclear danger, infinitely safer; from the point of view of structure, far more chaotic. In those days you had a Cold War; you had basic criteria of what would benefit one side or the other. Today you have a very amorphous situation. What exactly is NATO supposed to do? What do we want to happen in Bosnia, in Asia, in the Middle East, in the long term? Moreover, you have the economic and political organisations of the world at variance from each other. The economic concerns are global, the political firmly regional. And all these forces are moving at a time when the quality of political leadership is declining – because the leaders are too busy getting elected or re-elected.

In other words, we have inherited the ancient Chinese curse 'May you live in interesting times'. The world's political leaders are afraid of political or military involvement in the world's endemic conflicts because they don't want the body-bags coming home as in Vietnam or, more recently, Somalia, or because they don't want to take risks or to be blamed if matters go awry, or, rather less creditably, because they simply want to be popular and garner votes at home. This creates a vacuum in the search for world peace, part of which private military companies like Sandline should be able to fill.

Until Sandline was established I had spent most of my life as a professional soldier in the Scots Guards, one of the crack regiments of the British Army, a career which gave me the chance to see the world, to gain experience in a growing and diverse number of roles, to serve in dangerous places, including Northern Ireland, the Falklands and Bosnia, to take part in two wars and to rise to a respectable military rank. I can fairly say that life has not been dull.

This experience has given me a few precepts that I apply personally. First, I believe that your effectiveness comes totally from within your own efforts, and the excellence you obtain in whatever you do is directly proportionate to the effort you are prepared to put in. I know that war or combat is different for everyone but that is where a soldier develops his capabilities and finds his own strengths and weaknesses. As a soldier you have to draw on that, research your experiences, absorb what is useful, reject what is irrelevant or useless, add what is your own.

No one should be under any illusions about soldiering. Soldiering is about fighting and, if need be, killing. That fact can be cloaked in a wide range of fancy garments, or hidden by pomp and flummery, but when you get right down to it, soldiering is about hitting the enemy hard, before they can kill you. Soldiering is a means of getting your way by force and cunning, often in very dangerous places, and even in peacetime can involve living in difficult conditions, under considerable hardship and often at some risk to life or limb.

Soldiering, in short, is hard, dangerous work, a vocation which offers little reward in terms of either finance or thanks from the public the soldier has elected to serve – and soldiers know that. Kipling's words

'It's Tommy this and Tommy that, and throw him out, the brute
But it's hero of his country when the guns begin to shoot'

are as true now as they ever were. That is why, when I was commanding troops in the British Army, I always trained them for war fighting and why one of the offences I considered most serious was a soldier letting his rifle become dirty or rusty. I came down hard on such people, for a very good reason – if that weapon jammed in combat, they would die wishing they had kept it clean.

I am very patriotic – I really believe that Britain is best – but there is a revolutionary streak in there too and I can rarely restrain the attempt to find humour in a situation or to 'take the piss' out of the system. Evelyn Waugh's *Sword of Honour* trilogy was a bench mark in the development of my military philosophy. Having said that, I understand the importance of being organised and of employing method and I respect professionalism.

My service experience gave me a grasp of those military skills that Sandline markets to its clients all over the world in places where indigenous professional military skills are sadly lacking. That soldiering, and the lessons I learned from it, form part of the Sandline story and are therefore a part of the Sandline Affair.

The final part of this book is a personal view of the security situation facing the world, especially the Western world, as we enter the next millennium. A whole range of problems are coming on stream and these problems – disputes ranging from civil wars to quarrels over water rights, from international terrorism to genocide, from the destabilising of legitimate governments to the ethnic cleansing of entire populations – are not only not being addressed by national governments, they are often being actively ignored.

This cannot continue. I have seen a great deal of misery in the last few years and to let it go on without trying to do something about it is intolerable. If this book succeeds in getting a number of uncomfortable issues on to the agenda for public discussion it will have done a great deal of good, and if, in the process, I can explain how private military companies have a role to play in these situations and how a modern, corporate PMC differs from the rightly discredited image of the mercenary soldier, it will have filled a useful purpose. At the very least, I hope to make people think.

I have been told that the main difference between a book and, say, a television programme or a newspaper article is a matter of time and reach. The last two appear within a given country or circulation area, cause a stir or pass unrecorded within a matter of days or weeks, and are then forgotten. Books, on the other hand, tend to circulate all over the world and stay around for years for criticism or consultation. That is another reason for telling this story in book form, for the tale I have to tell and the facts that it reveals will, I believe, become ever more relevant as the next decade unfolds. First, though, let me explain what Sandline is all about.

Sandline is a private military company. Other people, with a rather wearying ability to miss the point or an inability to tell the difference, have called us mercenaries, or a corporate kennel for the 'Dogs of War'. PMCs exist to tackle those situations, mostly but by no means entirely military situations, which national governments are, for various reasons, unable to deal with themselves and where outside agencies, the UN or friendly nations, have refused to become involved.

This begs a number of questions, the first of which is that if national governments choose to leave a situation alone, should private companies meddle? The short answer is that the national government concerned – and legitimate PMCs only work for legitimate governments – have the right, and indeed the duty, in the absence of international intervention to find solutions that can resolve an internal situation at the greatest possible speed and the minimum cost in lives.

In Papua New Guinea and Sierra Leone, the two countries with which Sandline has been publicly concerned since the company was founded in 1997, the elected, legitimate national governments faced a situation where 'friendly' governments had either flatly refused to help or restricted their help to pious murmurs about diplomatic solutions and negotiated peace settlements. The objections to our participation in both Papua New Guinea and Sierra Leone came from outside governments, not from the national governments of those countries, who in each case desperately sought our help.

When the situation is fully considered – years of war, rape, looting, starvation and murder before a PMC is called in – one is driven to the old conclusion: with 'friends' like these, who needs enemies? If the threatened government feels that a PMC can help in such situations, who has the political or moral right to deny it that help, unless they are willing to step in themselves? Writing in *The Times* on the situation in Sierra Leone, Sam Kiley recorded what happened when the rebel RUF took over Freetown:

> Eastern Freetown has been razed by rebels. Their scorched earth tactics and the staggering level of their atrocities blight much of the countryside. Yesterday the rebels were seen cutting the hands off civilians fleeing from their path. Refugees talk of wholesale slaughter by the rebels, piles of bodies lying in the street and all-night partying by drug-crazed pre-teen killers. The rebels have to be stopped, and soon.

Was the legitimate government of Sierra Leone supposed to negotiate with people who chopped children's hands off, or sit down and confer with ten-year-old, drug-crazed killers? Having described the situation, Mr Kiley went on to suggest that Mr Cook, the British Foreign Secretary, should authorise the deployment of 'mercenaries' to help ECOMOG – the West African force helping the legitimate government – drive these rebels out of Sierra Leone. What the Foreign Office posture actually did was trigger a Customs and Excise investigation into Sandline International – and the killing in Sierra Leone went on.

The dilemma faced by those Third World governments who, lacking a wide range of options or resources to resolve internal military problems, choose to employ PMCs is illustrated by the reaction to Sandline's activities in Papua New Guinea and Sierra Leone. The public profile gained by Sandline in these operations fuelled debate and dissension over the very existence of PMCs, a debate which uses a lexicon of knee-jerk phrases to feed a set of misconceptions and preconceived ideas which obscure the real issue. That issue consists of two main elements: the moral and the practical. Should something be done in a given situation, should PMCs be used to do it, and do they have the resources to do it better than – not merely instead of – national military forces? The reader can judge after hearing the full story of our involvement in these countries, and this will be covered fully in later chapters.

The notion that PMCs are mercenary concerns only in it for the money is the one that attracts the greatest amount of heat, and a rather smaller amount of light, and leads directly to the moral arguments deployed against PMCs. First of all, is it right to go soldiering about the world for money? If PMCs are to be employed, should not their employment be regulated and their work overseen by some legitimate international body? Should not conflicts be resolved by negotiation and diplomacy rather than by force?

The short answer to all these questions is 'yes'. We work for legitimate governments and of course we expect to be paid for what we do, just like any other business providing a technical or a professional service. We would welcome some form of regulation and supervision provided we have some say in what form this takes and it takes into account the realities of the world we live in. And the main aim of PMC activity is to create a situation where negotiations can start and diplomacy can work by restoring the political balance, by restoring peace, by creating normality, and this too will be illustrated by our work in Papua New Guinea and the work of another PMC, Executive Outcomes, in Sierra Leone.

From this comes a further set of questions. Are PMCs effective and, since military services are not cheap, are they cost-effective? Are the real PMCs competently run, able to keep their bargains, able to work to a pre-agreed brief and not exceed it? Can they be useful on the international stage, settling a foreign dispute without severe political fall-out at home?

Although I run a PMC, I intend to examine this subject as objectively as possible in the following chapters and answer all these questions, though I will not be discussing the specifics of Sandline International operations in great detail. Client confidentiality precludes me from discussing current operations or those not already in the public domain. However, I will explain the difference between PMCs and the old-style mercenaries and reveal what Sandline is really about, what it will and will not do, and its corporate ethos. This will, I hope, dispel some of the myths that surround Sandline and move the argument on to more solid ground before I address some specific examples further on in this book.

To illustrate the difference, I can take the reader briefly through the Sandline ethos, which can be summarised by two quotes. The first is from T.E. Lawrence, Lawrence of Arabia: 'Use the smallest force in the furthest place in the quickest time.' The second is from the Chinese General Sun Tzu, writing in AD 500: 'The best general is he who wins a battle without firing a shot.' Sandline aims to solve the problem swiftly by supplying the best possible military services effectively and with the minimum impact on innocent bystanders.

We do not advocate the use of force. Indeed, the implied use of force can be more effective, as we demonstrated in Papua New Guinea by intending to use Russian attack-helicopters to sweep low over insurgent positions and transport ships; they did not fire but their arrival concentrated minds among the Bougainville rebel commanders, indicating that the war had moved on to a new dimension. Another effective element is psychological operations, a form of direct propaganda such as using aircraft equipped with Sky Shout loudhailers and flying over insurgent villages to spread the government message. All this has the aim of bringing the parties to the negotiating table. Having said that, if all else fails, we are prepared to use force and would support the military operations of a legitimate government, with the caveat that we remain within the law of armed conflict and show respect for human rights. This is not a pious intent, or put in here to enlist the support of readers. Experience has shown that a respect for human rights works in a military situation; if governments fight terrorism with counter-terrorism they lose all legitimacy and will probably – and deservedly – fail.

Sandline has five basic operating principles: we only work for legitimate governments; we will do nothing illegal, even for those governments; we will do nothing against key Western nations' foreign policies; we apply First World standards to all our military work, including respect for human rights; and we ensure client confidentiality.

First and foremost we are military consultants, particularly at the level of command, control, communications and intelligence. We can evaluate an army and its equipment, from private to general, from heavy artillery to boots. We can cost out their facilities at a time of financial stringency and suggest savings – do they really need all those barracks and all that real estate? We can – and it is one of our preferred tasks – supply training of any kind, from basic training for newly joined recruits right up to Special Force units, creating 'Behind the Lines' units like the US 'LRRPS' (Long Range Recce Patrols), and counter-terrorist forces, police as well as army. This might include the creation of police SWAT (Special Weapons and Tactics) teams. Since our niche in the market is at the command and control level, we can also supply intelligence support, evaluating and training intelligence personnel, both military and police, and if required we can assist in intelligence gathering.

In addition to our military package we offer a humanitarian one, and the recent experiences of UN officials and aid teams in Somalia and Macedonia indicate the need for this. Again, this is based on our military expertise, but it can cover the training or supply of convoy escorts or guards for food distribution points threatened by insurgents or thieves, staff protection and engineer work, such as repairing roads and bridges, digging wells and, of growing importance, clearing mines. This is a highly skilled and dangerous activity, one that calls for professional skills which Third World armies do not always possess and for which First World armies cannot always allocate resources.

Another broad question is why have PMCs emerged now, in the 1990s? The short answer is that during the Cold War, political and military matters were, as Dr Kissinger said, to a very large extent cut-and-dried. There were two power blocs: the Soviet Union, its satellites and the Warsaw Pact powers, and the West, the USA, Britain and their allies in NATO, SEATO and all the other defence pacts. Between them, these blocs contained most of the trouble, actual or potential – and created quite a bit of it, from Vietnam to Afghanistan. Anything that might really rock the boat, create serious instability and lead to nuclear conflict was, however, strictly controlled. Although there were periodic conflicts, mostly in the Middle East and Asia, these too were eventually resolved for fear of the escalator effect leading to a spreading world war.

Then the Soviet Union collapsed and the West declared a 'peace dividend' by dismantling its defences and running down its armed forces, before the leaders woke up to the fact that the world had actually become more dangerous. I shall have something to say later about the effect this had on the operational effectiveness of the British Army in the Falklands War and the Gulf War of 1990–91.

The 'peace dividend' was not paid to everyone. At the moment, in 1999, it is estimated by the UN that there are no fewer than forty-three wars of various sizes going on in different parts of the world, ranging from ethnic disputes in the Balkan state of Kosovo, and tribal wars and oppression in Africa, to civil insurrection in Turkey between the national government and the Kurds, and the ongoing situation with Saddam Hussein in Iraq.

The potential for violence in the future is almost limitless and with the USA unwilling always to act in the role of the 'world's policeman' and the UN's actions constantly stymied by a lack of resolve, or capability, or by blocking votes, something was bound to fill the gap. And so we see a growth in private military companies; it could be argued that PMCs are the inevitable outcome of the UN's failure to tackle long-term problems with sufficient resolve and adequate resources.

David Shearer, who headed Save the Children Fund programmes in Iraq, Rwanda, Somalia and Sri Lanka, is on record as saying, 'There is no doubt that these companies [PMCs] are effective. They have taken advantage of the increasing reluctance of Western governments to intervene in civil conflicts. The civil wars we are seeing at the moment are messy, brutal, nasty things that governments don't want to commit their troops to, but these companies are willing to take that political risk and may even contribute to stability.' Shearer also urged governments to start talking to private military companies, who, he said, are keen to be perceived as legitimate.

Ask why governments are disinclined to act and the answers are both varied and complicated. The Soviet Union has no money and plenty of problems at home. The European powers are too diverse, cannot always agree on policy and do not have the right manpower available, or the will to use it if they had. As for the USA, politicians there are hampered by what I have come to think of as the CNN factor – a deep-rooted concern about the reaction of the domestic voter. When US troops went ashore in Somalia in Operation Restore Hope in December 1992, their landing was delayed until it could be filmed as it happened and shown on US TV by CNN. So far, so good; the work of the US and other national forces, in suppressing the criminal gangs then at large in Mogadishu and in allowing the international relief operation to begin, was widely praised and gave everyone at home a nice warm glow every evening as the television news showed young American soldiers doing humanitarian work.

Then it went horribly awry. The parents of these young soldiers saw their sons under attack in the streets of Mogadishu by the people they had been sent to help. At least two US servicemen were butchered on TV, their naked bodies being dragged about the streets behind trucks – and all this on prime-time TV. There was an understandable public outcry – What are our boys doing in that place? – and within a matter of days the US contingent was withdrawn. The other national contingents soon followed. Somalia remains in anarchy, but who would willingly go back? Support for international intervention has declined and this has created a market for PMCs, for if the work has to be done, someone has to do it. The alternative is chaos.

Sandline is not a charitable organisation. What we do we do for money, and we expect to make a profit out of it. We would argue that PMCs, being profit-orientated, are necessarily cost-effective, unlike many UN operations. UN intervention in Angola cost $1 million a day – $365 million in one year – and achieved absolutely nothing. The South African PMC, Executive Outcomes, charged the Angola government $80 million over two years and got UNITA to the conference table, putting an end to the war in a matter of months. Readers may judge which amount of money achieved the better results.

So, to revert to the earlier question, is it immoral to work for money? Most people do, including the civil engineers and doctors who work in the Third World. Is it right to resolve conflicts by coercion, rather than by negotiation? If common sense ruled the world, everyone from judges to generals would be unemployed. Since the world is not so sensible, however, it often takes a certain amount of coercion, or more often the threat of coercion, to bring the parties to the negotiating table. If the end result is a peaceful, acceptable solution to the situation, why argue about the means? Besides, chapter VII of the UN Charter provides for the use of force 'to coerce conflicting parties to restore or maintain internal peace and security', and it is under this chapter that UN forces are deployed on peace-keeping operations.

Unfortunately, even some of the UN officials seem unaware of this, or unaware of what chapter VII means. The UN Secretary-General, Kofi Annan, speaking at a press conference in June 1997 to discuss civil war in Sierra Leone, declared himself horrified at the suggestion that the UN would ever consider working with a respectable mercenary organisation, arguing that there is no difference between respectable mercenaries and non-respectable mercenaries, which is simply nonsense. That view is hard to reconcile with UN actions in Somalia and Congo, where local militias, armed to the teeth, were hired and paid to protect UN officials and UN facilities. It should already be clear that PMCs are light years away from the popular 'mercenary' concept, but the issue remains.

Another frequent allegation made about PMCs is that they are 'not accountable'. Not accountable to whom? World opinion? Outside politicians? I can only speak for Sandline, but we are always accountable, to our own policies and ethos and to our client government, with whom we always have a binding negotiated contract. It is under the terms of such a contract that the new government of Papua New Guinea were ordered by the courts to pay the outstanding debt for our work on behalf of the previous PNG administration. To underline this principle of accountability on the ground, Sandline people are always enrolled in the forces, police or military, of the client state; in Papua New Guinea, all of us were appointed special constables and were subject to the same laws, rules and regulations that governed any other government servant. We did not operate as a private army.

It is also alleged that, in hiring a PMC, a government is abrogating its own responsibilities to the citizens or the electorate. A second's consideration will reveal that this is nonsense. A national government cannot abrogate responsibility for its own defence or the ethics and principles it stands for, but it does have a responsibility to be as effective as possible in maintaining the peace and security of the state, and therefore can hire experts if it feels the need to do so – experts who must be subordinate to the host government and fit within the existing military authority.

These allegations over practical matters are easy to answer, not least on the grounds of common sense. The argument usually then moves on to the moral issue and the accusation that PMCs are careless of human rights and are 'mercenaries' who go about killing people. This accusation is not supported by the facts. Indeed, I would argue that the presence of a PMC force in a country actually raises standards of behaviour among the indigenous forces, who are often riven with ethnic or tribal rivalries or hatred and are more than willing to extract compensation from the civilian population for past wrongs. PMC personnel, apart from being less involved and therefore more objective, will stamp on this sort of thing hard, partly because as professional soldiers they do not approve of it and partly because they know that brutality does not work. Respect for human rights is not widespread in Third World armies or police forces – and less widespread than it should be everywhere else – but teaching such respect is one of the features of Sandline training. The locals are taught higher standards of behaviour and shown that it is in their own interests to work on 'hearts and minds' activities with the local people. They discover that the results are cumulative: the better they treat the locals, the more support they enjoy, the easier their task becomes and, last but not least, the better they feel.

The fact that we take payment for our work clearly bothers some people, as does the allegation that we will take payment in kind, in mineral wealth, in gold or diamonds, in territory or mining leases. This allegation is not even true.

Sandline has never accepted payment in this fashion, and we have no intention of doing so. Our reluctance is more practical than moral, for I can see no fundamental objection to payment in kind. Hard currency is difficult to come by in many Third World countries – we have even been accused of depleting the national stock of hard currency – and if we were offered payment in coffee futures or diamonds we would probably consider taking it. But we are a military company, not commodity brokers. We would do so only with the greatest reluctance, for we simply do not have the expertise to get involved in these transactions. A mineral concession to me is worth nothing; it is a liability, likely to soak up millions before any return is seen, if one ever is.

Finally, there is the matter of transparency, the demand that all our activities should be open to public inspection and government intervention or regulation. Taking the last point first, where there are legal limits to our policies or actions we obey them, and we also impose limits by sticking to our own corporate ethos and sound professional military practice. We would welcome some form of regulation, not least so that we would then know where we stand and perhaps be spared the usual wearisome moralising – another point I shall return to. On the first point – often interpreted by the media as 'the public's right to know' – the answer lies in this page. This is a book about Sandline's activities and if I had anything to hide I would not be writing it.

One frequently expressed concern is that PMCs may step outside their stated, self-imposed operating principles and abuse their position of trust to the extent that 'the tail wags the dog'. In other words, if a government employs a PMC, before long it is no longer the client government which calls the shots but the PMC, which, having the control of command and weaponry, is in a position to alter its terms of employment and dictate to the host government. This is the rational reason, and were it a realistic one, there would be good cause for concern. The situation on the ground, however, dictates otherwise. Simply on the matter of numbers, PMCs lack the muscle to impose their policies on any national government, for the number of operatives deployed in any one place is very small – I cannot recall any instance where we have put more than a hundred people on the ground, and it is usually much fewer. Then there is the fact that professional PMCs work through the legitimate national governmental hierarchy, and on a contractual basis. There is no scope for illegitimate action, extortion or private coups. All this presupposes that the PMC ever wanted to act in such a fashion in the first place, but there are other, practical considerations.

Given that a PMC is a business, it is acknowledged that a fundamental law of successful business is that the supplier is only as good as his last contract. Ethical businesses first build a reputation and then work hard to protect it. If a particular PMC performed badly or unethically, exploited the trust placed in it by a client, changed sides, violated human rights or sought to mount a coup, then the company and its principals would find that their forward order book was decidedly thin. Discarding ethical and moral principles can therefore only be a one-time opportunity. The chance will not recur and the company's prospects would disappear; common sense alone makes such actions most unlikely. Such allegations should, I suggest, be proved rather than asserted.

Besides, the company and its clients also have their rights, and confidentiality is one of them. Provided their operations are legitimate, every company is granted a degree of privacy which is embedded in the national laws of the country where it chooses to incorporate or base itself. Why should PMCs be required to present a higher level of disclosure than their peers simply to satisfy the curious?

Regulation must work within the bounds of commercial reality. It is often the case that when a client has decided to take up their services, PMCs are required 'in-theatre' almost immediately. Any project-authorisation process must be capable of operating within this time constraint, for as far as the clients are concerned our lack of bureaucracy and our ability to streamline executive decision-making has a definite appeal. It might be pointed out that when the British Army's 'Rapid Reaction Force' was first deployed, it took months before it got out of Tidworth Barracks. I doubt if any client would wait that long.

However, assuming that this process was in position and worked, we then have to consider the matter of what happens on the ground as the PMC goes to work. It would not be enough to permit their deployment and give them *carte blanche*. The next step must be some form of operational overview, and again this is something we would welcome. In my opinion, no legitimate PMC would object to the attachment of an observer team deployed alongside it in the field, within certain limits. This team would work in the same way as the referee at a football match, i.e. not interfering with the action, ensuring their own personal safety by avoiding being hit by the ball (or the player), yet having the authority to caution participants if they are in breach of the regulations. Clearly, the analogy is not ideal. In the case of PMCs and their clients there are lives at stake, and it would be hard to imagine an observer carrying sufficient weight to ensure the removal from the field of personnel who break the ground rules (e.g. the terms of the Geneva Convention), a task that must be left to the local commanders. However, the PMC will be fully cognisant of the fact that their actions are being constantly monitored and will not want to be banned from 'playing in another game' in the future, or to find themselves in front of an international tribunal.

This suggestion has merit and might work, not least because it offers something to all the various parties. The observer force, by its very presence, can ensure that criticisms and suspicions often levelled at PMCs, such as unnecessarily prolonging their participation for excessive commercial gain, applying indiscriminate military techniques resulting in unacceptable civilian casualties and collateral damage, or violating human rights, can be independently monitored. By being present throughout the deployment and planning phases, the observer force will be fully conversant with the overall objectives, the chain of command, the directives and orders that are issued and the conduct of operations, thereby creating accountability for all actions of the PMCs.

Undoubtedly there are other options, many of which will be variations on those set out here. There needs to be a balance between the extent of oversight required at the 'international level', at the UN and in the media, that which can be practically managed on the ground and that which would be acceptable to PMC management and the client government without 'switching them off' the concept. At this stage, where no such organisation or system exists, it is sufficient to examine the options. In the meantime, the majority of legitimate PMCs are quite capable of continuing to operate and grow without the introduction of a regulatory regime.

PMCs will accept external regulation if it is manageable and adds to their commercial aspirations and operational effectiveness. Few businessmen of any kind welcome further regulation, but most sensible businessmen accept that in any business a degree of regulation is usually necessary. I would only suggest that since PMCs operate in an international setting and in high-risk, volatile situations, the sort of heavy-handed regulation employed in other areas of public concern might not be entirely appropriate.

Finally, however hard the high-minded or the politically motivated may argue to the contrary, the fact is that private military companies work. They resolve conflicts, they provide answers and they have proved useful in restoring peace and bringing the parties to the conference table. Because they work, there is a growing demand for their services.

The advent of PMCs and their obvious effectiveness has raised the suggestion that they have an effective role to play in international affairs, particularly when the traditional 'world's policemen' – the United States and Britain – are unable or reluctant to intervene or, in the case of the UN, are grossly overstretched already and none too effective on the ground because they operate to international mandates that are arrived at by compromise.

However, the development of PMCs also raises a number of understandable concerns. It is obvious that those PMCs which operate what British Foreign Secretary Robin Cook has called an 'ethical foreign policy' have their value. The profession of arms is not immoral, but there may well be a need for some form of regulation. Reputable PMCs would welcome this, but they would like to be part of the dialogue in forming these measures. From our point of view, there is a danger of overly prescriptive regulations which will negate much of the speed and flexibility of legitimate PMCs, thus putting them out of business. A more likely scenario is that it will drive the dubious companies underground, making their activities harder to monitor.

The profession of arms has a long and honourable history and I am proud of my part in it. I have now moved on into a new military sphere and that too is developing a history in which I hope to play an honourable part. To quote Sir Thomas Legg in his report on the Sierra Leone investigation in London, 'PMCs are part of the international scene and are here to stay.'

My experience with Sandline fully endorses that opinion. Since PMCs are here, and here to stay, surely the answer is not to moralise, restrict or criminalise their activities but to engage in a sensible dialogue and maximise the benefits of PMCs as part of the 'New World Order'? I won't pretend it isn't an uphill struggle, and we should never lose sight of the fact that nations cannot abrogate responsibility for their own security. PMCs cannot work miracles and their role will always be limited. However, in certain situations they can assist or enhance national forces and buy time for sanity, decency and peace to return once again to a land ravaged by war.

This being so, surely PMCs should be encouraged and supported, rather than criticised and condemned? Much of that condemnation stems from the fact that some people cannot discriminate between a PMC and the 'Dogs of War' mercenary concept and lack any knowledge of mercenary history. So, with Sandline now introduced, let us move on to examine the issues raised in this chapter in more detail, starting with a look at the history of mercenary warfare.

TWO

A SHORT HISTORY OF MERCENARY WARFARE

'And as for war, my wars were global from the start.'
HENRY REED

The *Oxford Dictionary* defines a mercenary as 'a hired soldier in foreign service', someone who serves a country other than his own, for pay. There is no mention in that definition of the obloquy that seems to have gathered about the word 'mercenary' in the public mind in recent years, when the term is taken to mean a hired thug who will serve any cause and do any dirty work, provided the price is right.

As accurately described in the dictionary, the word 'mercenary' does not worry me; my only objection is that, certainly as far as Sandline International is concerned, the implication that is so often grafted on to the word 'mercenary' is neither fair nor historically accurate and if it has to be applied at all it should be applied in the proper context. Sandline International does not consist of a group of mercenaries in the *Rambo* mould; we are a corporate body marketing military expertise, and in that respect we are directly descended from the classic mercenary companies of antiquity and the Middle Ages.

There is nothing wrong with soldiering for pay. During my life as a professional soldier I expected to be paid. As for serving foreign nations, there are no more respected soldiers in the world than the Gurkhas, yet the Gurkhas are subjects of Nepal, not Britain or India, two countries where the Gurkhas soldier for pay. They use their pay as other men do, to support their families. When people start using words like 'mercenary' in the pejorative sense, the true meaning is rapidly obscured. However, since the phrase is used so often, it would be as well to look at the entire business of mercenary soldiering to see just where Sandline and the modern private military company fit into the 'mercenary' framework.

Mercenary soldiering has a long and honourable history. Go back to the dawn of history, to the empires of the Egyptians, the Hittites or the Assyrians, and accounts can be found of mercenary soldiers. This history also has connections with the modern world, because throughout history, as today, nations and rulers have hired mercenaries because they lacked the will, or the technical skill, to do the fighting themselves. Mercenaries can be found in every nation: the Japanese samurai were mercenaries, the Swiss export industry in the sixteenth and seventeenth centuries was largely composed of mercenary soldiers, and the British used mercenary troops in many of their colonial campaigns, an example recently followed by the United States in Vietnam, where Nung and Montagnard tribesmen, supplied and trained by the CIA or US Special Forces, served against the North Vietnamese Army and the Viet Cong.

When something is both widespread and long-lasting, there must be some fundamental reason for its existence. In the case of mercenaries, the reasons why they have continued to survive and prosper down the centuries can be reduced to just two: efficiency and technology. In the Middle Ages the mercenary was simply more efficient, more reliable and better equipped than the reluctant vassal, who was obliged to serve his lord in the field for forty days a year but often did so reluctantly, with one eye on his crops and the other on the calendar. The feudal levy produced a large number of half-armed, ill-equipped, untrained tenants and peasants, most of them useless for military operations – and even they had to be paid and fed. Far better, therefore, to contract with a mercenary captain for the services of professional soldiers, trained troops who would stay in the field as long as they were paid, and who had the proper equipment and the skill to use it.

Many weapons then in use, either complicated ones like the crossbow or those which required years of training to achieve a useful level of skill and physical strength, like the English longbow, could only be properly employed by hired soldiers. Gradually, over the centuries, the employment of mercenary soldiers became the rule rather than the exception, and by the seventeenth century most wars, other than civil wars, were largely fought by mercenary armies. The ordinary citizen simply would not serve and the old feudal duty which made him serve had long since been abandoned.

Besides, to handle cannon or the musket, to have a grasp of infantry or cavalry tactics, to know the intricacies of siege-craft or how to order a line of battle were not skills the private citizen had the time or the interest to acquire. Again, these technical matters were best entrusted to the mercenary soldier, a man who fought for pay.

It was never just a question of money. Some men enjoyed soldiering and regarded it as a skill like any other, and a way to earn a living doing something they enjoyed and were good at. From the employers' point of view, mercenaries were hired because they could use modern equipment or had special skills, again as they are to this day. For example, in the Hellenic period, Darius, the Persian Emperor, hired a force of 10,000 Greek hoplites, heavily armed and armoured infantry, to assist him in his wars. The Greeks did good service, but when the wars were over Darius decided to reduce his payroll and massacre them, a fate avoided when the 'Ten Thousand' left Persia and set out to march home, an epic recorded by Xenophon. Mercenaries were, then as now, the victims of higher authority. At the start of the Christian era, Julius Caesar and his rival Crassus both raised mercenary forces of Gallic horsemen to augment their infantry legions, and many non-Romans were actually recruited, as mercenaries, into the legions; one of the rewards for years of legion service was Roman citizenship and a plot of farmland.

This process continued down the centuries. The Emperor of Byzantium had a mercenary force of axemen, the Varangian Guard, made up of Norwegians, Danes and, after the takeover of England by William the Conqueror in 1066, even Saxons. In every case, be it Greek hoplite, Gallic horse or Saxon axeman, the mercenary provided the recruiting army with some military asset it would not otherwise possess. These mercenaries proved their worth in combat and were loyal to their paymaster; the Varangian Guard perished to the last man in the defence of their Emperor when the Normans attempted to take over Constantinople.

Mercenaries or professional soldiers could be found in all the medieval armies. Many mercenary soldiers were trusted servants of the Crown, men like Sir Robert Knollys and Sir Hugh Calvalry, who served Edward III in his French wars. They expected to be paid but they stayed in the field as long as the money kept coming. The French also hired mercenaries, many coming from Italy; 6,000 Genoese crossbowmen opened the attack on the English line at the Battle of Crecy in 1346.

A major link with the modern military company came in the fourteenth and fifteenth centuries when the city states of Italy hired professional soldiers – *condottieri* – to fight their interminable wars. Some of these *condottieri*, like Fredrigo di Montifeltro, became dukes – Fredrigo became the Duke of Urbino – and were noted for their culture and humanism. One of the greatest of the fourteenth-century *condottieri* was an English knight, Sir John Hawkwood, who took a large company of men-at-arms and archers into Italy in 1360, where the citizens of Florence were so impressed by their glittering armour and clean surcoats marked with the red cross of St George that they named Hawkwood's force 'The White Company'. Thanks to the bows of the White Company, the Florentines gained some notable victories over Milan, Pisa and Bologna. Hawkwood was a man who kept his bargains, and when he died the Florentines gave him a splendid tomb which can still be seen in the Duomo.

These mercenary soldiers serving the Italian city states fought under a contract, a *condatto*. This was a document which laid out precisely the terms under which they were engaged: what arms they would bring, who they would fight, what length of time they must serve and how they would be fed, housed and paid. Mercenary soldiering was then, as it is now, a business and much like any other business, only with a slightly higher level of risk. It was not considered immoral or unusual for military experts like the *condottieri* to be called in to save the day if the city state or its ruler was in difficulty, and the connection with the modern, professional military company must be obvious.

Hiring the best foreign troops was both sensible and fashionable. The kings of France maintained a bodyguard of Scottish archers and when Charles the Rash, Duke of Burgundy, made war on the Swiss in the 1470s he hired the finest professional soldiers from every corner of Europe: English archers, Spanish sword-and-buckler men, French cannoneers. Unfortunately for Duke Charles, the Swiss infantry were formidable warriors and much in demand by medieval and Renaissance princes, who valued their discipline and their skill with the pike, halberd and battle-axe, and they beat him in three straight battles and killed him at the last one. The Swiss Guard still maintained by the Pope to guard the Vatican are a reminder of that fifteenth-century Swiss skill with hand weapons.

In the sixteenth century, Henry VIII of England and his rival François Premier of France spent fortunes hiring mercenaries, especially Swiss ones who, along with the up-and-coming Germans, were regarded as the finest soldiers in Europe, not least because while many countries were clinging on to the traditional weapons of sword, lance and bow, the professional soldiers had invested in early model hand-guns, muskets and field artillery and become proficient in their use. Mercenaries, then as now, sold their expertise in military technology as well as their professional skills.

In the seventeenth century, the Thirty Years' War in Germany was fought almost entirely by mercenary bands, and it is in this century that we see the rise of the professional general, officers who knew how to manage large armies in the field and win battles, feats beyond the competence of more aristocratic commanders. The Scots were to the fore here, and one Scottish general, Leslie, came back from Germany to lead Scotland's armies against Charles I. So we see a development in mercenary activity that can be traced on to some modern PMCs; not the provision of fighting men, but the supply of high-level skills and technical military expertise, the beginnings of command and control, and with it a grasp of logistics and communications to keep an army in the field, disciplined and fit and ready to fight.

The eighteenth century saw the start of the colonial wars and the American Revolution, where, in an attempt to match the tactics and fieldcraft of the American riflemen, Morgan's sharpshooters and the 'Green Mountain Boys' of Vermont and New Hampshire, the British recruited mercenary soldiers in Germany, particularly from Hess. These 'Hessians', bogeymen in early American history, were usually gamekeepers or forest wardens, well used to the woods and good shots – two reasons for American troops to fear them and US history to demonise them. The King of England also recruited from Hanover, but this was hardly mercenary activity, for the King of England, George III, was also the Elector of Hanover.

And so we come to the Napoleonic Wars, edging closer to the present day with no break in mercenary involvement. Both sides used mercenaries. The French hired Polish lancers and the British had a crack contingent of troops from Germany, infantry and cavalry, called the King's German Legion, a unit that fought with great distinction at many of Wellington's battles. When the wars ended, many of these unemployed soldiers – even some of the senior officers – found their way to South America, where one naval officer, Admiral Cochrane, became the founder of the Chilean Navy; history is full of examples of professional British military men offering their skills to foreign armies.

All this history must refute the notion that mercenaries are either a new phenomenon or are intrinsically bad. Many states owed their very survival to the skills and courage of mercenary armies, and as we entered the modern era, mercenary activity, far from declining with the growth of citizen armies, actually increased and gained official recognition.

The early years of the nineteenth century introduced the French Foreign Legion and Britain's much-admired Brigade of Gurkhas. I suspect that a number of Gurkha officers will take exception to my calling their superb troops 'mercenaries', but while no one can or would dispute the great service and loyalty the Gurkha soldier has shown to the British Raj over the last 200 years, they are subjects of the King of Nepal and serve the English Crown and State for pay. Personally, I think that perfectly right and proper, and I am sure all clear-thinking British people will agree with me.

The Gurkhas are splendid troops, and having served with them in the Falklands War I know just how good they can be, which is why their fighting skills are so admired and so sought after. India, which used to call the Gurkhas 'mercenaries' in the days of the Raj, now has over 80,000 Gurkhas in her army – and the Sultan of Brunei employs a further 2,000 as a personal bodyguard.

The warm relationship between the British Army and the Gurkhas began in 1814 when, following attacks by Gurkhas on British outposts – outposts of the East India Company in those far-off days – a British Army under General Gillespie invaded Nepal to teach these little men a lesson. It did not turn out like that, as the hillmen of Nepal revealed themselves as formidable fighters, but the British know how to soldier and the two sides, while fighting each other fiercely, soon began to develop a mutual respect. One Scots officer, James Fraser, said of the Gurkhas, 'They fought us in fair combat, like men, and in the intervals of actual combat showed us a courtesy worthy of a more enlightened people.'

This regard was mutual. There is an account of an injured Gurkha coming into the British lines during one battle waving a white flag and asking for medical treatment in order to go on fighting. The British surgeons duly patched him up and he returned to his own lines and continued the fight. The Nepalese War went on for two years, with much bloodshed but no bitterness, until peace was reached by the Treaty of Segauli in 1816, after which two full battalions of Gurkhas were enlisted into the Indian Army – and after 1947 into the British Army – to serve the British Crown, where the Gurkhas have had an honoured place ever since. The service given by these doughty hillmen is beyond all praise; they are formidable soldiers working to the simple code of the Gurkha soldier: 'It is better to die than be a coward.'

If the Gurkhas do not fit precisely into the mercenary mould, the same cannot be said about the French Foreign Legion, the 'Légion Etrangère', a mercenary force *tout court*. The Legion was raised by decree on 9 March 1831, when King Louis-Philippe authorised the formation of 'a legion, composed of foreigners, to be called the Foreign Legion'. France did not really need more soldiers; the main purpose of forming the Legion was to round up, recruit and ship to the war in Algeria the large number of stateless persons who had started to arrive in France after the end of the Napoleonic Wars and who were now thought to represent a danger to the state.

The Legion was disbanded and reformed time and again over the next few decades but it gradually became recognised as a disciplined, hard-fighting force – and one where heavy casualties did not cause too much upset among the French electorate. The Legion was not popular in France, at least outside the military sphere, but it was useful and highly regarded in army circles. The top six cadet officers passing out of St Cyr are still allowed to serve in the Legion, a much-prized appointment for a young officer.

The 2nd REP – 2ième Régiment Etranger Parachutiste – is now the crack unit in the French Army but the Legion has a superb fighting record in all its wars: at Camerone in Mexico, at the Chemin de Dames in the Great War, at Bir Hakeim in North Africa in the Second World War, at Dien Bien Phu in Indo-China in 1954, when the Legionnaires fought to the last round and then charged the Vietminh with the bayonet, and at a score of minor engagements in the years since, not least the rescue by the 2nd REP of Belgian citizens trapped by rebels in the Zairean mining town of Kolwezi in the 1980s. The Legionnaires parachuted in, beat off the enemy and rescued the citizens for the loss of five men killed and a score wounded. This was, of course, a gross violation of the sovereignty of another country – but the alternative was to do nothing and let the Belgians be massacred.

The Legion is a purely mercenary force. In theory, only foreigners are allowed to join, though in recent years some French recruits have been admitted, a trend that the old sweats greatly deplore. Every European upset brings recruits to the Legion; the Hungarian uprising of 1956, for example, brought Czech and Hungarian soldiers into the Legion, and Bosnian and Croatian recruits arrived in the early 1990s.

Once in and trained, the men are Legionnaires. Discipline is tough, even harsh, and the training is relentless, but the pay is good and a man who can soldier can find a home in the Legion. All a man has to do is be a good soldier – and be loyal to the Legion. Over the years the Legion has developed its own ethos whereby a man's usual and natural loyalty to his country is replaced by loyalty to the Legion, a point rammed home by the Latin motto on the Legion memorial at their depot at Aubagne in Provence: 'Legio patria nostra' – 'The Legion is our country'.

So, skipping lightly over the other wars of the nineteenth century where mercenaries were inevitably employed, we come to the present day and the 1960s, when civil war and massacre broke out in the former Belgian Congo, now Zaire, and the modern mercenary appeared on television and entered the public mind in a less than favourable light. The differences between the Congo mercenaries, the traditional forces mentioned above, and their descendant, the modern private military company will soon become obvious.

The Congo mercenaries did much to create the squalid modern image of the mercenary and created the popular notion that the mercenary soldier, as summed up in Peter Tickler's book *The Modern Mercenary*, is inevitably 'a freelance soldier of no fixed abode or loyalty, ruthless, undertaking short contracts for large amounts of money'.

This may in part be true of that time and place, but in the chaos and bloodshed of the Congo, many people, black as well as white, were glad to see a mercenary force arrive in their area and offer protection from rape and murder. The Congo troubles began in 1960 on the day after independence, when the Force Publique mutinied and began a campaign of rapine, looting and murder, largely directed against those Belgians who had not had time or the good sense to get out before independence. The UN intervened and were soon locked in combat with the local troops, especially those in the breakaway province of Katanga, ignoring the local slaughter in their desire to keep the Congo intact.

The first foreign soldier involved as a mercenary in the Congo was a Frenchman, Michel de Clay, who defended Elizabethville, the capital of Katanga, against the UN troops and defeated them. Before long he was joined by other mercenaries, including the legendary Bob Denard. This first war petered out, but in 1964 the Simba revolt began, a much bloodier affair led by one Pierre Malele, a man who believed in witchcraft and black magic. His warriors, the Simbas, began a ruthless campaign, murdering tens of thousands of people as they rampaged across the Congo and into Katanga.

The Simbas soon defeated the Congolese Army and Moise Tshombe, now the Katangese President of the Congo, having few friends in the outside world, called for mercenary help. This arrived in the form of 'Mad Mike' Hoare, who was hired to raise a force to fight the Simbas. Hoare recruited troops in South Africa and formed a crack unit, 5 Commando, to spearhead the fight, but there were also a number of Katangese units and before long Hoare had over a thousand men under command, most of them mercenaries, unemployed professional soldiers, who had come to the Congo because it offered them employment and action. Many of them were veterans of the Second World War; their ranks included an ex-Wehrmacht soldier, Siegfried Muller, who went into battle wearing the Iron Cross he had won fighting in Russia in 1943.

Hoare started well by rescuing a number of Belgian nuns held by the Simbas at Albertville, but it took outside intervention, a parachute drop on to the town of Stanleyville by the Belgian Para-Commando Regiment, soldiers of the former colonial power, to curb the Simbas there; the Belgian Paras arrived just in time to prevent a general massacre of the captive expatriate population. Matters went fairly well for the next two years before Tshombe was ousted from office by President Kasavubu. Kasavubu did not last long, being ousted by Mobutu in 1967, and the UN, who had been complaining since 1964 about the actions of these 'Congo mercenaries', persuaded President Mobutu to expel them.

By now Mike Hoare had left and 5 Commando had been disbanded. The two mercenary units left in the Congo in 1967 were 6 Commando, commanded by Bob Denard, and 10 Commando, under 'Black Jack' Schramme, the two units together totalling no more than a few hundred men. Seeking to play one off against the other, Mobutu asked Denard to surround and disarm Schramme's troops and turn them over to the Congolese Army – who would have cut the throats of the lucky ones – but Denard told Schramme about this plot and the two men joined forces to overthrow Mobutu – which, in view of what happened to the Congo during Mobutu's rule, may have been a good idea.

These two mercenary units fought the Congolese Army but were eventually forced to withdraw to the town of Bukuvu on the shores of Lake Tanganyika, where they surrendered to the UN. The survivors were flown out to safety, in spite of Mobutu's efforts to get them sent back for trial and execution in the Congo. Despite all their faults, however, the mercenary companies that fought in the Congo did at least prevent a bad situation from getting a good deal worse.

The mercenary scene then shifted to the former Portuguese colony of Angola, which descended into civil war almost as soon as the Portuguese left, though a War of Liberation had been waged before that and had endowed Angola with a quantity of weapons and a population inured to war. Angola has since been the scene of various military operations, including a successful small-scale operation by the South African PMC, Executive Outcomes, but in 1975 it witnessed a full-blooded civil war between the government, such as it was, and the rebel UNITA forces of Jonas Savimbi. Both sides were soon recruiting mercenaries, Cuba sent in troops and heavy weapons to help the Marxist MPLA government and the country was gradually torn apart in the fighting.

The significant feature of the war in Angola in the history of mercenary warfare is that it was here that the notoriety earned by a small group of thugs gravely damaged the reputation of mercenaries as professional soldiers, and it is that dire reputation that has since become imprinted on the public mind. These Angolan mercenaries were led by a Greek Cypriot from London, Costas Georgiou, who elected to call himself 'Callan', after a TV character of the time. Like a number of his men, 'Callan' had served briefly in the Parachute Regiment, from which the majority of them had been rapidly kicked out for various crimes and misdemeanours; they were, in fact, simply a bunch of young thugs looking for excitement, and they got more than they bargained for in Angola.

The story of 'Callan' and his gang in Angola is that of a farce descending into tragedy. A great many stories, some true, some pure myth, have grown up about the 'Callan' affair but the bottom line is that eventually thirteen of these mercenaries were captured and put on trial by the MPLA. All were found guilty of various crimes, including mercenary activity, and in spite of pleas for mercy from the Pope and Queen Elizabeth II, four of them, including 'Callan', were shot by firing squad. The rest served years in an Angolan prison, the last of them not being released until 1984.

Before that could happen, Mike Hoare was back in the news, taking a group of mercenaries to overthrow the government of the Seychelles in November 1981. This operation rapidly went awry and Hoare and his men were eventually obliged to hijack an Air India jet at Mahe and fly in it to South Africa, where, somewhat to their surprise, they were immediately arrested. Tried and found guilty of mercenary activity, Hoare was sentenced to ten years in prison, but was released after four.

These last incidents, taking place between 1960 and 1981, have provided the basis for the popular concept of mercenary warfare: a bunch of thugs attempting to subvert the legally elected government and leaving chaos in their wake. The men who take part are, in the main, discontented former soldiers whose only trade is soldiering, and they sell their services to the highest bidder.

Before we leave this area it is worth pointing out that these incidents left a legacy: the belief in the Third World that a few well-trained, white, professional soldiers – though a large number of Congo and Angolan mercenaries were in fact black – could make a real difference to the outcome of any Third World campaign. This had the effect of enhancing the reputation of even the crudest mercenary force and begs the question of whether those mercenaries were created by the unique opportunities posed by the post-independence circumstances in Angola and the Congo or whether they merely represented a re-emergence of the historic mercenary role in a corrupt and bastardised form. Certainly, during the post-independence phase in Africa in the 1960s and 1970s, it seemed to become accepted that the defence of the fabric of African society against the threat of rebellion largely depended on the rapid recruitment of mercenary forces.

Wars attract mercenaries like honey attracts bees. Professional soldiers from

Britain, the USA, South Africa, Australia and the Continent of Europe flocked to the former Rhodesia – now Zimbabwe – during the years of Unilateral Declaration of Independence to serve in such units as the Rhodesian SAS and the Selous Scouts. The same is true of the more recent conflicts in the Balkans, where former soldiers from a dozen countries were detected by the UN observers and the media, serving in the various forces as advisers, trainers or specialists.

As for those mercenaries who had fought in the Congo or Angola in the 1960s, they were soon back in the fray and seeking employment. Few of the world's trouble spots were active for long before some mercenary soldier appeared on the scene, offering to round up a few old friends and provide practical military help and trained personnel, at a price. It takes two to strike a bargain, however, and these mercenaries did not lack employment. All the old names – Bob Denard, Jack Schramme, Robert Falques – appear from time to time in the accounts of these flare-ups, but the Congo mercenaries are growing old now and the market for their kind of warfare has declined.

At this point it is necessary to underline the difference between the traditional mercenary, who was an honourable soldier working under contract for a legitimate government, operating a business within the profession of arms and selling his skill and technological expertise, and the excitement-seeking thug. The latter category is new, unacceptable, ineffective and rightly condemned. The professional soldier, on the other hand, with skills for hire to legitimate outlets is an entirely different kind of warrior. Times change, warfare becomes ever more technical and the weapons employed grow ever more sophisticated but the old, long-established and honourable tradition of 'mercenary' soldiering remains; as in ancient and medieval times, the modern professional soldier is hired as much for his technical competence as for his fighting abilities.

The supply of such military expertise often lies with governments, especially with those governments who have developed a large export trade in arms. The British government, while officially deploring 'mercenaries', still allows their employment in several client states such as in the Arabian Gulf, where the use of 'contract officers' to train local forces, lead them in operations and fly ground-attack aircraft in support of operations against dissidents is – or was – widely known and tacitly encouraged.

During the troubles in Dhofar and the Oman in the 1960s and 1970s, British Army volunteers were involved in defending forts and strategic sites against the dissident tribesmen, manning Vickers machine guns and three-inch mortars in support of the local militia action and taking part in front-line operations.

The war in Dhofar was one of the catalysts for my original thinking about Sandline. The Oman had long been of strategic importance to and a close ally of Britain. When Sultan Quabos came to the throne in 1970, he inherited the insurrection in the province of Dhofar which had begun in the 1960s when the local Dhofar Liberation Front, or DLF, had risen against their reactionary chief, Sultan Said bin Taimur. The DLF had then been infiltrated by a yet more radical group, the People's Front for the Liberation of the Arabian Gulf (PFLOAG), a Communist front with backing from the USSR and China.

On coming to power in the Oman, Sultan Quabos tried the diplomatic route, offering an amnesty to the rebel tribesmen – the *adoo* – and beginning a programme of civil works and aid to the local tribespeople. This did not work; the fighting escalated and eventually the local military and their British helpers became involved.

The Sultan's armed forces consisted of a number of regular units and their composition was interesting. The rank and file were Omanis or Baluchis, the latter recruited in Baluchistan, a province of what is now Pakistan. The units were generally commanded by serving British officers on secondment to the Omani Army, while the staff posts in the battalions were held either by additional seconded officers or more generally by 'contract officers', ex-British, Australian, Rhodesian or South African military personnel. This structure was the same in the Omani Army staff and in the small Omani Air Force. These Omani units were supported by regular formations from the UK, most notably from the 22 SAS Regiment and the Royal Engineers. These contract officers were, in effect, mercenaries.

The concept of indigenous troops being commanded by a mixture of seconded and contract officers working as a cohesive unit for a sovereign government against an insurgency, and being supported by regular forces from a friendly power, proved to be an effective mix; the Dhofar campaign was professionally conducted and ultimately successful.

On the subject of 'loan service' or seconded officers, the MOD in Whitehall maintains a Loan Service Department which seconds, or loans, British servicemen to foreign armies. They are integrated into the armed forces of the country they serve with, they wear the national uniform and they can go on operations. This was another facet of the marketing of military expertise. Here was an official government department exporting military skills, a function that might equally well be offered by the private sector. This too formed part of the inspiration for Sandline.

Unfortunately, I joined the British Army too late to go on secondment to the Oman, but I followed the course of the war closely, although it was not fought in the full glare of the world's media as it would be today. A number of books were subsequently written about the campaign and I later came in contact with several people who had served there, including my immediate superior at the NCOs Battle School at Brecon.

Even then, on hearing their stories, the thought was beginning to form in my mind – although at this stage it was still ill defined – that there was clearly a need for the skills of professional soldiers in such conflicts and that this work could be carried out without the participants gaining the lurid reputation of being unprincipled, ruthless 'Dogs of War', which by the '80s was already well established in the public mind as the true face of the mercenary soldier.

About the same time as the war in Dhofar was ending, the war in Rhodesia was starting up. A similar 'contract' concept was adopted by the Rhodesian Army, which readily took on the services of professional soldiers from other armies, from the UK, the USA, South Africa, New Zealand and Australia. Many of these highly trained and skilled soldiers graduated to one of the élite Special Force units, the Selous Scouts or the Rhodesian SAS. Again, the concept worked, and I am delighted that a number of veterans of this campaign are now working for Sandline.

During the late 1970s and 1980s, David Stirling, a former Scots Guards officer and founder of the SAS, was already trying to put this idea into practice with his Chelsea-based company Watchguard, which I suppose could be called the forerunner of the modern PMC. Watchguard became involved in the Yemen and in Africa and their methods and outlook also contributed to my thinking in setting up Sandline.

Private military companies – or seconded or 'loan service' officers – can claim an historic link with the mercenary companies employed by the Italian city states and the medieval rulers, not least in that they work only for established, recognised governments. They offer expertise where it is lacking, in the use of military technology, in the training of troops – including 'hearts and minds' training – and, certainly in the case of Sandline International, in the vital areas of intelligence, operational planning and command. These are high-level professional skills, the result of years of tuition, training and experience, and they have a value similar to that of the skills offered by the surgeon, the architect or the civil engineer. These skills have to be recognised as useful, not deplored as fundamentally undesirable.

The history of the mercenary soldier is chequered, to say the least, but on balance the mercenary has served a useful and honourable role in the history of the nation state. Without mercenaries and their military expertise many small nations could not have survived, and many countries, Switzerland and Germany to name but two, have a long history of mercenary soldiering.

It is only in more recent times, in the 1960s and 1970s, that the mercenary soldier has been labelled as an undesirable, a reputation that may say more about changing moral values and the complexity of political judgements than it does about the role and ethos of the mercenary soldier. One can only hope that the evident uses and professional skills of private military companies will restore the reputation of the mercenary soldier to its rightful place in history.

THREE

PRIVATE MILITARY COMPANIES

'An army may be likened to water: water leaves dry the high places and seeks the hollows; an army turns from strength and attacks weakness. The flow of water is regulated by the shape of the ground; victory is gained by acting in accordance with the state of the enemy.'
SUN TZU, *THE ART OF WAR*

Having described the traditional role of the military company and laid the 'mercenary' canard to rest, it is now necessary to describe the purpose of private military companies. Private military companies are organisations which do more than provide passive assistance in areas of conflict. The accent is on the word passive – PMCs are not passive; they do not stand about murmuring soothing words, and their operations extend beyond the guarding role. PMCs offer practical military help in an acceptable form to legitimate governments.

Before continuing and providing some examples, it would be as well to outline the differences between a legitimate PMC and a modern mercenary. A mercenary will be an individual, recruited for a specific task. He is not part of a permanent structure and has only a limited range of capabilities. There is no group cohesion; before the job he will not know his colleagues. He subscribes to no doctrine or collective training standards and his ideas on discipline, the rule of law and human rights may be well short of those required by the law of armed conflict. He is recruited without adequate vetting, his standards of competence are not checked and his motives are suspect.

A PMC, on the other hand, offers a packaged service covering a wide variety of military and quasi-military skills – a study of the chart will be helpful here. PMCs are permanent structures, corporate entities, which are run like a business. They have a clear hierarchy, are run on military lines and operate to high disciplinary standards and within the law of armed conflict, with a particular concern for human rights. In a well-regulated PMC, the involvement will begin with an analysis of the situation facing the client government and the preparation of a commander's estimate – a process known to an older generation of soldiers as 'making an appreciation of the situation', or, in lay terms, finding out what the real problem is and suggesting ways to solve it.

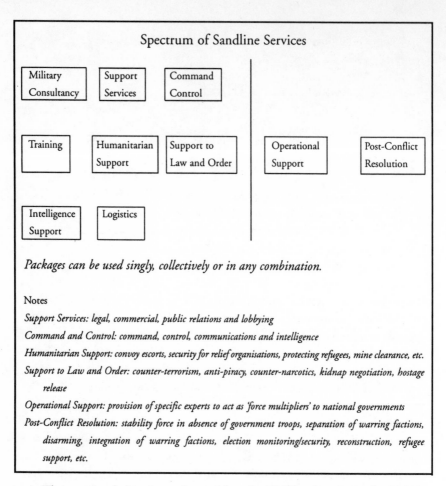

Spectrum of Sandline Services

Military Consultancy	Support Services	Command Control

| Training | Humanitarian Support | Support to Law and Order | | Operational Support | Post-Conflict Resolution |

| Intelligence Support | Logistics |

Packages can be used singly, collectively or in any combination.

Notes

Support Services: legal, commercial, public relations and lobbying

Command and Control: command, control, communications and intelligence

Humanitarian Support: convoy escorts, security for relief organisations, protecting refugees, mine clearance, etc.

Support to Law and Order: counter-terrorism, anti-piracy, counter-narcotics, kidnap negotiation, hostage release

Operational Support: provision of specific experts to act as 'force multipliers' to national governments

Post-Conflict Resolution: stability force in absence of government troops, separation of warring factions, disarming, integration of warring factions, election monitoring/security, reconstruction, refugee support, etc.

The commander's estimate is crucial to the PMC's ethos. In it, the PMC's senior executives will analyse the situation facing the client, examine what is feasible and suggest what might be done to resolve the situation. PMCs do not simply supply what the client asks for. The closest and simplest analogy is with the medical profession. The patient goes to the doctor and says he feels ill; the doctor examines the patient, organises any necessary tests and proposes a course of treatment that will cure the condition; he does not simply respond to the patient's request for a sick note and a bottle of pills. In short, as professional organisations operating in a highly technical field, PMCs expect to be consulted.

The range of PMC facilities at the disposal of any suitable client can be considerable. PMCs may provide training and equipment to extend the capabilities of the client's existing military resources, or provide them with whatever strategic or operational advantage is necessary to suppress their opposition, or, going even further, play an active role alongside the client forces, as 'force multipliers'.

A 'force multiplier' is something that makes a force more effective, a term best summed up by the use of helicopters during the Borneo Confrontation of the 1960s between Britain and Indonesia, when it was said that 'a battalion with helicopters is worth a brigade without them' – in other words, adding helicopter support increased the battalion's effectiveness by a factor of three. PMCs can be responsible for supplying trained manpower or equipment such as helicopters or battlefield radar, even deploying their own personnel into the field of conflict – but with the strict caveat that they are acting within the chain of command of the client's military hierarchy, and, certainly in the case of Sandline, that military hierarchy must be the arm of a legitimate government.

A PMC is, by this very definition, not in the business of providing arms to its client in isolation, and Sandline, incidentally, is not an arms-dealing company. Like any well-run PMC, we would prefer only to supply weaponry and systems within a wider package of training, support and operational use. To touch on the moral issue, we need to know what we are getting into, but the practical point to remember is that PMCs are not 'arms dealers' *per se* but packaged-services providers. Using the example of computers, well-run PMCs are not hardware providers. They deliver a workable package containing all the elements the client needs to make use of modern military technology, i.e. hardware, software, personnel, installation, training and implementation.

PMCs have permanent structures and are not created simply to fulfil the needs of one contract. They do not recruit unemployed hit-men for obscure operations or interview would-be gunslingers in the bedrooms of sleazy hotels. Within the limits of commercial and political discretion, their operations are open to view. They employ or have access to the services of a large number of ex-service personnel from First World armies and the client government employs this expertise through a single contract with the PMC and not through a series of arrangements with individuals or small, informal groups.

PMCs operate from established offices, delivering the necessary support services from within the company, e.g. marketing, sales, administration, accounting, personnel, procurement and so on – just like any other company working in the international arena. They make use of promotional literature to create awareness and do not operate 'in the shadows' as one might expect of the typical 1970s mercenary of the kind portrayed in entertaining films like *The Wild Geese*. Running a PMC is a business much like any other.

It might be argued, 'Yes, but it's a dirty business,' so let me add that, once contracted and deployed, PMCs operate as a military hierarchy with associated discipline, observance of the laws and customs of the host nation, and adherence to the principles of the Geneva Convention and the international law of armed conflict. PMC operations can and do include such humanitarian activities as mine clearing, support for relief operations, the rescue of civilians trapped in a civil war – Sandline rescued scores of such people in Sierra Leone in 1997 – and training of Third World forces in human rights.

This activity has its uses and should be given more official support. In their book *War and Anti-War: Survival at the Dawn of the 21st Century*, Alvin and Heidi Toffler suggested, 'Why not consider creating volunteer mercenary forces, organised by private corporations to fight wars on a contract-fee basis for the United Nations – the *condottieri* of yesterday armed with the weapons of tomorrow?' I might take issue with the word 'mercenary' and suggest that PMCs exist to end wars rather than fight them, but otherwise the suggestion has merit.

That said, the next question that needs to be answered is whether private military companies really can take on the role of the national armed forces? Do they have the equipment, the manpower, the resources and, most of all, the legitimacy? The answer will emerge as this chapter continues, for I intend to give a number of examples where the involvement of PMCs has been highly effective, even where the requirements have included the most sophisticated arms and equipment.

If mercenary forces have a long and honourable history, the modern concept, private military companies like Sandline International, can be linked to those organised companies of professional soldiers that served the city states, and forms part of an expanding international network of specialised military companies. Sandline International is only one of a number of companies specialising in providing various forms of military expertise and our competitors are spread all over the world, notably in the USA. When it comes to selling military expertise, Sandline International and all the other PMCs are in competition both with each other and with a large number of Western governments. The usual conflicts between the 'private' and the 'public' sectors arise in this business, as in many others.

The benefits of privatisation will become clear, but flexibility and a freedom from bureaucratic interference are just some of the assets PMCs have to offer. It would also be useful to look at the wider world of private military companies in order to put the present situation and Sandline International's operations into an accurate context. To do this we need to look briefly at some of the other PMCs, and in particular the South African company Executive Outcomes, or EO.

EO was established in South Africa in 1989 and rapidly became the world's largest private military organisation. Right from the start, EO fostered a clear, corporate image and kept its affairs in the public eye. As a step to that end, it was registered as a limited company with the South African Board of Trade and was organised on a corporate basis. EO activities were conducted on an open, day-to-day basis, without any attempt at secrecy.

The private sector cannot compete on turnover terms with national governments, where arms sales are counted in billions, but it is alleged that in

1995 EO had an income in excess of $50 million, which is not a small sum for a private limited company and indicates that their services were in great demand.

EO's range of military-oriented services steadily expanded to include the recruitment and contracting of military personnel for private work, the training of state armies in the developing nations, where such training is sorely lacking, and the planning and conduct of military operations, and it could equip its client for a wide range of military situations, even those involving the use of armour, artillery and aircraft.

EO's insistence on corporate respectability and accountability did not entirely dispel the 'mercenary' aura, but it certainly helped. EO's professional approach and the clear benefits which have been reaped by the countries that have employed the company, notably Angola and Sierra Leone, are undoubted. By declaring and then sticking to a clear set of rules – a corporate ethos – the organisation established a reputation that took it well away from the public concept of mercenary activity.

EO – which ceased trading at the end of 1998 – was in the service-provider industry, and in order to provide such specialised services EO maintained a regularly updated database estimated to contain the names and details of around 2,000 former military personnel, all highly skilled in various aspects of the military art. Having worked with some of them in Papua New Guinea, I can attest to their high standards of professionalism and personal conduct.

Given its base in the troubled continent of Africa, it is not surprising that EO personnel were often ex-members of the South African Defence Force (SADF) or the South African Police – and, or so it is alleged, their ranks even included former members of the military wing of the African National Congress, Nelson Mandela's ANC. But the company was more than an employment agency. Africa has plenty of warriors; what it lacks are competent professional soldiers, trained in all aspects of modern warfare, able to operate at the higher command level and offering a wide range of skills, including low-intensity operations and 'hearts and minds' activity. This is the business EO pitched for and its last brochure stated that the company was able to offer 'competitively priced, high-quality services and products tailored to our client's requirements . . . Executive Outcomes provides tailor-made packages for government armed forces, thus assisting in the creation of an environment conducive to peace and stability and a stable climate for investment.'

EO's first foray into a civil war was during Angola's 'third civil war' between 1992 and 1994. A UN contingent – UNAVEM – had been deployed in Angola for some years, but the war was marked by terrible atrocities and a great deal of misery which the UN force seemed unable to prevent. This was largely the fault of its mandate, by which UNAVEM III was tasked only for peace-keeping and prevented from peace-making – a not uncommon UN problem. Since there was no peace to keep, the UN force was impotent. UNAVEM lacked both the military capacity and the necessary UN mandate and could offer no worthwhile protection to humanitarian aid workers who were often harassed by UNITA rebels. The weaknesses in UNAVEM's mandate created a security vacuum in which chaos and murder reigned.

EO's first involvement resulted from a contract to recover the strategically important oil refinery and operating base at Soyo in 1992. This refinery had fallen into the hands of the rebel UNITA forces and EO were hired to turn them out and regain the plant intact; this task was completed early in 1993. The operation enhanced EO's reputation locally and encouraged the MPLA government of Angola to hire their services for the war against UNITA.

According to MPLA ministers, the company was hired to provide security advisers to protect vital industrial and military installations, but EO personnel also took part in the Angola fighting; the EO share of the later Angolan war effort was substantial and effective, not least in the provision of training and support. Some 500 EO personnel were engaged to train recruits to the Angolan Armed Forces (FAA) and some of these men were also able to advise and direct security sweeps and took part in operations. Rigorous training turned FAA's 16th Battalion into an effective, hard-fighting force, while EO also supplied aircrew, who flew Angolan Air Force combat aircraft, and Special Force soldiers, who conducted commando operations against UNITA's command centres.

Fundamentally, EO provided FAA with the military expertise that their army lacked. Apart from providing discipline and basic infantry tactics, the army was trained in night fighting and the use of explosives and provided with expertise in electronic warfare and air-assault operations. This gave the FAA a distinct edge over UNITA, which was forced out of its bases in the north-west of the country and cut off from supplies of food and ammunition.

By August 1994, rebel-controlled territory had decreased from 60 to 40 per cent of the country. Such FAA successes were largely credited to EO and the company was thanked for playing a significant part in forcing UNITA to the negotiating table, a step which resulted in the signing of the Lusaka Peace Accords in November 1994 – a highly satisfactory outcome for all concerned.

The company then became involved in a not-dissimilar situation in the West African state of Sierra Leone, where the government had been engaged in a relentless war with the rebel Revolutionary United Front (RUF) since 1991. Thousands of people had been killed, and tens of thousands wounded or injured. Almost five million people were living in refugee camps where disease and privation were killing them in large numbers. No help arrived from friendly countries or the UN, and by 1995 the National Provisional Ruling Council (NPRC) – the government – was under heavy pressure from the rebel forces, the country was in a state of anarchy and the government's authority had all but vanished. Driven to desperation, they contacted EO.

Having cut its teeth in Angola, EO made an appreciation and then moved fast. Some 160 operatives were deployed in-country, to reorganise and retrain the Sierra Leone Military Forces (RSLMF), and before long the company began to get results. The methods used in Angola paid off here, for apart from basic military training the company also provided instruction in counter-insurgency tactics which proved highly effective against the ill-trained RUF fighters. As a result, the RUF guerrillas were quickly driven from the capital, Freetown, and other population centres were regained by government forces.

After a series of defeats, the RUF rebels were forced to take part in talks that led to the November 1996 peace agreement, an agreement that enabled Sierra Leone to hold its first free elections in twenty-nine years. It cannot be denied, therefore, that EO made a direct contribution to the return of peace and stability and achieved a result that had eluded other means for nearly three decades. President Ahmed Tejan Kabbah, Sierra Leone's first democratically elected president in three decades, declared in 1996 that EO 'did a positive job . . . protection by other means. We didn't consider them as mercenaries but as people bringing in some sanity.'

Another comment comes from a UN source. General Ian Douglas, a Canadian negotiator for the UN, referring to his time in Angola, said, 'EO gave us stability. In a perfect world we wouldn't need an organisation like EO, but I would be loath to say that they have to go just because they are mercenaries.' EO would probably deny that they were mercenaries, but otherwise the praise is well earned.

Personnel protection and the guarding of plants are usually non-controversial; it is the military aspect of PMC activity that attracts attention. I consider that EO did a good job in both Angola and Sierra Leone. They defined a new kind of specialised military company, something quite unlike the groups of mercenary desperadoes led by Denard and 'Callan', groups with which they are all too often incorrectly compared. It cannot be denied that EO's activities in Angola and Sierra Leone made a significant contribution to peace and security by supplying the legitimate armed forces with the means and skills to mount effective military operations in a way that had previously been lacking. The argument that PMC involvement only exacerbates internal conflicts and leads to a continuation of the struggle is refuted by what EO achieved in Angola and Sierra Leone.

It is often alleged that PMCs seek to continue the conflict in order to line their own pockets and that, once in a country, they cannot be forced to leave. This allegation cannot be substantiated because it simply is not true. PMC work is limited by contract; once the contract has been completed – or if it is terminated by the client – the companies withdraw. They cannot be drawn into an ongoing commitment unless a further contract is offered – and if the client government wishes them to leave, they could simply ask them to do so under the terms of the contract. The importance of working to a contract is fundamental to the activities of PMCs.

If EO was the market leader until 1998, a number of other PMCs have been hired to assist the elected governments of countries outside Africa in the prosecution of anti-terrorist operations. In the Far East, the government of Sri Lanka, which has been engaged in a vicious war with the Tamil separatists in the north of the island for over a decade, engaged the British PMC Keenie Meanie Services (KMS) to train and direct government forces operating against Tamil separatists. This is an example of hiring specialist help, for KMS specialise in counter-terrorist and counter-insurgency training.

Some time in 1995, at the height of the Balkan troubles, another PMC, an American company called Military Professional Resources Inc. (MPRI), was hired by the Croatian government to train their army for a counter-offensive against Serb forces in Bosnia. Thanks to MPRI's expertise, the Croats were able to hang on to their remaining territory and contribute to the Dayton Peace Accord.

KMS's active participation in the Sri Lanka fighting did nothing to end the conflict. Ending a civil war is a matter that lies far outside the limited brief offered by most PMCs. Civil wars require political will as well as military solutions. Using the military option is only justified if it contributes to a political end and brings the warring parties to the conference table. Solving the underlying situation is fundamental to a PMC brief, and among the first questions wise PMC directors will ask – of each other as well as of the potential clients – is 'What are we getting into here?'. If what they are getting into does not improve the situation and cannot be seen as a clear step to that end, they would probably be well advised to stay out of it, if only in the long-term interests of their company.

EO's operations took place against the background of the chronic instability prevailing in Africa, especially in the so-called 'failed states', that increasing number of places where the UN and the major players in the Western world are now unwilling to get involved. This is regrettable, for nothing can be done to improve the lot of the African people until civil war and political corruption are ended and security and economic stability are restored. Only then can democracy be established in Africa and inward investment and foreign loans and all the benefits that flow from such activity be attracted. PMCs have demonstrated that it is possible to deploy professional, well-led and well-trained troops in a way that can make a real difference to the prospect of peace and stability. Consequently, the sub-Saharan African states will continue to be a market for PMCs until the UN and the international community recovers its nerve.

The outlook for further PMC involvement in sub-Saharan Africa looks promising, a fact which pleases me professionally even if it saddens me personally. The market for PMCs is stimulated by the failure of the world community to regulate international security and introduce that 'New World Order' which President George Bush suggested had arrived after Saddam Hussein was soundly defeated in the Gulf War of 1990–91. But in 1999, eight years after the end of the Gulf War, Saddam Hussein is still in power, and flaunting that fact in the face of world opinion.

Other dictators, in Africa, Asia and the Balkans, are equally intransigent and there is no sign that the UN or the other world leaders have the will to take them on, or any idea of how to do so in practical terms, combining ground forces with air power to achieve a quick and favourable result, even supposing the popular support from the public and the media were there to urge them into action.

There is, however, a constraint on PMC activity and, as I have said already, it is one which may inhibit the use of PMCs in the future – governmental interference. I have no quarrel with regulation, but any company, particularly one trading in the international market, has to know where it stands – and where it stands must not be on constantly shifting ground. At the moment, as the Sandline – or Arms to Africa – Affair demonstrated so clearly, the ground we are on is shifting not only between governments but between national governments and the UN, and even between government departments, where it seems that not only does the right hand not know what the left hand is doing, it will also move heaven and earth – and employ the lawyers – to stop the other hand from finding out.

In such a 'Court of the Borgias' atmosphere, where do the PMCs stand and how can they plan their future operations? At the very least we need to know what the rules are, but in the absence of that information it is only sensible to speculate on how the governmental-PMC relationship will develop. Governments hate private initiatives in what they deem to be governmental affairs. It sometimes appears that they would rather see chaos reign, economies destroyed and people die in huge numbers than see a private company come in and sort the matter out – even when the PMC has been invited in by the host government, which is surely entitled to make its own decisions and employ whomever it likes.

A typical governmental attitude seems to be, 'If we cannot do it, or do not want to do it, or cannot get the UN to do it, then we don't want it done at all. We will do a bit of hand-wringing and pass a few resolutions and impose sanctions and maybe send in a bit of aid, but that's it – and if anyone intervenes privately, and meddles in matters we regard as our domain, we will put them in jail.'

It may not be that easy. While these chaotic civil-war situations exist, the demand for the services of private military companies will continue – nature famously abhors a vacuum. With EO now closed, other PMC organisations may compete for the position of market leader. I may be overstating the decline of the UN and the Western powers in the security arena, but I have seen them at work in Bosnia and elsewhere. While the people on the ground are magnificent, the results have been frankly disappointing. There is wide potential for more PMC activity and more PMCs will enter the marketplace. My guess is that governments will not turn a blind eye and, rather more likely, will begin to interfere.

Success does not always breed success. In attracting praise from the countries they served, and by achieving results after years of failure, EO created a high level of 'concern' at both national and international level. This 'concern' centred on the issue of EO's 'lack of accountability' and the 'long-term impact' of their activities on the countries they worked in. These terms are little more than meaningless diplomatic waffle. Who are PMCs to be accountable to, other than their employers and the law of armed conflict? And as for the long-term effect of their activities, that can be limited by contract.

This so-called 'lack of accountability' seems to pose serious problems for some of our higher-minded politicians, although they want to have it both ways. On the one hand, PMC involvement in civil wars or low-intensity conflicts reduces the need for official intervention, and they are happy about that. On the other hand, they lose out on the chance to appear 'decisive' and 'caring' and fret that the responsibility will be on them if a PMC operation goes awry. They can, of course, do what governments usually do in such cases, even when they are directly involved. If it works, hog the credit; if it fails, plead innocence and pass the buck.

Governments can take comfort from the fact that ethical PMCs only work for legitimate governments. Clearly, given the human-rights record of some 'legitimate governments', this could still mean there is wide scope for error. Another part of the Sandline ethos is that we only work for the 'good guys', and we stick to that principle. Had Sandline existed during the Second World War, for example, we would have worked for the French Resistance, the Maquis, but not for the *de facto* Vichy government of Marshal Pétain, which worked closely with the Nazis. PMCs might end up working for international villains; however, such people have not yet been supported by any legitimate PMC – and the Serb mercenaries employed by Mobutu were not PMC employees. Furthermore, any such government should be the subject of a UN embargo, which would curtail or cut off the supply of PMC assistance. These basic provisions affect all business concerns trading in the international market and there is no clear reason why PMCs should be treated any differently.

International 'concern' – a euphemism for government interference – was reflected in EO's decision to withdraw from Angola in January 1996, which was brought about as a result of political pressure from Washington, who wished to see a US PMC – MPRI – provide services there. PMCs do not operate in a political vacuum, and international 'concern' may be strong enough to delay or even terminate an otherwise successful operation. As far as EO is concerned, this 'concern' may have led the South African government to pass the Regulation of Foreign Military Assistance Act, which, if enforced and extended elsewhere, represents a potential challenge to all PMCs and may have contributed to EO's decision to close.

This Regulation Act clearly reflects a popular governmental view: that security issues should be subordinated to politically accountable decision-making. We can agree with the principle, but to whose political decisions – those of the national government concerned, or those of some outside government which will not otherwise get involved? Perhaps these governments are anxious to suppress PMCs because the PMCs, by succeeding where they have failed, make them look bad before the electorate.

Fortunately, realism is making some headway. There now exists a willingness in at least some foreign-policy departments to accept the fact that well-run PMCs have their uses. This view was influenced by the fact that when the Sandline Affair broke cover in the UK, the majority of the political media were solid in their support of what Sandline International had done and were still doing.

Financial motives may not be better than political ones but they are not necessarily worse. While a PMC remains motivated by profit, those in control have to devote their time to their first duty, which is to their clients only. Of course, even though a PMC is a private company, its services cannot come cheap – sophisticated hardware and skilled personnel cost money – but the costs are in relation to the services provided and the results obtained. It has been alleged that in recent years the government of Sierra Leone paid sums amounting to some 25 per cent of its Gross National Product for PMC services. They may have spent a considerable amount, but the amount was approved by the International Monetary Fund; presumably the government of Sierra Leone and the IMF thought it was worth it.

There are some concerns over the sordid subject of money. It clearly depends on the individual point of view, but of all the motivations involved in international affairs I would argue that the profit motive is not usually the most sordid. I would go further and argue that the profit motive provides security for both the nation state and the international community.

Yes, an operation may be cancelled if we feel that the client is about to renege on the deal, but that is just good business practice. On the other hand there is no evidence, as some allege, that a contract may act as an incentive to prolong violence and justify a PMC's presence. Quite the contrary; our contractual terms are clearly defined – and if we do a bad job our reputation suffers, so we have every incentive to get on with the job and fulfil our part of the bargain. There is no evidence to support this allegation, and plenty to show that the successful completion of one job leads to another one, often from the same client government.

More and more people can see the potential for PMC activity. An article in *The Economist* in January 1999 posed a question that the powers that be have yet to answer: 'Is what these companies do so bad? Most of them draw a moral distinction between protecting people for profit and attacking them. Most mercenaries protect oil wells and embassies and fight battles only as a last resort.' A review of *Privatising War* by Mike Dewar points out, 'By and large these companies are run by experienced and capable ex-military men. Rather than label them as mercenary organisations, there is a need to engage with them. This would be the first step to controlling and regulating them. After all, there is no doubt that Sandline and the others could well prove useful to the UK and other Western governments.' The argument over PMCs is by no means only between the people running such companies and high-minded people in government and diplomatic circles; there are plenty of people who believe that in the current state of world affairs, PMCs have a useful part to play.

When considering these issues and allegations, it is important to remember that PMCs exist and function because a demand for their skills has been created by the international community's failure to meet the demands for assistance coming from many Third World states. It may well be that the issue of 'accountability' will have to be addressed and a code of conduct drawn up to enforce agreed standards, but some credit should be given to the PMCs in the meanwhile. Surely they have helped some 'failed states' by restoring, if only on a temporary basis, the fundamental necessities of peace and security? PMCs can deliver the necessary elements for a political settlement and subsequent restoration of the national economy, and if no one else can do it, why should their efforts be impeded?

It could also be argued that PMC action might offer the basis for the risk-reduced introduction of UN peace-keeping personnel who could then continue the work started by the PMCs. This process would offer some political leaders that element of UN involvement without which they become unhappy and uncertain. One might even go further and invite their governments to take over the task begun and carry it on with their own forces now that the risk of conflict and loss of life has been reduced by PMC action. If they were willing to do so, the success of our actions in places like Sierra Leone would be enhanced and the cost of establishing a new, functioning democracy as a basis for economic recon-struction could be greatly reduced – and the process speeded up at the same time.

If international governments continue to stay on the sidelines and remain reluctant to deploy regular professional forces on the ground in these places, how are such issues ever to be resolved? If they are not resolved, all the terrors – from tribal massacres to mass starvation and ethnic cleansing – will continue. Moreover, even if these governments find the resolve, they have so reduced their armed forces that they have difficulty finding the men, the kit or the money for long-term deployment. So nothing can be done on practical or economic grounds either. Is this what people want?

If this is what people want then the television companies should stop beaming horrors into our homes, presenting the electorate with problems their governments have no intention of solving, and government ministers can spare us their well-honed expressions of regret and their empty promises of action. The situation in many Third World countries is far too serious for soundbites.

If the UN, and the international community as a whole, continues to ignore its oft-vaunted responsibilities for solving or stemming civil wars and racial bloodbaths, it is hard to see where the involvement of PMCs like Sandline International or Executive Outcomes can do anything other than good. At the very least they should be allowed the chance to try. If we fail, blame us and point out our errors, but if the UN and the nation state armies still remain conspicuous by their absence in the trouble spots of the world, we should be allowed to ply our military trade and sell our expertise.

Any PMC must adhere to the law of armed conflict, as defined by the Geneva Convention, and show a respect for human dignity and human rights. Although our operatives are always enlisted in the forces of the governments who employ us, not least to ensure a clear chain of command, if one of our people were told, for example, to attack a village, an action which would unnecessarily endanger innocent lives, he would not do it. Such actions are outside the Sandline mandate and we will not permit them – and we would discourage our host government from such a course of action as well.

It has been suggested, most recently during the House of Commons Foreign Affairs Select Committee report on the Sandline Affair, that the law should restrict and codify the actions of PMCs. I am certainly not against the principle behind this notion, but who is to administer the law and what are the rules to be? The suggestion that a PMC should obtain permission for every job it undertakes and file a precise detail of its operational plan for approval by, say, the UN sounds a good idea in theory, but it would be quite impractical, if only on the grounds of speed and security.

Nor does there seem to be any great interest in regulating PMCs. In March 1998 Sandline International submitted proposals on how PMCs might be regulated to both the Under Secretary-General for Human Rights and the Under Secretary-General for Peacekeeping at the UN; copies of our proposals were also sent to the UK government. At the time of writing, more than a year later, we have had neither an acknowledgement nor a reply from any of these people.

In default of some official interest, Sandline is prepared to set up an Oversight Committee, a kind of non-executive board of directors, to examine client requests and check on the conduct of our operations. This committee would contain a number of senior and respected individuals from the diplomatic world, the military, the law and the media. Representatives from humanitarian organisations and relief agencies could also be among the members.

A first step towards regulation must be the setting up of a list of PMCs, a register. Were such a register to exist, it would have to be monitored and PMCs would have to subject themselves to a procedural audit process whereby the registration body – and this should perhaps be a UN function – conducts an evaluation of the company's compliance with a predetermined set of internationally defined and accepted operating practices and also examines the quality of the PMC's internal procedures, rather as the Legg Committee investigated Foreign Office procedures after the Sierra Leone débâcle. Such a process can be designed to be wide-ranging and rigorous. It can also be repeated at regular intervals to ensure that a snapshot assessment of compliance is maintained over time. The output would be a certificate issued by the registration body which the PMC could present to prospective clients as a demonstration of the acceptability of the company's underlying ethos and business practices.

The concept is an extension to registration and the audit should lead to inclusion of the PMC on a list of 'approved companies' maintained by the regulating authority. The authority would have the right to remove, suspend or fine a particular PMC if there was evidence to prove that the company had breached its now certified operating obligations and governing code. Bearing in mind the problems Sandline has had with the British government over Sierra Leone, this notion has a definite appeal, but it might even go further and include project authorisation. Prior to a PMC accepting an assignment, it would have to apply to the regulating authority for permission, setting out basic project details, a justification for its involvement and a statement of the parameters within which it would work. Again, given our experiences during the Sandline Affair, this notion has its attractions, but two issues need to be considered here: secrecy and speed.

The regulatory authority (the UN? national governments?) must be willing to undertake this work within the confines of accepted security measures, so that the intended mission is not compromised. This is simple common sense, for if, for example, a rebel or terrorist organisation were to find out about the possible involvement of a PMC, security would be gone and lives would be at risk – and the lives of our operatives must not be at risk. Secondly, PMCs, by their very nature, are able to deploy very rapidly, and that ability must not be compromised by bureaucratic delays.

The possibility that mercenary activity might be officially recognised was first raised in the 1960s and has been again in the decades since but it has not met with much sympathy from the UN or in the OAU – which, in spite of the fact that many members hire mercenaries, still maintains a rooted objection to their employment.

In 1997, for example, the US Defence Intelligence Agency (DIA) organised a conference entitled 'The Privatisation of Security in Sub-Saharan Africa'. The conference was attended by officials from the State Department, the Pentagon, the intelligence community and Organisation of African Unity (OAU), as well as representatives from several African states, large oil companies and private security organisations and PMCs, including Sandline, Executive Outcomes and the American company MPRI. In their post-conference report the organisers declared, 'The market for private, foreign forces will continue in Africa in an attempt to meet a perceived security void. The challenge is to make private forces effective, efficient and loyal to their clients.'

The conference pointed out that a number of international businesses and Third World states recognise that intervention by PMCs in African security situations is inevitable unless and until the African nations can guarantee such security themselves. The African states clearly recognise this for, unlike in the 1970s, when the Angolan government shot 'Callan' and his cohorts, there is no longer any clear consensus against 'mercenaries' – and Angola employed EO to protect their strategic assets and train their troops.

As a matter of declared policy, though, the OAU still maintains, 'The difficulty of controlling the operations of mercenary organisations leads to the possibility that they might be willing to offer their services to illegitimate causes. This would lead to a conflict of interests between the objectives of the international community to control 'rogue states' and the need for private security organisations to make a profit. The fact is that, at the moment, there is no clear, international consensus on the possibility of recognising and controlling organised mercenary activity, even in its new guise.'

The objective observer is driven to the conclusion reached earlier in this chapter, that the real objection to the use of PMCs by governments, and the eagerness of their critics to call them 'mercenaries' and tar them with a dubious reputation, arises from a deep-seated, official fear of any private involvement in what they feel should be a governmental responsibility. Those who are facing a situation where military expertise is needed and people are dying because of the lack of it cannot afford to be so high-minded, or so careful to preserve the official status quo. This brings me back to the quote which opens this chapter; circumstances alter cases, and armies – and politicians – must respond to the realities of the situation and seek solutions, rather than go on banging their heads against a brick wall.

Flexibility is called for. Victory will be gained by acting in accordance with the actions of the enemy and not, alas, by relying exclusively and continually on methods that have been tried and found wanting. The Sandline Affair of 1998–99 brought much of this into the open. I will not deny that the issues of transparency and accountability need to be addressed, but at least the bulk of the problem has been aired in this chapter and will, I hope, be fully understood by anyone interested in contributing to the issue.

We have now looked at the basis of Sandline and what it attempts to do, covered the history of mercenary warfare and, in this chapter, outlined the current state of play regarding the modern manifestation of private military companies. Having come this far, it is now time to go back to the reasons why I became involved in this business. To do that I need to cover my own military career and follow the path it took me, from the streets of West Belfast to the heights of Tumbledown in the Falklands War.

FOUR

STARTING TO SOLDIER

*'Know your enemy, know yourself, and you can fight a hundred battles
without disaster.'*

SUN TZU, *THE ART OF WAR*

I was born in the Queen Elizabeth Military Hospital in Aldershot – 'The home
of the British Army' – in 1952, so it is fair to say that I was born into the army.
My father was a military man, commissioned into the Dorset Regiment, though
he had really wanted to enter the Royal Navy. Poor eyesight had prevented a
naval career, however, and he instead entered the army, but he always loved the
sea and sailing, and our family photograph albums are full of reminders of
yachting holidays and times spent at sea.

During the Second World War my father volunteered for service in the Far
East, but the Indian Army was very short of officers after the early disasters in
Burma and the retreat through Manipur and he was hauled off the troopship in
Bombay and despatched to join the Royal Indian Army Service Corps (RIASC).
This did not please him at the time but he was luckier than he knew. The
troopship carried on to Singapore, arriving there only hours before the surrender,
and the men on board marched ashore and almost directly into harsh Japanese
captivity, which a large number of them did not survive.

Meanwhile, my father was making his way to the North-West Frontier of
India, where his unit of the RIASC were using mules to supply a Gurkha Brigade
on operations against the Pathan tribesmen. The Russians were said to be
probing forward from Central Asia into Afghanistan and what is now Pakistan,
so my father was able to take part in the last round of the 'Great Game', that
nineteenth-century contest between Britain and Russia for the control of India.

My mother was an adventurous lady. Before the war she had owned a motor-
racing garage and seems to have spent a lot of her time speeding about the
countryside in very fast cars and on very fast motorcycles. Her first husband,
Frank Simon, was a racing driver who joined the RAF, became a fighter pilot and
was shot down and killed later in the war. It is in his memory that my middle
name is Simon. My own father died in 1990.

I had a happy and interesting childhood, and if there is any truth in the claim that a man's future career is decided quite early on, then my childhood fascination with matters military may have been a portent of things to come. I had a large collection of toy soldiers, a fort and various items of service equipment, and since my father stayed on in the army after the war, soldiers were always around and part of my life. At this stage I was, as one might say, 'army barmy'. This pattern continued when I went to my school, Sherborne, in Dorset, a school with a long tradition of supplying officers to the army, the Royal Navy and the Royal Marines – a surprising number of Old Sherburnians served together in the Falklands War, including three in my own battalion headquarters. I joined the Royal Marine Section of the School Combined Cadet Force as soon as I arrived at Sherborne and can recall field days with the Special Boat Section (SBS) of the Royal Marines – the UK's maritime Special Force unit – at their base in Poole.

It might seem that a career in the military was stretching out before me, but it was not to turn out like that – or not yet. In 1968–9, when I was in my late teens, I rebelled. Young people tend to rebel and the 1960s – and especially 1968 – was a good year for rebelling. There were riots in London, a virtual revolution in Paris, President Johnson of the USA decided not to run again and the Viet Cong gave the US Army a real drubbing during the Tet Offensive and made it clear that the Vietnam War would go on for years – or until the USA gave up and went home.

This was a heady time to be a young man and I revelled in it, becoming a typical example of rebellious youth circa 1960s. I had long hair, wore a kaftan and, a particular treasure, had a shirt made out of a North Vietnamese flag, which went down very well at demonstrations. I was fashionably against the war in Vietnam and continued to protest when I went to spend a year in the USA.

Rebelling against everything I had been brought up to believe in did not go down well with my parents, who were amazingly tolerant and long-suffering, not least when I decided to give up education, abandoning the chance to go to Cambridge and read history. Instead, I took myself off to the USA for what would now be called my gap year. I based myself in Oklahoma City, travelled a great deal and worked when I needed money, as a waiter, a gardener, a disc jockey or at any other job that came along.

It was now 1970 and the USA was a fascinating place to live, in a state of social and political tumult. Martin Luther King and Bobby Kennedy had been murdered, tensions ran high and one had the feeling that the entire country was about to explode. One event I recall vividly was the trial of Lieutenant William Calley for his part in the My-lai Massacre in Vietnam, when a company of the American Division killed a large number of totally innocent Vietnamese civilians, including women and children.

This shocked me deeply, but I was amazed to discover that the US public at large – even those who were totally against the Vietnam War – supported Lieutenant Calley and rooted for his acquittal. I also met a large number of US Vietnam War veterans, many of them far more upset and traumatised by the cold reception they got on coming home than by any fighting they had experienced during their time in Vietnam. Looking back, this was another useful lesson: if you fight an unpopular war, the public at home, the electorate that sent you there in the first place, will not thank you for it. Far better, then, to carry the public with you – and this realisation awakened my understanding of the power of the media.

However, I cannot say that all my time in the USA was spent debating high-minded issues or puzzling over politics. I generally had a great time – until it was time to come home and address the question of what I should do for a living. During my time in the USA I had become interested in the law, so when I returned to the UK I decided to train as a lawyer. I liked the idea of the law and found it challenging and stimulating, so I enrolled at the Law Society's Guildford College of Law and began legal training.

I think I must have been confused by the 'single-stream' US system, which simply produces various kinds of lawyer rather than the two-tier, barristers-and-solicitors system that exists in Britain. As a result, I got into the wrong stream and trained as a solicitor when I suspect I would have been far more use and far happier and would have stuck with the process had I trained as a barrister. As it was, I became bored, though the law did have its lighter and more interesting moments. When I came to London to do my articles, I became involved in a fascinating fraud case my firm was handling, but most of my work was on the bread-and-butter of the solicitor's life – house conveyancing. Since this is more like working as an estate agent, I came to regard it as scarcely law at all.

To beat off the boredom, I had meanwhile joined the Territorial SAS Regiment, 21 SAS (Artists Rifles) in London. Here I made the interesting discovery that I really enjoyed soldiering and seemed to have an aptitude for it. It is debatable which comes first: did I enjoy soldiering because I was good at it, or was I good at it because I enjoyed it? In fact you have to manage both, since a lot of soldiering is instinctive and pretty uncomfortable, certainly in the place I wanted to be – up at the 'sharp end' with the fighting men, the front-line soldiers.

My father had by now retired from the army but he had a new job, working as a retired officer with a Guards Brigade in Rhine Army in Germany. When I told my parents that I had decided to give up the law and join the army, I suspect they sighed with relief. My father had certainly known for some time that the army was my natural bent and had somehow maintained a saintly silence until I discovered that fact for myself.

I wanted to join the Parachute Regiment, not least as a stepping stone to joining the SAS, but my father had many friends in the Guards and, while he had no objection to my joining the Paras, he introduced me to some Guards officers, who allowed me to join their battalion for a few days while they were on exercises in Germany. One of these officers was Captain John Kiszley of the Scots Guards, the son of our family doctor, a man who will appear frequently in this book. I liked the Scots Guards – it seemed a very decent regiment – and the upshot was that I was invited for an interview with Colonel Murray de Klee, a senior officer in the Guards Brigade and Regimental Colonel of the Scots Guards.

Colonel de Klee looked to me like a very tough old bugger; only later did I discover that he really was a very hard man indeed, and nobody's fool. He had served with the Guards Parachute Company which was with the SAS during the Borneo Confrontation in the 1960s, jumped with the Guards Parachute Company at Suez in 1956, created the Guards Squadron of the SAS and generally put himself in harm's way throughout his service career. Given all that – and my basic attitude to soldiering – it is hardly surprising that we got on well. Colonel de Klee urged me to join the Scots Guards and promised that the regiment would sponsor my application for entry to the Royal Military Academy, Sandhurst. This was too good to refuse and the upshot was that, after years of struggling against it, I finally joined the army.

Becoming an officer in the Guards is not easy. The first step is to join the Brigade Squad for two months' training at the Guards Depot as a recruit, serving with private soldiers, with no privileges of any kind. The discipline is ferocious and the training is deliberately made very hard. I got on well with my comrades, I look back on that time as valuable and I think that every officer should serve some time in the ranks. Only there can you learn, at first hand, how to value the men and what good people they are. I was now coming up to twenty-two years old and had already knocked about the world a bit, so I found some of the 'bull' harder to accept than some of the younger potential officers did, but there was nothing to do here but put your head down, keep your mouth shut and do your best. So, after passing out as a trained soldier, I was sent forward for interview at the Regular Commissions Board . . . and failed!

Failure came as a considerable shock. Failure was not an option I had ever considered and, apart from my own disappointment, I had to consider the effect on my family and on people like Colonel de Klee and my regimental sponsors, the Scots Guards. Looking back, perhaps I came across at the interview as cocky and too worldly wise – which may have been the impression I gave but was certainly not the way I felt. There was, however, a small gleam of light, because although I had been turned down, I was invited to come back and try again after a few months.

You have to learn to take these things and make the best of them, so I went back to Germany, stayed with my parents and took a German course. I was still technically in the army, so I was able to keep my military skills honed by going on exercises with various units, and I even went on an exercise with 21 SAS when they came out to Germany. One of my ideas at the time was to go to Dhofar in the Arabian Gulf and serve in the war there as a seconded officer. One of my SAS mentors, Colour-Sergeant F____, had been in Dhofar, had told me all about it and encouraged me to go there, but before anything came of that I was summoned back to the Regular Commissions Board for another interview . . . and this time I passed.

The Standard Military Course at Sandhurst, the one leading to an army commission, was then for six months. Needless to say, after that initial setback, I went to Sandhurst determined to do well and show them how wrong they had been the first time – and I did so, winning the Sword of Honour. I then did the Regular Careers Course, which took another six months, so it was a full year before I joined my regiment, the 1st Battalion, Scots Guards, at Chelsea Barracks in London.

The regiments of the Foot Guards – the Guards Division – are, first and foremost, soldiers in the British Army, taking their share of duties, as infantry battalions, wherever the British Army serves. In addition to that they are the Household Troops of the Sovereign and therefore carry out public duties in London, mounting ceremonial guards at St James's Palace, the Tower of London and Buckingham Palace, as well as taking part in ceremonial duties such as trooping the colour, the state opening of Parliament, state visits by foreign dignitaries and other state occasions. A spell on public duties amounts to a pretty full-time job, one that rotates among all the Foot Guards battalions, and that is what the 1st Battalion of the Scots Guards were doing when I joined.

I cannot say that I enjoyed public duties. The workload is unfairly shared and falls mainly on the soldiers, who have to spend long hours on guard and even longer hours cleaning their kit. It is – or certainly can be – a considerable drain on their basic military skills. We were also chronically short of soldiers at the time as the battalion was under strength and some of the officers did not pull their weight, coming in late and sloping off early. This was not what I joined the army for and, all that apart, it was also very expensive. There were a lot of dinner parties and lunch parties and other costs which really required a private income, which I did not have, and for all these reasons I took every opportunity that came my way to get away from London, do courses in various aspects of the military art and see the world.

The army is good for this sort of thing. I managed to get away for two months on a jungle warfare instructors' course in Brunei, returning in time for a little local excitement in London when the Fire Brigades went on a 'go-slow' and we were ordered to fill the fire-fighting gap manning antique 'Green Goddess' fire engines. I don't know how effective we were, but we all had a very good time.

And then, at last, came a small chance of action, when we were sent to beef up the security forces in Northern Ireland.

Like most soldiers who served in the British Army between 1969 and the Good Friday Agreement of 1998, I have done a number of tours in Northern Ireland. The background to all that and some of what happened during these tours will come later, but my initial impression of Northern Ireland and what came to be called 'low-intensity' soldiering will be recorded here.

My first visit was not on a regular, four-month Northern Ireland tour – these tours were later extended to six months – but a short opportunity, a sudden deployment to the province lasting a few weeks, and we went with minimal training. It offered, quite simply, a taster of life at the sharp end. It was thought necessary to increase the security coverage at this time as HM the Queen was intending to make a visit to the province and it was feared that the IRA would seize an opportunity to stir up trouble.

We therefore went out with just a week of pre-tour training, but fortunately we had all done some Northern Ireland training before; since Ireland was the most likely deployment at the time, everyone did it, along with a month of special training before any particular tour, the kind that is still repeated every time a battalion goes to Northern Ireland, no matter how many times they have been before. When it comes to soldiering in Northern Ireland, no one can afford to take chances.

We went out 'on attachment' to existing battalions, basically to beef up their manpower on the ground, travelling up to Liverpool and crossing to Belfast from there on a naval vessel. Those who had not been to Northern Ireland before were expecting bullets to be flying all over the place, but as we sailed up Belfast Lough it could not have been nicer. It was a beautiful day, with blue skies over soft green hills, and just for once it was not raining. On arrival, the battalion was split up into companies and the companies were sent on to units already in place and in the middle of their tours. My company was attached to the Gunners of 45 Commando Group, then based in West Belfast and having a pretty tough time.

45 Commando Group is a Royal Marine unit, normally based at Arbroath in Scotland. The core of the Group was, and is, 45 Commando, Royal Marines, a proper, green-beret Commando unit about 650 strong, trained in amphibious warfare, like all Marine Commando units. In addition to all that, 45 Commando was charged with a role in defending the NATO Northern Flank in Norway and spent four months of every year on the fringes of the Arctic Circle, getting about on skis and training in Arctic warfare. In this role they needed support from artillery, engineer and medical units – hence the 'Group' – and our hosts in West Belfast were not Marines but Commando-trained Royal Artillery men – Gunners – from 29 Commando Regiment, RA, serving in Northern Ireland in the infantry role. They made us very welcome and soon showed us the form.

Coming to Northern Ireland as a soldier is a strange experience. Northern Ireland is part of the United Kingdom – or United Kingdom of Great Britain and Northern Ireland, to give it its full title – and at first sight the link is obvious. There are the same shops, Marks and Spencer's and W.H. Smith's, the same street names, the same red letterboxes and telephone boxes; it may be a bit greener because it rains more over there, but the Six Counties of Ulster look just like the rest of the UK – at least to begin with.

The battalion disembarked at Belfast Docks, got into a convoy of trucks and headed off for our various destinations, through the suburbs and into the city. Here again was a surprise. Anyone watching the events then shown nightly on television news – rioting mobs, bomb explosions, buses on fire – would imagine that when they are not out terrorising each other, the good people of Belfast are at home, behind locked doors and hiding under the bed. Not so; Northern Ireland is extremely 'normal'. People were riding bikes, cursing the traffic, going to the shops, playing golf and taking their children to the park.

So far, so normal – but as we crossed into West Belfast, the Republican part of the city, the atmosphere changed. It was not simply the fact that our escorts, all armed, took a grip on their rifles and became alert, nor the steady rattle of stones thrown by the children that bounced off the side of the trucks, each stone accompanied by a chorus of jeers. It was not even the Irish Republican flags, the IRA symbols and heroes' portraits painted on the ends of the houses, or the Irish colours decorating the paving stones. All these helped increase the tension, but it was the air of relentless, sullen hostility seen in the faces of the people in the streets, from the youngest to the oldest passer-by, some mixture of hatred and resentment, that seemed to well out of the ground and dampen our spirits; by the time we got to our destination, we were pretty subdued. The saddest thing of all, and perhaps the most depressing, was that these people were British.

They lived under British law and took advantage, even full advantage, of all Britain had to offer in the shape of education, housing, social benefits and health provisions. There was no reason for the violence, for they could even become Irish citizens and attach the province to the Republic if enough of them wanted to and swung the necessary number of votes – and yet they hated us. Some of the soldiers had been there in the early days, but even those like me who were there for the first time could see that this was serious. The first thing I did when we got out of the trucks was to get the Guardsmen together and tell them to watch out for themselves and each other.

That first brief visit to Northern Ireland was an eye-opener. Soldiering in Northern Ireland is something better imagined than described, for it is quite unlike soldiering anywhere else. The tension is constant and staying on your toes and fully alert at all times is essential. The work itself is relentless. A soldier's day in Northern Ireland is an endless round of 'tasking' – day patrols, night patrols, guards, VCPs (vehicle control points, that is, stopping and searching cars and trucks), more guards and more patrols, day after day, night after night, with no overtime pay or weekends off – and that is when nothing in particular is going on.

During this three-week visit – it was hardly a tour – there was quite a lot going on. The IRA were trying to take over the streets and there was one gunman about, a very good sniper, who murdered a number of soldiers. I remember that on one night there was a real 'punch-up' when one of the 45 Commando Marines, Marine Bewley, was shot right through the throat. He had not done up his flak jacket to the very top, and the bullet went right into the gap and killed him. This IRA gunman was moving from place to place, firing on the soldiers, and on the same day some other IRA men threw a blast bomb or a grenade at a military police team and wounded someone else very badly.

The Marines did not like this sort of thing, not at all; one of their people had been killed and they were really up for a fight and were determined to sort the IRA out. Orders came down from Commando Headquarters telling us to 'lift all known hoods', all the IRA 'players', an action that would have caused absolute mayhem had we gone out to do it.

The Commando intended to put everyone on the streets except the guard platoon and I remember that we were detailed off to load boxes and boxes of 'baton rounds' – rubber bullets – into the back of the Land-Rovers. Everyone was carrying full magazines, lots of them, but sanity returned and the operation was called off. A lot of IRA people were 'lifted' – brought in for questioning – over the next few days, and we had three weeks of that before we were sent back home again, leaving the Marines and the Gunners to get on with it.

Soldiering in Northern Ireland is very hard work. It is good training and it did the British Army a lot of good, especially in small-unit handling and NCO training. The campaign was essentially a 'corporal's war', largely conducted at section strength – say, ten men – but more often by teams of four men. It was also character-building, not least in finding the patience needed to put up with the aggravation that comes in such a politically charged situation: the constant abuse, cat-calling and stone-throwing, to which the soldiers must not respond, as well as the ever-present risk of being shot or blown up.

For the duration of their tour the soldiers do not go out of their barracks or whatever police station they are based in unless it is on patrol, in the company of their fellow soldiers, carrying a weapon and with a bullet in the breech of their rifles. They do not go to the pub, the shops, the cinema. They used to, in the early days, until the IRA got into the habit of luring them out of safety into some dark corner and shooting them in the back of the head. As it is, any soldier who does not keep his wits about him in Northern Ireland stands a very good chance of being murdered.

Off duty, you clean your kit, clean your weapon, watch a video if you still have the energy, and sleep. Mostly you sleep, catching up on your rest before the shake on the shoulder wakes you up for the next task. Then you go out again, into those wet, dark and dangerous streets, for another round of duty.

FIVE

LEARNING TO SOLDIER:
FROM NORTHERN IRELAND TO THE
FALKLANDS WAR

'Leadership is a matter of intelligence, trustworthiness, humaneness, courage and sternness. Discipline means order, a chain of command, logistics.'

SUN TZU, *THE ART OF WAR*

After that first brief visit to Belfast, I went back to London with the battalion and we returned to the usual grind of public duties. What I needed and wanted now was more operational experience, and this arrived when, eight months after our first visit, the 1st Battalion, Scots Guards, were sent back to Northern Ireland for a four-month tour of duty.

This tour began with an intensive period of preparation for the entire battalion. This training is a superb introduction to life in Northern Ireland and what the soldiers can expect to meet on the street from the IRA and the local people. This preparation takes months and covers basic tactics, patrol drills, organisation and an update on the current state of play, both generally in the province and in the battalion's own designated operational area.

One memorable part of the training is the time spent at a special centre in Kent, where a replica Irish village has been constructed, right down to the shops, pub and social centre. This village is populated by training staff in civilian clothes and with Ulster accents, including servicewomen acting as housewives, and they give the troops a particularly hard time. The women stage riots, hurl stones, bang dustbin lids to warn the terrorists that patrols are coming in, use language their mothers would flinch at, snipe and bomb – with blanks and small charges – and generally replicate the life we would have to endure during our four-month tour of duty.

There is also a great deal of 'reading in', studying maps of the countryside and the streets, marking in the homes of the known terrorists and generally getting a grip on the current situation. Having more time to prepare this time around, I also took the opportunity to read up on the Irish question and find out exactly what we were doing there in the first place. As with everything else in that benighted country, the answer was easy to find but hard to unravel. However, since this campaign lasted almost thirty years and caused the deaths of more than three thousand people – not counting the tens of thousands injured, mutilated and beaten, and they are still being killed, kneecapped and beaten as I write this in 1999 – it seemed only right to put the problem we were facing in the streets and fields into context.

Like a lot of soldiers, I have a certain amount of sympathy for the ordinary Catholic citizens, the people who live on one of the Ulster housing estates, but none at all for the IRA thugs and murderers who prey upon them and whom they are obliged to protect. Most of the death and misery over the last thirty years has been caused by the Republican terrorist movement, the Provisional branch of the Irish Republican Army (PIRA), and a large number of British soldiers have lost their lives, or been seriously injured, in an attempt to contain the violence until the public came to their senses or their leaders got tired of the whole bloody business and worked out an acceptable compromise.

At least that is what I thought – and so another plank went down for what was to become the Sandline platform. The role of the army was to create the right political atmosphere or to hold the ring until the powers that be found an all-embracing solution to the underlying problem. This was certainly the situation in Northern Ireland, where there was no military solution to this age-old dispute. It is one of Sandline's fundamental principles that a military solution is but the first step. That solution provides the security and the circumstances from which an embattled government can resolve the underlying problem from a position of strength rather than weakness.

Serving in Northern Ireland also brought us into contact with the media, especially the foreign media, on whom a lot of the blame for the continuation of the IRA campaign can be laid. The media sometimes tend to exaggerate and distort; it is, for example, also a matter of wonder that after more than a quarter-century of conflict, large parts of the world, especially the USA, Australia and Canada, still regard Northern Ireland as a British 'colony', where the inhabitants are prevented by force from uniting with the Republic of Ireland to the south. They have also been led to believe that Ulster, or Northern Ireland, or the 'Six Counties' – three names for approximately the same tract of land – is a daily battleground where the common people are held in subjection by a British Army of Occupation, who slug it out with the local population in order to maintain British rule. The fact that the vast majority of the population, Catholic as well as Protestant, are perfectly content with British rule somehow escapes their notice.

The IRA have caused trouble in the province since the 1920s but the present round of Troubles dates back to 1969 when, after the police broke up some civil-rights marches with considerable brutality, rioting spread across the province. When it became clear that the Royal Ulster Constabulary could not contain the violence, the British Army had to be committed to the streets. In the early days, the soldiers were made very welcome, and those who served in the province between 1969 and 1971 still recall the friendly reception they received, especially in Catholic areas: smiles, cups of tea, plates of sandwiches, invitations inside the houses to watch the rioting on television. Halycon days indeed, but they did not last; the IRA moved in and relations with the troops began to sour.

The riots in the North led to disputes in the ranks of the IRA. The IRA leadership noted that civil rights had proved more effective in arousing interest in Northern Irish affairs than forty years of sporadic terrorism and they felt the time was right to join the democratic process, allowing their political arm, Sinn Fein, to stand for election and, if elected, to take seats at Stormont, the Dáil, even at Westminster on the platform of ending partition and pressing for Irish unity. Had this course been adopted, a great deal of death and misery might have been avoided.

The younger, left-wing, Marxist element of the IRA totally disagreed with their leaders. They felt that the time had come for a renewal of the 'Armed Struggle' in the North, and this dispute created a major split between the old Official IRA/Sinn Fein and the New or Provisional IRA/Sinn Fein. Most of the deaths caused by terrorism in Ireland and Britain over the last thirty years can be laid at the door of the Provisional IRA.

And so the situation was when my battalion, the 1st Battalion, Scots Guards, arrived back in Northern Ireland in the summer of 1978. The worst of the Troubles were over, or so it seemed, and the province had settled down to what Reginald Maudling, a British politician, had once called 'an acceptable level of violence', whatever that means. The IRA had established a tradition of greeting a new battalion with an incident and bidding them farewell at the end of their tour with another incident, and so it was with us. On the day we arrived in East Tyrone after a six-month training cycle, maybe eight months after our first visit, the IRA shot and killed a policeman.

I was based in Cookstown with 'C' Company, 1st Battalion, Scots Guards, and our patch included some very dangerous places: Galbally, Capa, Lough Neigh, Coalisland, hard territory where the IRA Active Service Units – ASUs – of East Tyrone were very professional and usually very active. This was a four-month tour, and it was, on the whole, pretty quiet. We had a number of incidents but nothing too serious. I had the view that if we let the opposition know right at the start we would stand no nonsense and would hit back if they started anything, they would watch their step, and so it proved. As a result we had a pretty quiet time until 14 November, almost at the end of our tour, when I got blown up by a car bomb in Cookstown.

This was a pretty memorable experience. I was the standby platoon commander, and I was in the operations room when we got a call from the RUC saying they had a suspect car bomb in Cookstown High Street. This surprised me, because unattended cars are not supposed to be left in public places like High Streets in Northern Ireland, for one very obvious reason – they might be carrying a bomb.

The RUC had had a call from someone saying that a car was parked outside Alexander's drapery shop in Cookstown High Street with its headlights on. The bomb warnings actually went to that shop and one or two others and they passed them on to the RUC, who passed them on to us a few minutes later. This was at about eleven o'clock in the morning and I immediately went down to the High Street, taking with me my signaller, Guardsman I____, who was wearing a shirt, denim trousers and bedroom slippers; he had been sound asleep when the call came in, and in that sort of situation you do not hang about to get your boots on – you go.

The street was still crowded, so the public warning had either not been given or not been grasped. Therefore the first thing we had to do was to get all the civilians off the street, just in case it was not a hoax. The RUC and several of our sections were soon on the ground and together we set about clearing the street. I have a record of the incident and I see that callsigns 33A and 33C assisted the RUC in clearing Milligan's Supermarket, and callsigns 33 (me) and 33E arrived in the main street and assisted the RUC in clearing it. While we were doing so we caught sight of the car with its lights on and all callsigns were warned of the probability of a car bomb. Guardsman I____ and I went running down the street, telling people to take cover, that this was not a joke or a hoax, and we were still doing that at 11.42 a.m., when the blue Peugeot exploded.

I was about thirty feet from the car when it went up. The bomb was a 500-pounder, a Semtex primer and a main charge of agricultural fertiliser – a powerful combination. All I can recall is a massive bang, being thrown to the ground and a great cloud of yellow dust. Guardsman I____ was blown into a doorway but I did not have a scratch – no concussion, no cuts or bruises, nothing. The car was completely destroyed but somehow the debris, the glass and flying metal, had missed us.

What they had done was put a massive amount of homemade explosive under the back seat and in the boot, with an ignition charge, probably Semtex, to set the whole thing off actually resting on the back seat. In the event, only the ignition charge exploded, but even that was enough to reduce the car to fragments. Had the main charge detonated, Guardsman I____ and I, and most of Cookstown High Street, would have been vaporised. The most amazing thing is that no one was injured.

An investigation later revealed that the car belonged to a Mr McGurk – who was none too happy about what had happened to it. Mr McGurk claimed that his car had been hijacked the previous evening, 13 November, at around 11.30 p.m. by two men in white masks, one armed with a hand-gun. He said they told him that they wanted his car and he could get it back the next day, after 1 p.m., from the car park at the Kildress Inn. He also claimed that they told him that if he reported the theft or told anyone, he would be shot.

That was the only real incident during the tour, apart from the shooting of the RUC man when we arrived. We did a lot of observation posts, watching for two brothers who were high on the wanted list, spending hours and hours out in the freezing cold without getting sight of them. Otherwise we lived in a fortified police station and were continually on operations. We worked a three-day rotation: three days on guard, three days on patrols, three days on standby and so on. I did turn and turn about with the platoon sergeant and we did 'stags' – guards – in the ops room, manning the ops desk. From there you went out on patrol, on foot or by helicopter, all over the company patch. Then you went on standby platoon, with your kit on, ready to go. There were other men at ten minutes' notice and others at half an hour's notice; half an hour's notice was pretty good, because you got a chance to catch up on your sleep.

There was no going out. We lived in a place about half the size of a football pitch, a hundred of us or more, for four months. Life on the street could lull you into a false sense of security. The towns and villages were mostly Protestant, except for little villages on the east part of East Tyrone. You saw the occasional IRA hood; Cookstown is a market town and they came in to do their shopping, so we knew who they all were. We did have another incident when the SAS shot one; he came to a weapons hide the SAS had been watching and they had him. The countryside was beautiful but, here again, you had to watch your step and remember your drills: check your movement carefully, stay spread out, stay alert. You were vulnerable all the time if you did not do that.

And then you might have to go into the Murder Triangle, at Capa, Galbally, places like that, hard Republican areas, and there things changed considerably. In there you thought you were going to be shot at or bombed or attacked all the time – and that was very good. I used to take my men in there to sharpen them up. That is one of the problems with this sort of low-intensity warfare; it is hard to keep the men on their toes, but absolutely vital to do so if they want to stay alive. You have to keep the men alert, keep them vigilant, keep them looking for the hoods and alert for those anomalies, those tiny departures from the norm that are often the only hint you get that something is up. This is quite hard work and very tiring; when you came in after a patrol you were absolutely knackered. It went in a cycle: the first month you were green but keen, and everyone was on their toes. In the second month you were on top of the job and very useful. Third month you were cocky, and that was dangerous. Fourth month you were tired, and that was very dangerous.

During my time in Northern Ireland my next job was discussed. I was now a lieutenant and they wanted to send me to another battalion as assistant adjutant – a desk flunky. I said absolutely not. Instead I was posted as an instructor to the NCOs Tactics Wing at Brecon in the Black Mountains of Wales. This is a rugged assignment and, if I could not be with a front-line unit, I could not have wished for a better posting. It was one which taught me a great deal.

Sometime in his service, every infantry NCO in the British Army and the Royal Marines has to attend the Tactics Wing at Brecon and do a battle course. There are two basic courses for NCOs at Brecon: the junior NCOs' battle course, for corporals, which teaches tactics up to the platoon level, and the platoon sergeants' battle course, which takes senior NCOs – sergeants and above – and teaches tactics up to a company level, in the context of a battalion battle. This is above the level at which sergeants are supposed to operate, but the course is based on the sensible notion that they may have to take over the company if all the officers are killed and therefore ought to know what to do if that happens.

I was sent to instruct on the platoon sergeants course, each of which lasted eight weeks and contained about fifty students. These are broken down into syndicates of twelve men, instructed by a colour-sergeant. There were about three or four courses a year and in my two years at Brecon I must have taken about three hundred students through the mill, including Sergeant McKay of 3 Para, who later won the Victoria Cross in the fight for Mount Longdon in the Falklands. Most of the students were in their twenties, with one or two in their thirties, and we worked them hard. The subjects taught included tactics, leadership, survival, field administration, kit and equipment scales, fitness, duties of a platoon commander, battle procedure and orders drills and a whole lot besides, at speed and in the harshest conditions we could contrive. The old army adage, 'More sweat, less blood' was heavily underlined at every stage and the students came out of it as well-trained and well-tested leaders.

It has been said that, just as the Battle of Waterloo was allegedly won on the playing fields of Eton, so the Falklands war was won on the wet wastes of the Sennybridge training area, Dartmoor, and the Brecon Beacons. The terrain is not dissimilar, the weather equally vile and the battle course as close to the real thing as human ingenuity could make it; there is full regard for safety, of course, but otherwise there are no holds barred. There is the bare minimum of classroom instruction, with most of the training taking place out of doors, in all weathers and a lot of it at night. I think every army in the world should have a similar institution to Brecon. It is a first-rate training establishment and of inestimable value to the British Army.

As far as I was concerned, instructing at Brecon taught me a great deal. I learned the importance of having a good ethos for your unit, of working hard on training that had a point to it, of pushing drills to the limits of safety and also of taking good care of your soldiers. All of these are things that every officer and NCO is taught, but Brecon showed how to achieve all this and still win battles.

These battle courses are not, of course, restricted to the NCOs. There is one for the officers at the Infantry School at Warminster, but the terrain there is more gentle and the instructors at Brecon were always pressing to have the officers battle course shipped up to Wales. I spent two happy years at Brecon and at the end I was second-in-command of the senior command course and an acting captain, which I considered pretty good going in four years. Brecon provided the formative years of my military thinking; before it I had been the new boy, but at Brecon I was instructing the backbone of the infantry, so I had to be pretty good myself.

Looking back, it also provided the ethos of Sandline, making the point that professional standards among soldiers – along with good training, hard training, realistic training – are absolutely vital. Training is the basis of all good soldiering, and when Sandline was formed, the thought that Brecon put into my head came back: what I needed were professionals, good soldiers with this sort of training behind them – and the training standards taught at Brecon should be the standards applicable in Sandline training contracts.

I still had a hankering for special operations and the way into that was via the SAS, so during my time at Brecon I applied to take the SAS selection course. The course is notoriously gruelling and largely consists of carrying ever-heavier rucksacks over ever-longer distances, up ever-higher mountains and at ever-greater speeds. If it rains or, better still, snows, this is considered a bonus.

The selection course was at the end of 1981, after the Iranian Embassy siege had been brought to a rapid conclusion by the SAS. As a result of all the publicity, the SAS regiment had hit the headlines and the entire army wanted to be in the SAS. The selection course was huge, with scores of applicants from every regiment and corps in the army, but I managed most of the trials and tests without trouble, completing all elements of the initial course, and therefore I thought I had passed. However, when I marched in to be told the verdict by the then commander, Lieutenant-Colonel Mike Rose, I was told that I had failed. I was tenacious enough, but too slow, so I was out. Their standards are absolute; there are no exceptions.

This was a real blow, for I had set my heart on joining the SAS. Mike Rose was very nice about it, saying I was a marginal case, and they let me down gently by letting me join their combat survival course, which I have no hesitation in calling the best course I ever went on in the army. The contents of the course are classified so I will not divulge them here, but two of the elements, how to survive capture and resistance to interrogation, came in very handy when I was in deep trouble some years later in Papua New Guinea.

So my time at Brecon was up, I had not got into the SAS, and the Scots

Guards, not unreasonably, wanted me to come back to the battalion and do some work. I therefore returned to the 2nd Battalion, but I was not there for long either, being posted away almost at once to take a course at the Junior Division of the Staff College – a step, perhaps, to higher things.

The British took their time deciding that the army needed staff training. The Duke of Wellington preferred to do all the planning himself during the Napoleonic Wars and said that whenever he was not around to do so, matters usually went awry. This had an element of truth in it, for two years after his death the British Army marched off to the Crimean War where the staff work, such as it was, was lamentable. The soldiers were not properly fed or clothed or supplied with tents, blankets or supplies; everything except courage was in short supply. The entire campaign was a total balls-up, and since the media were now on the scene, in the shape of Mr William Russell of *The Times*, something had to be done.

It took another fifty years to actually do it, but by the time the First World War broke out in August 1914, the British Army had a trained staff. Unfortunately, it was rather a small staff – only 900 Staff College-trained or staff-qualified officers (those who had held staff appointments and not actually done much harm) for the entire army – and when the army expanded there were not enough staff officers to go round. But at least the point was made and the modern British Army sets great store by proper staff work – and anyone who has ever suffered from bad staff work will appreciate why. As a result, although my personal preference was for a field appointment, I was more than willing to go to the Junior Division of the Staff College and see how the whole thing worked.

Here again, although I did not know it at the time, this training in the fundamental elements of command, control and logistics was to prove extremely useful with Sandline International when we found ourselves dealing with Third World forces where such wonders as good staff work – planning, command and control, the use of intelligence and so on – were unknown. To put their role in civilian terms, the staff are the managers of the army; if the staff are up to the mark, the army works, the soldiers are happy and victory is achieved. If not, chaos and defeat are guaranteed.

The Junior Division course is a precursor to the full Staff College course. The junior course is for captains, to prepare them for Grade 3 staff appointments, or those who will go on to serve as adjutants and operations officers with their battalions. These two, the adjutant and the operations officer, are the battalion commander's right-hand men, but they operate in different situations; the adjutant is the power behind the throne in barracks, whilst the operations officer is the commanding officer's chief aide in the field. This course lasted twelve weeks and I came out of it a fairly well-rounded military animal.

The army provides endless opportunities for people to get on, but they are not thrust upon you; you have to go after these chances, seeking out those postings and courses that appeal to you. On the other hand, it is not a good idea to spend too much time away from your regiment, seeing the world, doing courses and having fun. If you want to get on, you have to make a plan and stick to it.

My plan was to become a competent, useful and experienced soldier as quickly as possible. So far, this plan was going well. I had done Sandhurst, done regimental duty, been to Northern Ireland twice, done the platoon commanders' battle course at Warminster, was a jungle warfare instructor, had been an instructor on the platoon sergeants battle course and had done the SAS selection and combat survival courses and now the Junior Division staff course. All this in five years, and I was a captain.

I then went back to the 2nd Battalion, which was terribly under strength, as combined operations officer, training officer and support company commander, being paid as a major, which was the rate for the job – and very nice. And so, in early 1982, with a great deal of training and useful experience behind me, I went to the Falklands War.

SIX

THE FALKLANDS WAR

'Freedom is the sure possession of those who have the courage to defend it.'

PERICLES, 429 BC

On the day that Argentine forces invaded the Falkland Islands, Friday, 2 April 1982, I was Captain of the Guard at the Tower of London. This is one of the most traditional public duties for the Brigade of Guards but not one renowned for memorable events. The Tower of London is a national treasure and a popular tourist attraction but it is also a military garrison, as it has been for centuries. After the crowds have gone home the Guard continues, culminating at 10 p.m. each evening, 365 days a year, with the Ceremony of the Keys, when the yeomen warders go round the Tower, locking the gates. That apart, there is not a lot to do and the time is usually spent visiting the museums and galleries, reading, catching up on paperwork or watching television. That evening, however, was different.

When I got back to the guardroom after the traditional ritual with the keys, I discovered that all was not at all well in another part of Her Majesty's wide domain. The soldiers not on guard were all gathered around the guardroom television, watching the news, and in a high state of excitement. Something was going on in the Falkland Islands, Argentine troops had invaded British territory, the Royal Marines of the garrison were fighting back and there was a lot of shooting going on. At that time I had only a vague idea where the Falkland Islands were, or why the British forces would be involved in combat with a seemingly friendly country like Argentina.

Other even vaguer reports of Argentine scrap-metal merchants invading South Georgia and being evicted by the crew of HMS *Endurance* a few weeks before came into my mind, together with one's stereotyped view of Argentina: a military dictatorship, polo players, beautiful women, racing drivers, excellent beef and so on. It was hardly high on the list of national enemies, certainly compared with the ones I had been dealing with most recently, the IRA, and the Soviet threat. Even so, as professional soldiers, if our country was going to war, wherever it was, we in the Scots Guards wanted to be in it.

It is hard now to recapture the excitement that swept the country in the early stages of the Falklands War. I know that after we dismounted the Guard at the Tower I went home and, like everyone in Britain, spent the rest of the weekend glued to the TV screen. Britain was in ferment, there was a constant round of news bulletins giving accounts of the fighting in the islands and resolutions at the UN and, following the over-running of the island and the expulsion of the British Governor and the Royal Marine garrison, a 'task force' was formed to get the islands back. This task force was largely composed of 3 Commando Brigade, Royal Marines, and since the retaking of the Falkland Islands would clearly be an amphibious operation, for which the Royal Marines were specially trained, this was fair enough. However, when two army battalions, the 2nd and 3rd Battalions of the Parachute Regiment, were added to this mix, we began to feel that the Guards could not, and indeed should not, be left out.

On the other hand, it did not cross my mind that a battalion currently employed on public duties would get involved. As I have mentioned previously, the snag with public duties is that they take up a great deal of time and keep the battalion in central London, where the opportunities for infantry training are, to say the least, limited. In the 2nd Battalion, Scots Guards, we had, in fact, always done our best to keep up with at least the basic weapon-handling skills and the physical fitness, but we were, as usual, under strength and lacked a great deal of field equipment. Even so, within a few days rumours spread that we might be going to the South Atlantic with 5 Brigade if a second brigade was deemed necessary, though this was probably collective wishful thinking.

The Land Forces Commander in the South Atlantic campaign, Major-General Jeremy Moore, said later, 'No one can imagine the kind of pressure the Household Division can exert when they want something,' and this pressure clearly paid off when, on 5 April, two Guards battalions, the 1st Battalion, Welsh Guards, and the 2nd Battalion, Scots Guards, were tasked for the South Atlantic. Some days after the Argentine invasion I was summoned to the orderly room and told that we would probably be going and that we must get the battalion on to a war footing as quickly as possible.

I was, it will be recalled, the battalion operations officer, so getting the battalion ready to go was part of my brief. I was also the training officer and the OC of support company, and that alone was a problem, for we did not have the men or the kit to provide the support we were supposed to provide. As anti-tank weapons, for example, we had the Wombat, the 105mm anti-tank gun which was large and cumbersome and not the sort of weapon that you can manhandle across country; it had to be towed – and towing vehicles were clearly not going to make it to the Falklands. Our commanding officer, Lt-Colonel Mike Scott, was moving heaven and earth to get us the kit we needed, but it took time and at the moment we were simply not equipped to go to war. I shall have some comments to make on this state of affairs later.

I therefore wrote out a 'shopping list' of all we needed and everyone in the unit went out to find it. Items ranged from more rifle magazines to rucksacks – we were determined not to take the totally useless large pack. In the end we got them, but we had to buy them from retail stores all over London and the Home Counties, some green, some blue, all colours, whatever they had; all the colourful ones were eventually repainted green and black on the *QE2*, using up all the paint we could find in the ship's paint locker.

We also wanted more machine guns. Normally there is one per section; we wanted two per section. We had six 81mm mortars; we needed eight. We needed more sniper rifles and M79 grenade launchers; we needed Clansman radios, which were in very short supply; we needed winter clothing. We needed things we did not have and more of things we did. That a British battalion should be so short of basic military equipment was a national disgrace, and in the end we had to use our initiative.

We ordered some Milan anti-tank weapons and beefed up our company firepower by acquiring some .5 Browning heavy machine guns. Where these came from I do not know – perhaps from some long-shut warehouse in an Ordnance factory. They were no longer on general issue but we were very glad to see them. When they arrived they were still in their packing grease and wrapped in heavy brown factory paper, but we cleaned them up and boiled them out, which took two full days, and set the men to training.

We also needed more men to flesh out the ranks of the battalion, but this was a smaller problem, for rumours had spread and we were inundated with volunteers from the other Guards regiments. We took the pick of the crop: Grenadiers, Coldstreamers, Irish Guards. These battalions were also extremely helpful in lending us kit and making good our deficiencies from their own stores, where our battalion quartermaster, Euan Lawrie, was working miracles. So, with surprising speed and great enthusiasm, the Scots Guards girded themselves for war.

In that busy period there was no time to wonder why a battalion of the Guards was so short of men and equipment that we were reduced to scrounging what we needed from other parts of the army. The short answer is that the services are kept chronically short of cash and are the subject of endless 'Defence Reviews', which is a popular political euphemism for yet another exercise in making bricks without straw. These reviews always say that the 'teeth' arms will not be affected; the 'cuts', when they are eventually owned up to, are only supposed to remove excess 'fat' and reduce the logistical 'tail'.

This is, of course, claptrap. After endless Defence Reviews, there is precious little fat left to remove, and if the logistical tail is continually reduced, eventually the army cannot function; it does not have the kit or the competence to maintain troops in the field. This fact, so savagely brought home to us in April 1982, taught the government nothing. When the British Army was ordered to send a force to fight in the Gulf War of 1990–91, it was necessary to cannibalise all the tanks in Rhine Army to get one small armoured division – just two brigades – in a suitable state to fight the Iraqis.

As a nation, we simply cannot go on like this. These *ad hoc*, make-it-up-as-you-go-along methods are tolerated because, with a lot of sweat from the soldiers, we have so far managed to go to war and pull off a victory, at least against Argentine conscripts and Saddam Hussein's reluctant warriors. One day, however, if the British government persists in sending its ill-equipped, under-strength army into action, we shall meet a foe who actually knows how to fight and is properly equipped . . . and then it might be too late.

Our participation was still in the speculative stage but at some point in these proceedings I accompanied the CO and the battalion second-in-command to Aldershot and met the commander of 5 Brigade, Brigadier Tony Wilson, MC. This seemed to be a secret meeting. We had to wear plain clothes, tell no one where we were going and travel down in unmarked cars. When we got there we met the battalion commanders of the units currently in 5 Brigade, including Lt-Colonel 'H' Jones of 2 Para. 3 Para had already gone, so we were to replace them.

The commander of 3 Commando Brigade, Brigadier Julian Thompson, had told the powers that be that since the Argentines now had upwards of 10,000 men on the islands, he thought he would need a bit more muscle than the Commando Brigade had on its own if he was to land in the Falklands and boot the Argentine invaders back into the sea. When asked how many battalions the Commando Brigade's logistical element could support he said five, and he was given first 3 Para and later on 2 Para to augment his strength. These two units, with the 7th Gurkha Rifles, currently made up 5 Brigade, which was based at Aldershot. The idea was that when these parachute battalions went off to join Brigadier Thompson on Ascension Island, from where they would sail south to retake the Falklands, Tony Wilson's brigade would be given battalions of the Scots and Welsh Guards and follow 3 Commando Brigade south, if required. This meeting at Aldershot was to clear the air and agree details of the handover and integration of these Guards battalions into 5 Brigade.

This was the first time I had met Brigadier Wilson and 'H' Jones, who struck me as a typical Parachute Regiment officer – enthusiastic, full of ideas, a highly professional soldier, impulsive, clearly not inclined to suffer fools gladly, the sort of man who would have made a good brigade commander. That thought may have been in his mind as well, for there was a certain air of impatience in the way he spoke to Brigadier Wilson. I met Hew Pike of 3 Para some time later. He was very different, quiet and thoughtful, and a very capable officer; his unit had already gone to join the Commando Brigade, while Jones's unit was still awaiting the order to go. Jones clearly wanted to get back to his unit, get his men committed and head south towards the action.

In due course the 2nd Battalion, Scots Guards, and the 1st Battalion, Welsh Guards, became part of Wilson's 5 Brigade. We needed field training and a chance to work together as a brigade and get to know each other, but before we did that there was a lot more slaving to do back at battalion headquarters. Some of the battalion officers must be mentioned at this point. The CO, Lt-Colonel Mike Scott, was a tower of strength, with the wit and wisdom to listen to his officers. Then there was Major Iain McKay-Dick, the second-in-command; John Kiszley, the senior company commander, who was very tough and very experienced; and the HQ company commander, Richard Bethell, a very experienced officer. One of the debates we were having was over what we should do with a man of his background and experience, and he was marking time before his next posting.

Richard Bethell was wasted running HQ company, which, though vital, is largely concerned with logistical support and communications; an officer like Richard should have had a rifle company. I recall having a long talk about this with the CO, who decided, rightly, that it would be unfair to the present company commanders and bad for morale if one of them were replaced simply to find Richard a job. This was so, but Richard was too good to lose and our solution was to put him in charge of forming and training the recce platoon, the ideal place for his well-honed SAS skills.

The kit and volunteers were starting to arrive and the men were being slotted into their companies and learning the basic drills, but we still had to get the battalion organisation on a war footing. Civilians should know that an infantry battalion in 1982 numbered about 650 men, mustered in three rifle companies, a support company and a headquarters company. Since we had been on public duties and were under strength anyway, we did not have a recce platoon, one of the main components of a support company.

So, gradually, we got ready. One of the things we lacked was a set of standard operating procedures (SOPs), a basic set of instructions covering all the standard routines for working in the field in war. Fortunately, my time on the junior staff course came in handy here, but it took a lot of evening and weekend work to get these discussed, agreed, written up, circulated and understood. In the meantime we went up to Sennybridge in Wales for some hard brigade training.

Going to war certainly concentrates the mind and opens the training coffers. We were given everything we asked for: full ammunition scales, all the range facilities and a team of outside umpires so that the brigade officers, instead of umpiring their colleagues, could do their own jobs and get their various acts together. We attempted to make the exercises, which went from platoon and company right up to the full brigade level, as realistic as possible, with bags of support weapons and live firing.

All this culminated in a full brigade exercise, an 'advance to contact' in ideal conditions – bleak, undulating country, pouring with rain, freezing cold – which put everyone from the brigadier down through their paces under the steely eye of the chief umpire, Brigadier Bernard Gordon Lennox of the Grenadier Guards, who went on to be a general and whose post-exercise debrief flayed the skin off some of the officers, which was pretty uncomfortable but right on the mark. There was also the traditional snag, which, though it never led to anything, is still interesting in illustrating how the regular army thinks. Our brigade contained two Guards battalions, and there is a rule in the British Army that this should have made us a Guards brigade and required the appointment of a brigadier from the Brigade of Guards. As I say, nothing came of this, but there was a murmuring in the Guardee dovecotes as we packed and repacked our kit to leave Sennybridge and go to war.

It had now been decided that we were going to the Falkland Islands but it had not yet been decided what we would do when we got there. 3 Commando Brigade would go ashore and seize a bridgehead, and it seemed to be assumed that when we arrived we would take over the bridgehead and hold it while Brigadier Thompson and his merry men went on to Stanley and won the war. We were not too happy about this, for we wanted a more active role, but meantime we had a quick spot of leave, a long weekend for everyone, before, on Wednesday, 12 May, we went to Southampton and boarded the *QE2*. Incidentally, just before we sailed, I was quietly informed that I had passed the entrance examination for the Staff College, so I went on board in good spirits and determined to come back.

If you have to go to war, you should try to get there on a luxury liner. One young officer said later that it was a ridiculous way to go to war, but I rather liked it. The entire brigade, plus Major-General Jeremy Moore's headquarters, were crammed on to the *QE2*, some 5,000 men in all, but the crew were kindness itself, the wine cellar offered a wide choice of vintages, a band played in the evenings and, at least as far as Ascension Island, we all had a wonderful time.

We worked hard, of course. There were maps to pore over and meetings to hold and the training round continued. The wooden decks began to splinter as platoons of heavily equipped soldiers pounded round and round, trying to stay fit; and after dark the men crept about practising night movement. I recall a platoon of Gurkhas practising night movement in daylight, all of them wearing blindfolds and going around in a conga, holding on to each other. We also did a lot of first-aid training and everyone had the chance to fire the 84mm Carl Gustav anti-tank weapon and the smaller and lighter 66mm. Some of this training was done wearing Arctic mittens, which felt a bit strange when we were crossing the equator.

As operations officer, my task was to do the planning, so I was kept busy working out what we might be asked to do and the best way to do it, but there was still time to find out exactly what the British were doing in the Falklands and what this war we were going to was all about.

The basic reason is that the Falkland Islands are a British Crown Colony but the government and people of Argentina think they belong to them and want them back. Since the population of the island is only 1,800 people, all British and mostly sheep farmers, this seems a strange thing to go to war over, especially at the end of the twentieth century. Indeed, the Argentine writer Borges described these two much-reduced nations battling out the Falklands War as 'like two bald men fighting over a comb', since the basic issue was not worth men's lives – but there turned out to be more to it than that.

To get to the bottom of the situation, I had to go back a bit. The Spanish–American Empire fell apart in the early years of the nineteenth century, when most of the Latin-American countries gained their independence. Argentina claimed all the Spanish colonial territories in her area, including a group of islands, 600 kilometres from the mainland, known to the Spanish as las Islas Malvinas and to the British as the Falkland Islands.

The British claim dates back to 1690, when the islands were visited by Captain John Strong of the Royal Navy, who named them the Falkland Islands after Viscount Falkland, the Secretary of the Navy. The next significant group of visitors were Breton whalers from St Malo; the inhabitants of St Malo are known as the Malouins, and the Argentine name, Malvinas, is a corruption of this Breton word. To stop further incursions, the Spanish established a small garrison at what is now Stanley.

Over the next century the islands were visited by seamen from Spain, France and Britain but the next step towards the Falklands War of 1982 was taken in 1811, after Argentina gained its independence and the Spanish garrison withdrew. The Argentines did not occupy the islands until 1826 and these troops were kicked out in 1831 by the United States because they had interfered with American whaling ships. The Argentines came back in 1832 but in 1833 the British frigate HMS *Clio* arrived, sent the Argentines packing, revived John Strong's claim of 1690, hoisted the Union Flag and declared that the islands were British. The British claim to these inhospitable, windswept islands therefore dates back at least to 1833, almost 150 years before the Argentine Army invaded in 1982.

It is hard to see why the Argentine people are so obsessed with the Malvinas issue and so keen to get the islands back. Perhaps there is no reason. Perhaps it is simply part of the national character, that these islands were part of their historical inheritance and they intend to possess them. That too is strange, as most of the Argentine population are not Spanish by origin; over 80 per cent are Italian. Indeed, there is a Latin-American joke that an Argentine is 'an Italian who speaks Spanish, lives in Latin America . . . and wants to be an Englishman'.

The motives of the junta generals were not entirely high-minded and patriotic. For the previous ten years they had been conducting a 'Dirty War' – a very dirty war indeed – against liberal and social elements in the national population. This 'war' – state terrorism is a better word for it – was now so unpopular that the junta feared for the future, but the recapture of las Malvinas would be acclaimed and would swiftly restore their popularity. With all this to play for, the junta sent its ships and men to capture las Malvinas.

The British garrison, sixty Royal Marines and some of the Islands' Self-Defence Force put up a stout fight for most of the first day, 2 April, killing a number of the invaders without loss to themselves, but more and more Argentine troops came ashore and that evening the Governor of the Falkland Islands, Sir Rex Hunt, ordered the Marines to stop firing and lay down their arms.

That evening Buenos Aires went crazy. The party was still going on a few days later when the news came that the British had taken this invasion of their territory by a supposedly friendly nation most unkindly and were sending a task force, of ships and aircraft and fighting men, to take the islands back. We were now part of that task force and, given all the circumstances, I thought the task worth while.

The holiday atmosphere changed at Ascension. On the way we had diverted to Freetown – a place I was to become all too familiar with some time later – to refuel. We were not allowed ashore but when we came alongside the refuelling depot there was the famous joke of some man yelling out, '20,000 gallons of four-star and make it snappy!' I did get ashore at Ascension, where we did a certain amount of cross-decking and combat loading, shifting supplies to other vessels and getting our own supplies into the right order. Then we sailed south into the war zone, the ship moving fast and blacked out, everyone doing anti-aircraft drills . . . and suddenly it was serious.

The mood on board was, I suppose, pretty 'gung ho', helped by an endless supply of rumours – that a submarine was after us, that we were being shadowed by Russian spy ships (which we were) – and by a lot of rather tasteless jokes in *Private Eye*. 'Kill an Argie, win a Metro'. But the more serious among the soldiers were simply determined to do a good job and detested the idea that we might be stuck in at the beachhead as garrison troops. Personally, I always thought we would have to fight. The American Secretary of State, Al Haig, was shuttling about, trying to find a compromise to stop the fighting, but I knew that would not work; sooner or later I was sure we were going to go in.

By this time the war on the ground had started. The port of Gritvyken in South Georgia, which had also been taken by Argentina on 2 April, was taken back by the British on 25 April, just twenty-three days after it had been seized by an Argentine force. 3 Commando Brigade went ashore at San Carlos on 21 May, established a bridgehead fifty miles from Port Stanley, the island's capital, and were already pushing out patrols towards the centre of the islands. On 28 May, when we were at Gritvyken, trans-shipping from the *QE2* to the rather more Spartan *Canberra*, 2 Para attacked Goose Green and Lt-Colonel 'H' Jones gained a well-earned but posthumous Victoria Cross. All this reached us on the radio, the details being filled in later from messages sent back by Brigadier Julian Thompson and forwarded by the fleet. As we lacked precise information, rumours flourished.

We heard about Goose Green at Gritvyken and that night we sailed for San Carlos. It was a very rough night, almost a full gale, and it was quite a relief to get into San Carlos bay and get off the ship. In spite of the weather we had an impromptu sing-song in the ship's lounge, led by John Kiszley playing the accordion, and later on he went into the sick bay and repeated the performance for the wounded. These included a number of Argentines, who seemed to appreciate John's playing as much as we did.

We went ashore on 6 June in broad daylight, which was a bit of a surprise after the air attacks, but the Argentine jets did not arrive and we got ashore unmolested. We then moved through the area held by 40 Commando out on to the slopes of the Sussex Mountains, where we dug in – or tried to. The snag was that we struck water at about a foot down and that was that. Even so, we told the Guardsmen to keep on digging; even a foot of cover can make a difference under shell fire or air attack.

My particular problem was to put together a battalion HQ. Under normal circumstances we would have got all the battalion trucks and Land-Rovers together, under camouflage nets and in cover, and so have a place to plan and lay out the maps and house the radios and generators and so on. It is pretty hard to run a battalion lying on your belly in the wet, but needs must; we had no transport up on the hills, or tents, or any of the comforts of home, apart from the ones we could carry. Digging a big hole did not work either, as it promptly filled up with water – and the last thing we needed at the time was a swimming pool. In the end we constructed an HQ out of ponchos and groundsheets; it was not very rainproof or well concealed, but it would have to do.

Anyway, we were not there long. When you are in a battalion, the broader picture is often obscured. I had enough to do anyway, and the Brigadier never came up to tell us the form. However, it appeared that 2 Para, following their return from Goose Green, had been sent back to 5 Brigade – so each brigade now had four battalions – and had gone up to a place called Fitzroy and Bluff Cove, some thirty miles up the coast from San Carlos as the helicopter flies, and a lot further by sea. The problem was that the CO and the brigade commander had not told Major-General Jeremy Moore about this exciting *coup de main*, and General Moore suddenly found that a portion of his force was stuck out on its own, well ahead of the rest of us and in urgent need of supply and support. I would hazard a guess that Major-General Moore was not best pleased.

I later heard that 2 Para had actually pinched the helicopters and told the pilots to take them forward, which may have seemed like a good idea at the time but presented the rest of us with a problem. There was a great shortage of helicopters since a number had been lost in action and more in the sinking of the *Atlantic Conveyor*. Therefore the only way to get large numbers of troops and adequate supplies up to Fitzroy and Bluff Cove was by sea, but the sea route was a good deal further, Argentine aircraft were active and movement by sea, unescorted, was a considerable risk. The recce platoon of the Welsh Guards tried to march overland across the Sussex Mountains to join them, but they came back after a day or so, utterly shattered.

As a first step, the next day I was sent on a recce to Bluff Cove by helicopter, flown by Captain Sam Drennen, formerly of the Scots Guards, now of the Army Air Corps, in company with Lt-Colonel Johnny Ricketts, CO of the Welsh Guards, who was very anxious about his recce platoon. This was a comfort in a way, as it was now clear we were going to go up to the front and 40 Commando, to their disgust, were going to have to stay behind and guard the beaches. The flight up was tricky as there was low cloud over the Sussex Mountains and Sam stayed only a few feet off the ground, following fence lines and gulleys until we found a saddle in the mountains and crossed over to the southern side where the weather was marginally better.

At Bluff Cove Settlement we met 2 Para, then commanded by Major Chris Keeble. I also met an old Brecon hand, Colour-Sergeant Dave Fenwick, a very good man, and he told me the form. 2 Para were clearly delighted with their victory at Goose Green and their morale was first rate, but they all seemed very tired and in need of a rest. There was no bravado or exaggerated stories and my overall impression was of a tough unit whose men had matured rapidly after the events of the previous days, and I was to see the same thing happen within the ranks of my own battalion before the week was out. That recce completed, we now had to get back and brief the battalion. The flight back was a nightmare: it was snowing, visibility was down to zero, and we came back at ground level, skipping over the fences, and just made it back before we ran out of fuel.

As the only alternative was to fetch 2 Para back to San Carlos and start again, it was decided to send the rest of 5 Brigade up to join them and we duly embarked on HMS *Intrepid*, one of the big landing ships, on the night of 5/6 June. Being on *Intrepid* was quite wonderful after a week in wet trenches. We had real bread and I ate a whole loaf, which was delicious. There were hot showers, we had a drink in the bar, we got our clothes dried – it was quite marvellous. It was another terrible night, raining and stormy, and halfway up, off Lively Island, we had to get into the smaller landing craft utilities (LCUs) and go on in those, which was even worse. I had one bit of luck when, at the last moment, I decided to take my Goretex jacket. There was a bit of rapid fumbling among the kit bags we were leaving behind at San Carlos but I had it when we got into the LCUs and swiftly put it on. I won't say it saved my life, but it certainly helped. The second-in-command, Iain McKay-Dick, was in the wheelhouse with John Kiszley and Major Euan Southby-Tailyour of the Royal Marines, who was doing the navigation by radar, but I was on deck and it was terrible out there. Everyone was drenched by rain and sea spray, the landing craft was rolling over rough seas, there was a howling wind . . . it was ghastly.

We also had a particularly nasty moment when we saw a warship steering towards us in what seemed to be a distinctly hostile manner. I said to Richard Bethell, who was out on the deck with me, that if this was an Argentine warship we had had it. I recall having the men mount a general purpose machine gun (GPMG) on the rail, determined that if we were to be sunk we would at least make a fight of it, but it turned out to be one of our own frigates, HMS *Arrow*, coming back from the gunline where she had been bombarding some Argentine positions.

That was a grim moment, but the worst feature of the trip was the weather. The soldiers did not have proper waterproofs and their kit was simply not adequate for these conditions. Many of them were teetering on the edge of hypothermia by the time we got to Bluff Cove and could get them ashore; this was at about five in the morning but it was still dark and we got there about two hours late, pretty good going in the circumstances. I would like to add that the Guardsmen were magnificent – wet and chilled but full of jokes and quite undaunted. Having got ashore, we took over the positions at Bluff Cove that had been held by 2 Para, most of them sheep-shearing sheds, which did at least keep the rain off and give us a chance to dry our clothes and kit. We were still there two days later when disaster struck the Welsh Guards at Fitzroy.

This was quite early in the morning and the first thing we knew about it was when we heard the sound of jets coming in fast and low. Our first thought was 'Harriers – and where are they?'. Bluff Cove Settlement lies at the seaward end of a wide valley – and we saw two Skyhawks, Argentine Skyhawks, coming down the valley like bats out of hell. The entire battalion opened fire on them with every weapon we had: rifles, GPMGs, Brownings. Up to then the battalion had not fired a shot, but in the next two minutes we got off no fewer than 18,600 rounds of ammunition . . . and we hit one, taking off the tailplane and shooting it down.

They banked round the headland at the end of the valley, turning towards Fitzroy; seconds later we heard the sound of bombs and saw a great pall of smoke rising over the hills. That was the *Sir Galahad* with the support company of 1st Battalion, Welsh Guards, on board; they lost a lot of good people that morning.

The Fitzroy disaster was a real blow, but it did not depress the troops or hold up the war. General Moore now had his two brigades up and was pushing hard for Stanley. To get there we had to cross a ring of hills surrounding the capital, hills with names like Mount Harriet, Two Sisters, Wireless Ridge and Mount Longdon, all of them well defended by troops who had weeks to prepare their positions. A commando or a parachute battalion was detailed off to take each one of these and the Scots Guards were allocated another one – Tumbledown.

SEVEN

THE BATTLE FOR TUMBLEDOWN

'The man who comes back through the door in the wall will never be quite the same as the man who went out.'
ALDOUS HUXLEY, *THE DOORS OF PERCEPTION*

What happened to the Welsh Guards at Fitzroy and shooting down that Argentine jet over Bluff Cove put the battalion on its mettle, eager to get stuck in and sort the enemy out. We stayed at Bluff Cove for just over a week, from 5 June to 13 June, taking the chance to dry our kit and get organised before we went into the field again. This does not mean we were otherwise idle.

During those days we did what any front-line battalion would do in such a situation. We sent out patrols to dominate no man's land and we attempted to locate some Argentine artillery positions somewhere to our front and track down what was believed to be a mobile Exocet missile launcher, which, if it ever existed, was a definite threat to our offshore shipping. The important thing was to stay active. In war you must never become defensively minded. Even when the situation is static and you are in a defensive position, you must be as aggressive as possible. Our aim was to keep the Argentines on the back foot while we waited for the next phase of the war, and whatever part we had to play in it.

As a step towards these ends we decided to send the recce platoon forward to hunt down that Exocet missile launcher. They would occupy an abandoned group of farm buildings called Port Harriet House, about five miles forward from our front-line positions, and set up a patrol base. This decision turned out to have some bearing on what happened later when we moved on Tumbledown, but it proved an interesting exercise on its own account.

The decision to put the patrol into the only houses in the area was controversial but on balance the right one; it may have been strange to put them in such an obvious feature, but the weather was foul and the terrain bleak and no one could stay out there for long and remain effective without shelter. The choice was between putting out patrols for a few hours, or a day at the most, or finding somewhere they could occupy for longer. The latter is what we finally decided to do.

The patrol consisted of the recce platoon, commanded by Captain Rory Scott with Colour-Sergeant Allum as his second-in-command, and consisted of eight Guardsmen, divided into two four-man patrols, plus some of our supporting sappers from 9 Parachute Squadron, Royal Engineers, there to blow up any Argentine guns or Exocets we happened to find. These Para sappers were a great asset to the battalion and superb soldiers. The patrol was inserted in Scorpion light tanks of the Blues and Royals, and the first useful bit of information they sent back told of the existence of a large Argentine minefield, straddling the Fitzroy–Stanley track, just below Tumbledown.

Then, some days later, a helicopter dropped in at battalion HQ containing an SAS patrol commanded by Corporal Nobby Noble of G Squadron, 22 SAS, and formerly of the Grenadier Guards. Nobby knew what we were up to and had dropped in to tell us that he was going to take his patrol forward by helicopter that night and establish an observation post at Port Harriet House. Had he flown straight on without telling us and arrived there after dark, he would probably have met with a hot reception from our own soldiers, so a very nasty incident was narrowly avoided.

His arrival was useful, as we wanted to resupply our people at Port Harriet House and had no objection at all to adding four SAS men to the strength of our recce platoon, or helping them deploy in any other way. Given the short distances involved in the Falklands, the range over which Special Forces could deploy was much reduced, thus creating a closer link between the operational and tactical levels. Before the landings, our Special Forces – SAS and SBS – had a number of strategic tasks, attacking the Argentine outpost on South Georgia or the Argentine air base on Pebble Island, but later their role became one of trying to make a significant input at the operational level, such as the *coup de main* attempt to seize Mount Kent and the attempt by G Squadron to take out the Argentine mobile reserve and its helicopters.

We decided that the best way to get up to Port Harriet House – killing two birds with one stone – was to take Nobby and his team, plus the stores, up to the house in two civilian Land-Rovers, battered, muddy vehicles which were owned by the farmers who worked at Port Harriet House. These farmers were now at Bluff Cove but were very anxious to get back to Port Harriet and have a look at the buildings and their sheep and insisted on driving the Land-Rovers.

We made quite a little party. There was Richard Bethell, who was currently looking after HQ company, the recce platoon commander from the Welsh Guards, who wanted a look at the ground, the two civilians, Nobby's SAS team and myself. We got togged up in whatever civvy clothes we could find – at least from the waist up – and off we went, driving slowly up the track. We had been going along steadily for about an hour when there was an almighty 'bang' – as the leading Land-Rover went over a mine.

I thought – we all thought – we had run into an ambush. We were stuck in a minefield in a narrow valley, the perfect spot for an ambush, and as we piled out and went for cover, myself yelling 'Ambush left!', I was expecting a hail of fire to sweep down on us. Instead Richard Bethell yelled out, 'Freeze!' Such are the benefits of military training that we all stopped, like statues, and started to peer around. The ground was carpeted with small, green, surface-laid anti-personnel mines, the sort that can easily blow your foot off – and had just blown the front wheel off the leading Land-Rover. We could not move. There was no safe place to run to or take cover, and had anyone set up an ambush we would have been dead. As it was, I think we all felt rather foolish, but we were also relieved and we burst out laughing at our predicament – stuck in a minefield and having to find a way out.

Getting sorted out took a little time. No one had been hurt but the first Land-Rover was wrecked and those in it had to walk very carefully back down the tyre tracks and join us. Hanging about in a minefield did not appeal and the noise could have attracted Argentine patrols, so, very carefully, we reversed the second Land-Rover out of the valley and set out back to battalion HQ. Once back there we needed to think again about how to resupply our recce platoon.

The problem was that radio batteries are very heavy and do not last very long. Those the recce platoon had taken with them had run down and we were therefore not getting any information back from the platoon, which made the whole exercise rather pointless. The second problem was how to resupply them without tipping off any Argentines in the area to the fact that we had people in Port Harriet House. In the end we decided to send in the batteries by helicopter. Again this was high risk; the helicopter would sweep in and land briefly, for just long enough to hurl out the batteries and pick up Captain Rory Scott, whom we needed to debrief. If the helicopter was quick, the Argentines might not realise it had actually landed and need not suspect there was anyone at Port Harriet House at all.

It was a high-risk idea and it did not work. As the helicopter landed, a missile of some sort was fired at it, and as it took off again, bearing Rory Scott, mortar fire began to fall in and about Port Harriet House. Clearly, our patrol had been rumbled. All hell then broke loose. Elements of an Argentine company began probing the platoon position, the first burst of Argentine fire hit and destroyed the platoon radio, cutting off all communications, and Colour-Sergeant Allum, a very capable soldier, wisely elected to make a fighting withdrawal, back to our own lines. This they did, though in the process Allum was badly wounded in the arm and they had to abandon a lot of kit. Meanwhile, back at battalion HQ, we were trying to put together a rescue party, urged on by Rory Scott, who was naturally going frantic; his soldiers were back there and he wanted to get them out.

We decided that the quickest and most effective rescue force would be a couple of Scorpion light tanks from the Blues and Royals which had just been attached to us. By the time the Blues and Royals, led by Rory Scott, met the returning platoon, Colour-Sergeant Allum had had two more men wounded, but we went up and met them coming in. The recce platoon had put up a really good show, came out intact and brought back a lot of useful information about the minefields surrounding Mount Tumbledown, a long, rock-strewn ridge close to the outskirts of Stanley and the next task for the battalion. Rory Scott deserved a decoration for this whole episode but was just another victim of the post-conflict incompetence and bureaucracy.

By now the British forces, 3 Commando Brigade, Royal Marines and 5 Infantry Brigade, a 'light division' commanded by Major-General Jeremy Moore, were closing in on Stanley. Moore knew that once Stanley fell the war was over, but the Argentine positions on the hills around Stanley were strong, well manned and supplied with plenty of heavy machine guns, offering the chance for supporting fields of fire between the various Argentine positions. He therefore decided to pinch out the Argentine positions in two, or perhaps three phases. The first phase would involve 3 Commando Brigade which, with 40 Commando left at the bridgehead in San Carlos, now consisted of 42 and 45 Commandos and 2 and 3 Para. Having been in action at Goose Green, 2 Para were in brigade reserve and the first-phase attacks would be made by 42 Commando attacking Mount Harriet, 45 Commando taking Two Sisters and 3 Para taking Mount Longdon.

Mount Longdon dominated Mount Tumbledown, which was the objective of my battalion, so Longdon had to be taken before we moved on Tumbledown. The idea was that after we had taken Tumbledown, the 7th Gurkha Rifles would pass through us and take Mount William and the Welsh Guards would then take Sapper Hill, which is inside the boundary of Stanley, the island capital. Then, in the final phase, 2 Para would come up and take Wireless Ridge . . . and we would all sweep down on Stanley and end the war by driving any surviving Argentine soldiers into the sea.

Tumbledown was a typical Falklands feature, a rocky ridge rising to some 700 metres (2,000 feet) above the surrounding countryside and running from west to east for about three kilometres. To add to the physical problems, the north face of Tumbledown was very steep and unscalable, and the more open south face was covered by machine guns from the ridge. The Tumbledown position was therefore of considerable size and was well defended. We had had intelligence reports which said that the Argentine defenders, from a good unit, the 5th Marine Battalion, had heavy machine guns on the western end of the feature, a rifle company in the centre and another company at the eastern end.

We had air photographs, which neither confirmed nor refuted these reports, and we later learned from Argentine prisoners that the 5th Marine Battalion's actual dispositions were a standing patrol of twelve men on the western end, a platoon of about forty men in the centre and a further forty men at the eastern end. This was far less manpower than we had been told, but the real strength of this position lay in the supply of support weapons. These consisted of no fewer than ten sustained-fire 7.62 machine guns, twelve 60mm mortars, a platoon of 120mm mortars and one of 82mm mortars. A further complication was the nature of the ground. Thanks to the steep slope on the north face and the machine guns covering the southern one, our options were clearly limited to an attack on a narrow front, directly along the ridge.

Things rarely go as planned in battle – or, in military parlance, no plan survives the first contact with the enemy – and so it was here. The original brigade plan from 5 Brigade was for 2nd Battalion, Scots Guards, and the Welsh Guards to march up the Fitzroy–Stanley track, using that track as their axis of advance, before we veered off the track and put in a frontal, uphill attack on the south face of Tumbledown. Quite apart from the fact that no one in their right mind makes frontal attacks on heavily defended positions if they can possibly avoid it, we now knew that that advance to the 'start line', from where the attack would be launched, would take us through the big minefield that the recce platoon had discovered, the one that had damaged our friendly farmer's Land-Rover.

Therefore, on 10 June, Mike Scott went back to brigade headquarters and talked the brigadier out of this plan. We then had to come up with another one, one which we felt comfortable with. The final plan called for us to assemble behind Goat Ridge, which lies to the west of Tumbledown and leads up on to it. From Goat Ridge we had a clear line of approach and we could attack in echelon along the crest of Tumbledown from there, clearing the mountain as we went.

We also decided that this attack needed a diversion, something to attract the Argentine defenders' attention as the battalion moved up on Tumbledown. This would be provided by Richard Bethell and all the men we could spare from HQ company, about thirty of them, who would make a noisy demonstration along the Fitzroy–Port Stanley track, attacking what we thought was an Argentine outpost, firing tracer, letting off grenades and flares and generally kicking up a fuss to the south as the main attack went in from the west. The idea was to make the Argentines think that the attack was coming in that way, and we subsequently found out that this is exactly what they did think, though this diversion effort was not without loss. Two of Richard Bethell's men were killed and ten were wounded, some seriously by mortars and mines. This change of plan forced a twenty-four-hour delay as we had to move the battalion by night from Bluff Cove to the assembly area west of Goat Ridge, which had already been secured by the Marines of 42 Commando. This delay caused some resentment in the Commando Brigade, but Mike Scott made the right decision. He said we were not ready and would not bow to the pressure put on him by the chain of command.

We were briefed for the attack on the night before we moved to the assembly area, the Orders Group (or 'O' Group) taking place in one of the sheep sheds at Bluff Cove, an event I will always remember. None of us had been in battle before, or at least not in a real battle, as this promised to be. The hut was lit with candles and storm lanterns and a fire we had lit in an oil drum – it must have resembled the scene on HMS *Victory* when Nelson was briefing his 'Band of Brothers'. There was a definite tension, a sense that this was not an exercise and there was to be no more 'frigging around'. People were really paying attention to all that was said, making copious notes, asking sensible questions. As operations officer, my job had been to write the plan and set up this 'O' Group, and it did convince me that the British Army way of doing things does actually work, if you follow the rules and adhere to the system. We had faith in the 'School of Infantry' approach to tactics, but we also intended to use our own initiative.

The basis of the plan was for an attack 'in echelon'. We would advance along Goat Ridge and on to the western end of Tumbledown, one company up front and leading the advance, the rest in echelon behind – in other words, deployed in the rear, and slightly to one side, of the company ahead. The order of advance was 'G' Company, commanded by Major Iain Dalzell-Job, which would open the game and break into the Argentine position. 'G' would be followed by the Colonel's 'Tac-HQ' (Tactical HQ) consisting of the CO, the RSM and the battalion staff – signallers, runners, the fire-control parties including the mortar officer and, among one or two others, myself. The fire-control parties are worth noting for we had two, one from the artillery and another from the Royal Navy, all of them carrying radio sets and supposedly in contact with the guns and our supporting bombardment ship offshore.

We also had some damned good signallers from 36 Signals Regiment and those excellent sappers from 9 Para Squadron, Royal Engineers, under a fine NCO, Sergeant Strettle. There was also our transport officer, Captain Ronnie Patterson, who was in charge of logistics. Since we had no transport, Ronnie looked after the soldiers who brought up our supplies – the 'humpers and dumpers', as they were called – but Ronnie was a fighting soldier and he insisted on coming along, although he should have stayed back at battalion HQ. Finally, there were two journalists, both armed with typewriters, A.J. McIlroy of the *Daily Telegraph*, and Tony Snow of the *Sun*. I told them they could come along if they wished but they would have to keep out of the way and they duly marched with us to Tumbledown. That made quite a big party, perhaps fifteen or twenty in the Tac-HQ. There was also an 'Alternative Tac-HQ', which would remain at the assembly area under the battalion second-in-command, and come up if anything dramatic happened to the CO.

Once 'G' Company were in the enemy position, the next company, Left Flank, commanded by John Kiszley, would pass through the Tac-HQ and 'G' to take the main Argentine position in the centre of the ridge. Finally, Right Flank would come up to drive the last of the Argentines off the ridge and secure the position. That was the plan as laid out in Bluff Cove before we moved up to Goat Ridge and began the wait for 'H' hour – the moment of attack. Guards battalions do not identify all their companies by letter – 'A' Company, 'B' Company and so on – and the practice of calling them 'Left Flank' and 'Right Flank' dates back to the time when the infantry attacked in line and the two ends, the flanks of that line, were held by the grenadier companies.

We were going to attack at 0100hrs Zulu (GMT) or about 2000hrs local time, as soon as it got properly dark. During the day the battalion recce group, the staff and the company commanders went up to an observation post on the edge of Mount Harriet for a close look at the Argentine positions, the ones we were due to attack that night. This was now in the hands of 42 Commando, but something must have alerted the Argentines, for they started to shell our assembly area behind and then the little group of British soldiers they could see on the crest of Mount Harriet. They had 105mm and 155mm guns and there is a significant difference between the two – the 155mm packs a real wallop. When the shells started dropping too close we decided to pull back, all of us quietly wondering whether we should be phlegmatic and walk or act normally and run like hell. These guns were firing from somewhere close to Stanley and at least one was taken out by a Harrier jet with a laser-guided bomb. I saw the Harrier come over and drop the bomb, which looked like a little aeroplane as it flew off towards Stanley.

Waiting for 'H' hour was a testing time. I had brought a cigar off the ship and decided to smoke it before we set off on the grounds that it might be my last chance to smoke one, but when I got it out the aluminium case had been dented and I could not extract the cigar. We checked our equipment God knows how many times, tried and failed to get some sleep, and at last it was time to go.

I wasn't frightened, but I was apprehensive. I knew I could function and was more worried about making things work than about myself – and anyway, once we got going it was a lot easier. The first distraction was that I could not find Ronnie Patterson; when the time came for us to move off, he was not there. I stormed off to look for him and found him rolling around behind a rock, cursing and wrestling about. At first I thought he might have been grabbed by some Argentine infiltrator, but I waded in and discovered that he simply could not get his kit on; it was fifty-eight pattern webbing, soaking wet and the straps were frozen. I gave him a hand and a good cursing, and we were finally ready to go. This incident has subsequently become an old-soldiers' joke between Ronnie and myself. Ronnie is the last person to be late for an action, but I cannot resist pulling his leg about this one.

'G' moved off first. The role of the battalion HQ is to command the entire battle and we were wary of the Colonel 'H' syndrome, of letting ourselves be sucked forward into a company battle, so we let them get clear before we followed. We went along, quite slowly, behind 'G' and they secured their objective on the western end of Tumbledown without firing more than a few shots. Their arrival did make the Argies awake to what was going on – our opponents were from the 7th Marine Infantry Regiment – and if they were indeed conscripts, they seemed to know what they were doing and they brought down heavy mortar fire on 'G' and on the Tac-HQ position. Everything was well under control, however. We were getting on with the attack, getting our 'sitreps' (situation reports) back to brigade and putting up with the fire that was gradually increasing.

It was about then that I made the discovery that I do not like artillery or mortar fire. Such fire is too random, especially in the dark; you do not know when it is coming, or where the bombs or shells will land – but we were busy and there was no real time to worry about it then. Left Flank came through and we were following them forward to a nest of rocks when a salvo of Argentine shells, six of them, landed on the left of the ridge. A minute later another six-shell salvo landed to the right of us and Roger Gwyn, our Royal Artillery battery commander, yelled out that we had been 'bracketed' and the next six shells would be right on top of us. We sprinted forward over the dark, tumbled ground and had got into the rocks when, as predicted, the next salvo fell just behind us.

However, we had not entirely got away with it. There was another explosion, right in front of us. Everything went red and we were all thrown to the ground. I can remember thinking 'Fuck this for a game of soldiers' and checking carefully to see if everything was still there, like both arms and legs – it is a curious fact that you always check your balls first.

Apparently none of us had been hit, but then I saw the RSM, Ronnie Mackenzie, crawling about on the ground and I asked him if he was all right. His answer was to snatch the night sight from my rifle and start peering through it at the ground. 'I was just unwrapping my last Mars Bar,' he told me, 'and I am not going to move until I find it.' It transpired that one shell had hit the ground just forward of the crest and exploded just in front of us but under the soil; if it had cleared the crest and landed in the rocks it might have done a lot of damage. But there was no time to speculate about that either, for that is when the trouble really started.

Most of these Argentine positions, on Two Sisters or Harriet or Longdon, were more or less the same: a long, narrow ridge, littered with big rocks resting on open moorland. These rocks created small caves perfect for machine-gun nests, and the open ground offered a good field of fire for snipers. The Argentines had had plenty of time to dig in and had excellent night sights, far better than anything the British Army could provide, and these factors now started to take a toll. John Kiszley had put his company in with two platoons up – about sixty men in the first attack – and they quickly bumped into the enemy. As soon as the Guardsmen moved forward they came under heavy machine-gun fire from well dug-in and concealed positions, and there were also snipers out there, tucked into nooks and crannies in the rocks, all equipped with those excellent night sights.

There was one particular sniper, a very good shot who, in a matter of minutes, shot two Guardsmen dead, each with a bullet through his cap-star. Another man was hit in the stomach by a phosphorus round. We were not wearing helmets; this was a night attack and to aid identification in the dark and avoid any subsequent turmoil or confusion we wore berets – anyone in a helmet would be an Argentine and could be shot on sight. That apart, the British helmets are useless anyway; they cut your peripheral vision and are a needless distraction. And so the company moved forward and the sounds and sights of battle – shots, bursts of machine-gun fire, shouts and screams, the banging and echo of grenades and 66mm rockets, tracer bullets bouncing off the rocks – began to fill the darkness up ahead.

The Argentine soldiers were putting up a very stiff fight; they held Left Flank and started to battle hard to hold the crest of the hill. Left Flank had got halfway into the enemy position, but then they were stuck and the battle went to and fro below the crest. There were two young officers up there with the leading platoons – one of them, James Stewart, was just out of Sandhurst – and they and their soldiers were using grenades, 66mm rockets and rifles to try and get forward under a barrage of fire from positions they could not locate. This was a time for 'fire-and-movement'; the battle-winning weapon on Tumbledown that night was the GPMG, and we did not have enough of them, even if we had far more than the usual number. This was the crux of the battle, a real, bloody, infantry affair fought by the junior officers, NCOs and men, at close quarters, using rifles, bayonets, shovels and whatever came to hand.

The company commander was my old friend John Kiszley. He needed artillery support and got his fire-control people on to it – the ones in contact with the guns and the Navy. For some reason, even with everyone trying their best, it seemed to be impossible to get the guns firing accurately on to the crest of the hill and into the enemy positions, and that was especially frustrating when the Argentine artillery and mortars were spot-on.

One of our supporting artillery pieces was right 'off-register' and dropping shells all over the place, the Naval support was not on hand and, meanwhile, we in Tac-HQ, apart from trying to find out what was happening up front and what we could do to help, were getting pestered by Brigadier Wilson on the brigade net, who kept asking for 'sitreps' and asking if we needed help. Perhaps this was understandable but the CO, Mike Scott, had enough to do without all that and eventually I took over the set, said, 'Nothing heard, out,' and shut down the link.

The CO was not bothering John Kiszley, knowing that John had his hands full and could be trusted to get on with the job. Eventually, after what seemed like hours, John or his forward observation officers got some shells falling on the ridge. It was a long line of shells, a great burst of artillery fire up ahead enough to keep the Argentines' heads down for a few vital seconds. For what happened next John Kiszley should have got the Victoria Cross.

Kiszley got up, yelled, 'Come on, Left Flank – who's with me?' and made for the crest, and his soldiers fixed their bayonets, got up and streamed after him. They took Tumbledown at the point of the bayonet and that broke the deadlock, though the Argentines kept on firing until the Guardsmen were right among them, shooting and stabbing with their bayonets. John Kiszley's beret was shot off, a bullet hit his compass case, two more hit his ammo pouches, and by the time he reached the crest he had no ammunition left and only four men were still with him. All the rest of Left Flank were scattered up the slope behind, but they had knocked the stuffing out of the Argentines and taken Tumbledown.

The battle still went on. While Left Flank were consolidating the position and sorting themselves out, Right Flank came through them as planned and started to clear the back of Tumbledown. That was the time when Lieutenant Robert Lawrence, one of the best of the platoon commanders who had led his men through the position and killed a few Argentine soldiers, was shot in the back of the head and very badly wounded – he later received a very well-earned Military Cross. They finally drove the Argentines off the hill and by daylight we could see them streaming back into Stanley, looking more like a mob than soldiers.

That was when I realised that the battle was over and we had won it. It had lasted eight hours, ending just before daylight, and had cost the Scots Guards eight men killed and forty-three wounded. Among the dead were Drill Sergeant Wight, killed fighting in the recce platoon diversion attack, Sergeant Simeon, Lance-Sergeant Mitchell and Guardsmen Denholm, Stirling and Tambini. The shelling was still going on and there was still some sniping from Argentine soldiers tucked away in the rocks, but we had taken a number of Argentine prisoners, including an officer who was very willing to show us where the minefields were, and the firing slowly petered out. The prisoners, from the 5th Marine Battalion, were pretty scruffy, but they fought harder than some of those we had met in the first phase of the attack.

The aftermath of a battle is not a pretty sight. As I looked around the hill that morning, a line from George Herbert's poem 'Death' – something I had studied for my A levels – came into my mind: 'Thy mouth was open, but thou could'st not sing.' There were bodies littered about and an amazing mass of kit all over

Tim Spicer as a student at Staff College

Blue beach, Falkland Islands, 1982. Left to right: Roger Gwyn,
John Kiszley, Tim Spicer, Mike Scott, Iain Dalzell-Job

Tim Spicer and Tony Buckingham

Crossmaglen, South Armagh, 1986

Lt-Colonel Mike Scott and Captain Tim Spicer, ops officer, planning attack on Mount Tumbledown, Falkland Islands, 1982

Royal review of the Scots Guards, Edinburgh, 1992

Commanding the 1st Battalion, Scots Guards, Germany, 1992

Belfast, 1992

Commanding the 1st Battalion, Scots Guards, Belfast, 1992

Tim Spicer with RUC Commanders, the Battalion Second-in-Command and the
Commander of C Company, Belfast, 1992

Climbing Mont Blanc, 1993

the hill and in the various caves and crannies in the rocks. There were dead men in there too, including one or two of ours. We started to clean it up a bit, found a few booby traps and generally hung about on the hill, resting and waiting for orders.

We had the Argentines on the run now and the Gurkhas were coming up to pass through us and take Mount William. We had worked out that since an Argentine does not pronounce the letter 'j' as we do – 'j' is pronounced like 'h' in Spanish – a good password was 'Hey, Johnnie', as in Johnnie Gurkha – though that caused a tragedy. One of the Gurkha soldiers did not know the password and was wearing a helmet so, taking him for an Argentine in the early-morning gloom, one of our soldiers shot him dead.

As it got light we saw more and more Argentines making their way back into Stanley from the surrounding hills and we called down artillery on to them or engaged them with our GPMGs. We did not want to go after them and fight them in the streets of Stanley so we mauled them while we could; street fighting is very hard on infantry and we would have destroyed Stanley in the process.

We also had to bring in the bodies, taking them back to the Tac-HQ position and putting them in body bags. The wounded were everywhere but, fortunately, on the way out we had done a lot of first-aid training and this certainly saved lives. Drips were fixed up, wounds were dressed and many of the injured were treated by the battalion pipers, who specialised in first aid. The only real problem was getting the seriously wounded back to the Regimental Aid Post (RAP); the ground was very rough and everyone turned to carry the wounded back to where our medical officer Colonel Alan Warsop could go to work on them.

The Argentines were putting down artillery and mortar fire and Guardsmen Reynolds and Malcomson were killed when bringing in the wounded. Casualty evacuation was greatly aided by the arrival of Sam Drennen in his helicopter. He lifted the wounded back to the RAP and, as the CO said later in his diary, 'We owe many lives to him.' Medical work in the Falklands War was very good and everyone who got back to the RAPs survived.

We were also waiting for news of Richard Bethell and how he had got on with the diversion attack. Richard had assembled a force of about thirty men for this attack, and his original plan was to move along the Stanley track attacking any enemy positions he could find, using the Scorpion light tanks of the Blues and Royals to provide supporting fire. In addition, since the Scorpions were equipped with excellent night sights, they could actually help the recce platoon locate the enemy positions. Then, after the Scorpions had hosed the enemy with fire, Richard and one or more of his three assault groups, the other two commanded by Drill Sergeant Wight and Sergeant Coull, would go in.

This recce proved useful, for, as expected, he found that the ground on either side of the track was heavily mined. Only the track was safe, and they eventually made their way forward through the 42 Commando positions on Mount Harriet, coming under artillery and mortar fire as they did so.

On the night of the attack they moved forward at 18.15hrs local time, some two hours before the main attack was due to start. It was pitch dark and starting to snow and at 20.15hrs, with no enemy yet detected, the leading Scorpion ran over a mine and had its front sprocket-wheel blown off. No one was hurt and, somewhat to everyone's surprise, there was no reaction from the Argentines, no shelling, no mortar fire, no questing tracer. However, time was passing and the diversionary attack had to start before the main one went in; it was necessary to find an Argentine position and attack it.

Ten minutes after their advance began again, Richard spotted the first Argentine position, a stone-built machine-gun post, or 'sangar'. As they moved up on it – drawn on by snores from some Argentine sentry – they detected two more sangars nearby, and they were within a few feet of the first sangar when an Argentine soldier looked over the wall and saw them. Richard immediately opened fire, fire was returned and the assault went in.

In that attack Drill Sergeant Wight and Lance-Corporal Pashely, one of our sappers, were killed and four other men were wounded, but the three Argentine sangars were taken. Then the assault group came under fire from a line of enemy trenches to the south. Richard immediately attacked, then led Sergeant Coull and Drummer Wand in a fierce and aggressive assault through the enemy positions. For the next hour or so they cleared these positions with rifles and grenades.

This went on until 02.15hrs, more than two hours since the recce platoon had come on the first enemy position, and there was still no sight or sound of our attack on Tumbledown. Richard decided to go firm where he was, get the wounded out and bring up more ammunition and the troop Scorpions. The Scorpions could not move, so in the end Richard decided to pull back a bit and await events. Then Tumbledown lit up as the rest of us went in.

Their advance continued, though not without loss, as three men were injured by mines, two of them losing legs. All these men were helped to safety by Richard and Piper Duffy, who cleared a path through the mines in the dark in order to reach them; the wounded were evacuated back to 42 Commando's RAP and then to Teal Inlet. Of the thirty men Richard Bethell took into this attack, two were killed and ten wounded, including Richard himself, heavy losses for such a small force, but the attack served its purpose and kept the Argentines worried about their southern flank as we came in from the west. Like Rory Scott, Richard deserved a medal, but thanks to the peculiarities of the system he did not get one.

The morning after the battle wore slowly on, with everyone feeling more and more tired and wondering what would happen now. Would the Argentines fight on? Would we have to go in again? Then our rucksacks arrived and we were able to dig out our sleeping bags and look around for somewhere to sleep. I crawled into my bag, found shelter somewhere in the rocks and was sound asleep when one of the signallers shook me by the shoulder and said, 'They've surrendered.'

EIGHT

THE TIME AFTER TUMBLEDOWN:
1982–91

'Thank God that's over; now we can get back to some real soldiering.'
REMARK ATTRIBUTED TO BRIGADIER 'BONEY' FULLER, ARMISTICE
DAY, 11 NOVEMBER 1918

Tumbledown was a slow, stamina-testing infantry battle that doesn't make history but remains indelibly impressed on the memories of all those who took part. We stayed up on Tumbledown most of that day, slowly getting organised, having something to eat, poking about around the battlefield, sorting through the detritus of battle before moving back to Fitzroy, though some of us managed to take a look at the capital.

Stanley was a total shambles, full of troops, with lots of Argentine soldiers moving about, gradually being herded into temporary POW cages before they were shipped out to Uruguay and home. I can recall Mark Bullough and me liberating a bottle of champagne and drinking it by the sea wall and then getting into a slight confrontation with a staff officer at Government House, where the Argentine regiments that had invaded the Falkland Islands had laid up their colours. These included the colours of the 7th Marine Battalion, the Argentine force we had fought – and thrashed – on Tumbledown. I explained to a staff officer that I was the operations officer of the Scots Guards and I felt that these colours should rightly become the property of the 2nd Battalion, Scots Guards. He did not agree and I was told that, under the terms of the cease-fire, the Argentine soldiers could take their colours home. I therefore contented myself with taking some souvenirs from the desk of General Menendez, the commander of the Argentine troops, and went off back to the battalion.

This immediate post-war period in the Falkland Islands was a curious time. I cannot say that anyone was eager to have another battle. Far from it; everyone was extremely glad the fighting was over, deeply sorry about the friends we had lost, worried about the wounded and personally grateful to have come through it in one piece. On the other hand, and in some strange way, we missed it.

The last few weeks had created a tremendous bond, a great sense of comradeship among those who had been there and a definite sense of irritation with those who were now arriving and who, through no fault of their own, had missed the fighting. I know I am not alone in thinking this; many veterans of the Falklands, and any other war, will say the same thing. The fighting had been terrible, the discomfort considerable, but life afterwards seemed, for a while at least, flat and dull and lacking in colour and excitement. I suppose the adrenaline that had kept us buoyed up on Tumbledown was now gone, and without it we all felt deflated.

After the battalion came off Tumbledown, we went back to the sheep sheds at Fitzroy and embarked from there on the ferry MV *Norland*, the ship that had brought 2 Para to the Falklands, where the ship's company made us very welcome. Our general mood was one of 'let's get civilised again and sort ourselves out'. Hot food and hot showers and a chance to get dry and cleaned up certainly helped, and there was even a bar on board, which was especially welcome. A number of us, perhaps about thirty all told, including myself, had contracted a form of 'trench foot' caused by long hours in wet, freezing boots, and my toes were so swollen and painful I was forced to walk about on my heels.

The *Norland* crew were marvellously hospitable, and since they had been there throughout the war, in and around 'Bomb Alley' at San Carlos, they counted as 'one of us', but we also met a number of recent arrivals and had nothing to say to them. There was a definite feeling of 'them and us' between all ranks of the battalion and the new arrivals, a feeling which was not helped by wondering what we were going to do now. To go back to the training round seemed stupid, and after we were put ashore at Port Howard in West Falkland, it was hard to work up any enthusiasm for the daily round of work. We did a certain amount of patrolling and worked out the positions of a number of Argentine minefields, but our big concern was to avoid becoming garrison troops. We all wanted to go home and were simply waiting about, killing time, until the order to move arrived.

Meanwhile, we enjoyed the hospitality of the Navies – Royal and Merchant – who were very good to us. We went on board the carrier HMS *Ark Royal*, where we met Captain Jeremy Black and HRH Prince Andrew and a lot of other veterans, told our war stories and kicked our heels until finally we sailed on *Norland* for Ascension Island. This was a very pleasant voyage, playing sport and eating well, with lots of sunbathing on the upper decks, though I was appointed 'OC Loot' and charged with rounding up the large quantity of captured weapons that the Guardsmen had acquired and brought on board.

We had been told that no weapons, other than our own personal weapons and battalion equipment, would be allowed back into the UK and that the Commando Brigade's loot had already been seized by Customs. There was a big scene about that, with signals flying all over the place regarding captured weapons. There were some marvellous weapons among the loot and we knew that if we ever parted from them we would never see them again, but in the end a great quantity of Argentine weaponry was collected from the Guardsmen and went into a container – and, sure enough, we never saw it again.

On Ascension we met the Queen's Own Highlanders, who, poor devils, had now been tasked to garrison the Falklands. They had had a very bad time, having been put on standby for the war but missing the action, and they were naturally pretty depressed. We flew home from Ascension, all of us pretty cock-a-hoop, looking forward to getting back to our families and going on leave.

When we got back we were immediately given six weeks' leave – and suddenly things were not right. The leave was too long, far too long, and it marked the end of a very close relationship between all ranks of the battalion. A number of us, probably most of us, were still a tight-knit group; some of us even decided we would go on leave together. We simply did not want to break up the group and have to account for ourselves to our families and friends. We did not want to talk in any detail about the war and what it was like to people who had no idea of what we had been through.

Naturally, our friends and families were interested and full of questions. They meant well, but they had not been there and could not understand that we did not want to talk about it. It was not a happy time, there was a lot of domestic friction, and I for one did not enjoy my leave, mostly because I could not relax. I don't suppose any of us were too easy to live with at that time, a number of marriages broke up and there was all sorts of domestic drama.

Dinner parties were a nightmare, with constant questions like 'Did you kill anyone?'. Questions like that are crass, and intensely irritating. How do you answer a question like that and, anyway, why do they want to know? I know I found it all very irritating and I suppose I was in a pretty bad temper most of the time. It would have been far better if we had been given a week or two's leave at the most and then put back into regimental duties and a busy training round, something that would have given us a chance to decompress and get back to working in the normal world.

Eventually our leave ended and we reassembled in Chelsea Barracks, from where I was quickly posted to the Guards Depot for a spell instructing on the Household Division's Centralised Courses. This was quite traumatic, breaking up the team at Chelsea Barracks, though the Falklands spirit was fading and it was no longer the same battalion. Even so, I did not want to go. The Depot course was a mini-Brecon, covering all the basic infantry skills, especially drills and leadership in battle, at various levels from section commander to platoon commander, and although this was an excellent course, I suppose we – those of us who had been in the recent war – had an 'attitude problem' and found some of it boring and even out-of-date.

The British Army way of training men for war was pretty good then, and I think it has got better since. The proof of the pudding is that the Falklands War, as I have said before, was won on the Sennybridge training area and the Brecon Beacons. I was an absolute believer in the benefits of hard, realistic training, but when you have just been to war, what do you do next? The Guards Depot is a marvellous institution, the place where they turn civilians into soldiers and then into Guardsmen. It makes them very tough, but the process inevitably requires a certain amount of bullshit – for want of a better word – and at the time I had no patience for it.

The training did not seem to relate to the war we had just experienced. I wanted to apply what I had learned to what we were now doing, and to see that those things that had gone wrong on Tumbledown did not go wrong again. However, we worked on and taught the syllabus and did what we were supposed to do, and I managed to introduce a new advanced military skills course, covering such subjects as heavy weapons – mortars and machine guns and anti-tank – sniping, foreign weapons, explosives, demolitions, close-quarter battle and combat survival, using live ammunition with plenty of field firing, which the soldiers really enjoyed.

For me, though, it was in general a somewhat unhappy time. I felt like a cuckoo in the nest, trying to do everything in terms of war fighting but also trying to fit into this rather rarefied atmosphere at the depot, and I did not really enjoy it. I then heard that the 2nd Battalion were going to Cyprus. This seemed a better option than instructing at the depot and I got Mike Scott to get me out of there and back with the battalion. I had passed the Staff College exam before leaving for the Falklands and was down to start the course in October 1984, so I was able to spend eight months with the battalion in Cyprus. This was good fun, with a lot of water sports, a lot of adventure training – which is a very valid form of training if there is no enemy on the immediate horizon – and a lot of spare time.

I was now a major, probably the oldest recce platoon commander in the army, and this got me involved in one incident that took place at that time, the decision to pull the UK peace-keeping detachment out of the Lebanon, which was then in the middle of civil war. BRITFORLEB, as it was called, was a pretty small outfit, fifty-odd soldiers with a few armoured cars, and the idea was that we should sail over to Jounia, a port in the Lebanon, in a Cypriot 'RoRo' ferry, and put the recce platoon ashore as a protection party while BRITFORLEB got on board.

This was not as easy as it sounds, for the likely opposition, groups like Hezbollah, could get hold of tanks and heavy weapons. We clearly needed anti-tank weapons or at least GPMGs, but we were told, 'No, you can only take rifles,' so this promised to be a typical shambles. We did not even have rules of engagement, covering what we could or could not do, but fortunately the whole scheme was called off and BRITFORLEB were taken out by helicopter.

I took some leave and travelled about, but eventually my time with the battalion was up and I returned to the UK to start my course at the Staff College. Staff officers are the people who make things function at brigade, division, corps and army level, even at the Ministry of Defence, and all taking the staff course are majors or captains, all in their thirties and marked out for promotion.

The staff course is an extremely good course, well up to university level, the military equivalent of the sort of course offered by ISNEAD at Fontainebleau. It could be said that this is the Harvard Business School of the military world – and the business of the military world is war. The course begins with three months at the Royal Military College of Science at Shrivenham in Wiltshire, which offers a thorough grounding in military technology. I have to admit I found this part rather boring, except for a chap called Dan Rasshon, 'Mr Small Arms', who knew all about weaponry and was really very good. That was followed by a year at Camberley absorbing the minutiae of staff duties. The Staff College is a very good institution, very well run, and designed to teach staff procedures in headquarters. The range of topics covered is vast, from writing training programmes and analytical studies to understanding tactics at the higher command level and the value of joint operations.

The course was very intensive and very hard work – ten hours a day and plenty of homework – but I thoroughly enjoyed it and came out in the top 5 per cent of the course. I had already acquired a good knowledge of minor tactics and lots of practical experience and this course really put the gloss on it. At the end of the course, provided you pass and can put 'passed Staff College' in your records, you have four years before your next promotion, in my case from major to lieutenant-colonel, of which you are expected to spend two years on the staff and two years on regimental duties – and you must get four good annual reports to qualify for that promotion. It did not matter which came first, but you had to do both, and I wanted to go to the staff and apply the knowledge I had recently acquired. Instead I went back to regimental duty with the 1st Battalion, Scots Guards, as a company commander, to Elizabeth Barracks at Pirbright, where I was immediately detailed off to command the 'Escort to the Colour' at the trooping the colour ceremony on Horseguards Parade.

This was not what I expected at all, especially from my friend John Kiszley of Tumbledown fame, who was now my commanding officer. At first I thought it was a joke; it was no secret in the brigade that I hated drill and regarded public duties as a form of purgatory. Public duties are detrimental to the fighting ability of the Foot Guards because they take up an immense amount of training time, though in a way they are good for group cohesion. A Guards battalion can stay on public duties for up to four years, which is far too long, a constant round of kit-cleaning and sentry-go at Buckingham Palace or St James's.

The showcase event in the public duties programme is the annual trooping the colour, and though I did not want to do it, I decided that we must do it well – and we did. We got a lot of hard-earned praise, and people said it was one of the best escorts they had seen in years. Then, such is the variety of a soldier's life, we came straight off the Horseguards Parade and went into training for a tour in Northern Ireland, where we were the resident company in Crossmaglen, in the so-called 'bandit country' of South Armagh.

This began with the usual pre-tour recce to visit the in-post company of the resident battalion. This came from the Royal Anglian Regiment, and they were not too happy at this time, as the IRA had recently killed their company commander. We took over from them a few weeks later, and I decided to let the IRA know where we stood, right from the start – that if they started anything with us we would, within the limits of the law, go back at them with everything we had.

This is the time I went down to the Sinn Fein office in Crossmaglen, accompanied by a very tough colour-sergeant, laid my rifle on the table and told them what we were about. I said that we would follow up hard on any incident, that we were not thugs and not law breakers but were thoroughly professional, and that if the IRA were looking for trouble, they need look no further, because they had found it. Getting this point over certainly helped, because we had a relatively trouble-free tour, although we had a number of significant incidents.

I liked Crossmaglen. It offered real soldiering – you had to be on your toes twenty-four hours a day, and our opponents in the South Armagh Active Service Unit (ASU) were one of the most experienced bunch of terrorists in Ireland, and very well equipped. They had mortars, 12.7 machine guns, plenty of explosives, even a flame-thrower. Most of these weapons were kept south of the border in the Irish Republic and brought across when they were needed for an attack. You had to keep on the *qui vive* all the time and search continually for bombs; we found no weapons but we did find a certain amount of explosives. A few bombs went off, but did no damage.

We were based in the police station at Crossmaglen in hardened shelters, proof against mortar fire, but we did a lot of patrolling out from there as well as providing the base for the series of fortified observation towers that had been established along the Irish border on patches of high ground. Our patch, our 'tactical area of responsibility', as it was called, was an area of about forty square miles so we had 'B' Company – the surveillance company – in the station as well. There were about 200 of us in all and I was the overall commander.

The attitude of the local people can be best described as mixed. Most of them were nationalists in sentiment, not pro-IRA but, at best, neutral. The rest varied up to being very pro-IRA, people who would inform on our movements and support the local ASU, and the hard-line terrorists and their immediate supporters would always try and catch you out. There were about thirty or forty of these and they were formidable, but we did not lose a man – which made it a very successful tour.

We came back to Britain in January and I was immediately posted as chief-of-staff of 11th Armoured Brigade in Germany, which could hardly have been more different from anti-terrorist work in Northern Ireland. My boss was Brigadier Jeremy Phipps, a cavalryman formerly of the Queens Own Hussars but also ex-SAS, and a kindred spirit. I knew of him, although we had never met. We got on very well and I had a very happy time working with him, though his opening remark was memorable. 'You come highly recommended,' he said, 'but one thing you must remember. This brigade is my train set. You can play with it, but it remains mine.'

The 11th Armoured Brigade was part of Rhine Army (BAOR) and equipped with Chieftain tanks and armoured infantry units in APCs (armoured personnel carriers). Brigadier Phipps was initially concerned that as I was a foot soldier I might not have the mind-set for mechanised warfare, a view of which I was able to disabuse him quite quickly. Phipps knew a lot about armoured warfare and, from his SAS time, knew a fair bit about creeping about in the undergrowth, but I was able to offer my background as a soundly trained infantry officer. In turn he taught me about handling mechanised units, so it worked very well.

I was his principal staff officer, responsible for operations and training. Another officer, Major Chris Stearn, was the deputy chief-of-staff and responsible for personnel, logistics and administration. Chris was a very good guy. I had met him at the Staff College and he was a professional logistics man. I knew nothing about logistics and we had a good relationship, combining into a good double act to back up the Brigadier. The Brigadier was confident enough to ask for advice when he needed it and listen to it when it was offered.

As far as my career was concerned – and for Sandline clients later – this was a good move, for it gave me valuable practical experience in armoured warfare and in the organisation and command of large units. I was responsible for running the HQ in the field, for updating the brigade war plan for fighting the Russians – if need be – and since this was the time when the IRA were attacking servicemen and military bases in Germany I was also responsible for liaison with the German police and security services at Minden Garrison and for the massive security operation being mounted against the IRA. This involved the expenditure of millions of Deutschmarks and lots of intelligence work, all very good experience.

I wanted to do this; it was a number-one job, at that time, for a major on the staff. There had been some talk previously that I might become military assistant to the chief of the general staff, a job I was short-listed for and would not have minded doing, but this work in Germany was much more practical and a very good career move, with a lot of exercises and planning. It was very good for building up experience and confidence in staff work.

Brigadier Phipps left after about a year. His replacement was none other than Iain McKay-Dick, formerly second-in-command of the Scots Guards in the Falklands. He had taken over as my CO in Cyprus, so I knew him well, and I stayed with the 11th Armoured Brigade until the end of the year, by which time I had served my post-Staff College time and had got my reports. I had done well, I was moving up, and at the end of the second year I was promoted to lieutenant-colonel. Like every other professional soldier, I was waiting to command a battalion in my own regiment.

I was now on what was called the 'Pink list' and slotted to command a battalion. Mike Scott, who was now the Regimental Colonel of the Scots Guards, told me that I was definitely going to get a battalion but I had to do more time on the staff first. Before I left Germany there was more discussion about my going as military assistant to the chief of the general staff, who was entitled to have a lieutenant-colonel in that position, but the brigadier intervened in some way and I was posted instead to the directing staff at the Staff College.

This was also a pretty good job and I did not complain about it, but I really wanted to go to the Ministry of Defence. That was the right career move and would have broadened my experience. I was also a bit fed up, as I seemed to have spent a great deal of my service career as an instructor and I felt that I really needed to move on and develop my skills in other roles.

I was now thirty-eight and a recently promoted lieutenant-colonel. I had spent my early career seeking action and I had been lucky enough to find it. I knew I would command my battalion and I hoped that would be in Northern Ireland. But the army is an escalator, not a ladder; you cannot afford to hang about and simply hope that the right job comes along. To move up you must be in the right place at the right time. As you grow older you get to the age and rank where the opportunities for hard training and operations are slim, and by that time you must have developed and demonstrated a capability in other fields. As a lieutenant-colonel you get one crack at commanding a battalion, and if you are lucky that will be on operations. If you are made up to brigadier you might command on operations, but primarily from that time on your career will be staff-oriented. I had now reached that level and needed more staff experience.

However, the Staff College it had to be. This posting turned out to be very interesting and extremely hard work. The directing staff at Camberley work even harder than the students, either marking work or setting tasks, and life on the directing staff is, in short, pretty grim. The interface with the students was great and the work was important, training the next generation of senior officers for the army, but otherwise it was simply hard graft and pretty tedious.

Even worse, I thought I was stagnating. The Gulf War popped out of the blue and the Deputy Commandant of the Staff College, General Rupert Smith, whom I got on very well with, had gone off to command the 1st Armoured Division in Germany just before the Gulf War started and was sent to command in the Gulf, where the 7th Armoured Brigade had been sent to support the US Marines. One or two people were sent to the Gulf from the Staff College, to fill various staff appointments, and as the situation got more serious word came back that we at the Staff College had been 'ring-fenced' to replace battle casualties among commanding officers, if the balloon finally went up.

In the meantime, some of us were used as a 'think-tank', considering various options in the war against Iraq, but the rest of us simply had to soldier on. Just before Christmas 1990, though, my lobbying finally paid off and I got out of Camberley. I had been agitating for a move for months – I had even written to Rupert Smith, who was by now commanding the 1st Armoured Division in the Gulf, saying I would be happy to come out as his driver if that was the only slot he could find. Things were now hotting up, as the air war had begun and the ground offensive was pending, and every soldier naturally wanted to be out there.

That was not to be, but I ended up at the Joint Forces Headquarters at High Wycombe, where I worked in the Joint Planning Group, which consisted of a naval officer, an RAF officer and myself. We were the 'think-tank' for the commanders; this work was highly classified, but basically we worked for Air Marshal Paddy Hine, the Joint Force Commander, and General Mike Wilkes, the Ground Force Commander, either examining options and suggesting alternative strategies or analysing problems that came in and suggesting solutions, depending on the available military assets.

I was there when the SAS patrol 'Bravo Two-Zero' went adrift, and ultimately I went out to Saudi Arabia and met General Peter de la Billiere. I also went into Kuwait on about the third day after liberation, flying in a Hercules through a dense cloud of smoke from the burning oil wells which the Iraqis had set on fire before they pulled out. While I was there, I also ran into the 1st Battalion, Scots Guards, which I was due to take over shortly. They had been involved briefly in the Gulf but it had been a very depressing deployment. They had been serving in Germany as armoured infantry when the Gulf War began and were first stripped of their own front-line equipment to equip other units in 7th Armoured Brigade. They were then ordered to the Gulf themselves and as a result went out under-equipped, and when I met them they were in Blackadder Camp in Dahran, serving as a reinforcement battalion and most unhappy. This is yet another example of the British Army being under-equipped for an emergency and sending troops into a war zone totally unable to make an effective contribution to the conflict. It was necessary to strip most of the tanks in Rhine Army to send two tank brigades to the Gulf, and here we had a crack battalion stripped of its equipment to equip another battalion. There ought to have been more than enough kit available to equip both battalions, without these desperate, last-minute, hand-to-mouth measures.

When the war ended and the command structure stood down, I did not want to go back to the Staff College. I had heard on the grapevine that General Peter de la Billiere, though due to retire, was to take over a new job acting as Middle East Adviser to the British government, acting as liaison with the rulers of the Gulf States, most of whom he knew and all of whom knew him, since he had been out there during the Gulf War. General de la Billiere needed a military assistant in this role and I got the job. We set up an office for him in the office of the Director Special Forces HQ in London and got on with it. It was really just a liaison office but we had a budget and we did a lot of flying around the Gulf, meeting the rulers and 'flying the flag'.

I did this for three months and then Brigadier Jeremy Phipps, now Director, Special Forces, asked me if I wanted to move down the corridor and work for him. The task he had in mind was that I should help distil lessons learnt from the Gulf. Much of this involved close liaison with the Special Force community in the UK and around the world and a full appreciation of their strengths and weaknesses. I cannot say much about this work, or about my time at Special Forces HQ, all of which is highly classified, but that kept me occupied for the rest of that year, until I took command of my battalion.

NINE

WEST BELFAST, 1992

'There lay the green shore of Ireland. We could see the towns, towers, churches, houses. But the curse of eight hundred years we could not discern.'

RALPH WALDO EMERSON

I was still working for the Director, Special Forces, when the time came for me to take command of the 1st Battalion, Scots Guards. To command a battalion of his own regiment is one of the highlights in any officer's career, and before taking over command I had already gone to Germany to visit the battalion at Hohne and look it over.

The soldiers of the 1st Battalion were not happy, and with reason. They were supposed to be an armoured infantry battalion, but all their Warrior APCs had been taken away to equip another battalion. They had then been royally mucked about in Saudi Arabia when they were sent there for the Gulf War. After the Gulf War, when their Warriors did come back, they were promptly taken away again and handed over to another battalion, so the 1st Scots Guards were armoured infantry without armour. None of this had been well handled, and morale was on the floor.

As our next task was to go into training for a six-month deployment in Northern Ireland, this was serious, for in Northern Ireland morale is very important. A happy battalion is an efficient battalion, and fortunately the intensive pre-tour training did a great deal to cheer everyone up and it also got the battalion to a high pitch of efficiency. I had some very specific views about training for Northern Ireland and some tactical ideas which I wanted to try out on the ground when we got there, but to make them work I needed soldiers who were keen and willing – and very well trained.

Training for Northern Ireland has been almost a routine task for any infantry battalion since the Troubles began in 1969, and although there is a basic training package – the Northern Ireland Training and Advisory Team package – covering all the basic skills the troops have to know or acquire, a battalion commander has a considerable amount of latitude, not least on the attitude his battalion should adopt to the task they are given and how they should handle the situation they face on the ground. My intention was to present the unit profile which I always thought appropriate in Northern Ireland: highly professional, always restrained and controlled, but letting the opposition know from the start that we would react swiftly and aggressively if the situation called for it.

It was very important that the battalion should be at peak efficiency, since on this tour we were tasked to take over West Belfast. West Belfast is a strongly Republican area, so the battalion had a high-profile role, in the heart of the province, right in the public eye. We also had to take into account the wider objectives of the anti-terrorist campaign and remember that even apparently trivial incidents which might seem unimportant at the time can quickly expand from the tactical to the strategic level and have a wider impact, especially if they are taken up by the media, who monitor what happens in Northern Ireland very closely. And finally, of course, there is the political angle.

We were going to Northern Ireland at a very interesting time. The seeds of the peace initiative had already been sown and we were clearly going to get closely involved in that, so even before I left the Director Special Forces HQ I spoke to the battalion and went to see the powers that be in Belfast, to look over our designated area, to meet the resident battalion and to see Brigadier M. of the Parachute Regiment, who was commanding in this sector. M. went on to be a very successful general, and was someone with whom I immediately saw eye-to-eye.

We intended to carry the war to the enemy – the Provisional IRA – and use our initiative. At this time the army was essentially 'holding the ring' for the police, the Royal Ulster Constabulary (RUC), and there seemed to be nothing new, no tactical innovation, no initiatives; what our job came down to was simply attempting to keep the lid on the conflict. I wanted to try out a couple of ideas which might take matters further than that, and one particular idea was to integrate the system of static, overt observation posts (OPs) that already existed in Belfast with the rest of our extensive surveillance apparatus.

I broached some of these ideas with the Brigadier but we both knew that using fresh initiatives in West Belfast was difficult. This area was in the full glare of the public eye. What happened in West Belfast caught people's attention, not only in the rest of the UK but right across the world. Everyone knew about Belfast or Derry, even if they were less aware of the situation in East Tyrone or Coalisland or many of the other equally tricky places. Therefore we were on a very dodgy wicket, for if things went wrong they could go very wrong and everyone would be aware of it. There was a very efficient PIRA Active Service Unit in West Belfast at this time, which also had to be taken into account.

There was also a tactical problem. I do not believe in placing my soldiers' lives at risk when there are any means to prevent it and there was a rule at this time that weapons could carry a loaded magazine but there must be no round in the chamber – in other words, the weapon had to be cocked, and a round put into the breech, before it could be fired. I felt this put the soldiers at a disadvantage, particularly when dealing with a terrorist who could choose the time and place to initiate an incident.

The soldier has enough to do when he suddenly comes under fire. He has to find out where the shots are coming from, even while diving for cover. He has to find out what has happened and assess the situation before he can respond, and if he has to charge his weapon he is losing vital seconds at a very difficult time. The result is that he will lose the initiative if he has to cock the weapon before he can return fire. Rapid response is what terrorist gunmen fear most; if they know there will be a pause before the soldiers return fire, it gives them a clear advantage.

I took this matter up with M. and he agreed, but unfortunately he was leaving and I knew that I would have to convince another Brigadier, Brigadier A., of the need to carry cocked and loaded weapons. I had never met him but I needed to sort this out and get the point covered in our training. Although this rule came down from HQ Northern Ireland, I am glad to say we got it changed and we did not have a single round let off accidentally – a 'negligent discharge' is the term employed – at any time in training or during our tour. The weapons are always carried with the safety catches applied, but fear of negligent discharges was the reason for imposing the unloaded-weapons rule in the first place. In the past there had been an awful lot of negligent discharges, any one of which could result in soldiers or innocent civilians being killed, but you will not have rounds fired accidentally if the soldiers have been properly trained in weapon handling. I told the battalion right at the start, 'There will be no negligent discharges – there is no excuse for them.'

To sharpen up on their weapon handling, we imposed a rule that the soldiers were to carry their weapons at all times when on duty, with safety catches on but with a 'blank' round in the chamber in barracks or on exercises and a live round on the ranges during the six-month training period – just to get them used to the idea that their weapons were loaded at all times and triggers and safety catches were not to be fiddled with. I was prepared to treat any negligent discharge, even with a 'blank', as a real one and come down hard on the offender. Our training was hard but effective and after the chaos in the Gulf the soldiers were eager for a change, a fresh start and a new challenge. Morale improved as the training phase continued and we eventually went off to Belfast in fine form.

My first task on taking over command was to set up a surveillance platoon whose tasks were, firstly, to support the police mobile units – generally known as 'The Blues' – and, secondly, to man the four sector OPs in West Belfast. All these

OPs were on top of tower blocks; one was on a hospital, another was on top of Templer House in the Ardoyne, a very tough area. They were all vulnerable as you had to approach them through hostile streets, but the idea was to match our OPs and surveillance activity with the 'Blues' patrols, which covered the whole of Belfast and were well in tune with IRA activity.

To help this process, all company areas were matched with the police areas. My opposite number was a police superintendent and each company commander was tasked to work closely with his local police inspector. This integrated police and army network worked very well. The idea was that the surveillance platoon would man the OPs for a certain time but, to give them a change, they would also go out on patrol with the police mobile units. It was a new concept and it had to be handled carefully, with a lot of special training. The officer I put in charge of the surveillance platoon was Lieutenant Jeremy Orwin, one of the youngest platoon commanders in the battalion. Jeremy was promoted to the rank of captain and told to make the concept work.

I hand-picked a number of people to help him, including Colour-Sergeant McCavera, QGM, who had extensive surveillance experience in Northern Ireland, and I let Jeremy run a selection course to find the right men and got the blessing of the brigadier to support him with additional equipment, especially photographic equipment. While that was going on, I had to train the rest of the battalion. The ethos of that training was a concentration on basic infantry skills, because if you have your basic skills right and impose your Northern Ireland procedures on top of them, you are well on the way to efficiency and safety when you get on the ground.

I also laid a lot of emphasis on fitness training. Soldiering in Northern Ireland is physically and mentally demanding. You have to be on your toes all the time and that is much easier to manage if everyone is physically fit – and that included all the battalion stalwarts, the drivers and storemen and clerks, who often tried to avoid anything that resembled physical effort. We were going to be in West Belfast throughout the summer and the marching season in July, carrying a rifle and wearing a jacket with heavy bullet-proof plates in it, plus a helmet. Going out for four-hour foot patrols or being on your feet for operations lasting anything from six to twelve hours is very demanding. It requires physical fitness of the type required for interval training – the ability to be on the move, sometimes trotting, sometimes running, always alert, never still, sometimes for hours on end.

I instituted a very rigorous fitness programme and made fitness lessons CO's parades, which in the Foot Guards means that the CO is going to be there and therefore everyone has to either be there or get my permission to be excused – which they might get if they are dying, but not otherwise. The doctor and the RSM, Phil Jackson, took care of the sick, the lame and the lazy and the message that this was serious and I meant it soon got around. We had a very good PTI (physical training instructor) and between us we soon got the battalion in very good shape. I was fortunate to have a very good team to help me run the battalion, but in particular I was lucky to have an outstanding RSM in Phil Jackson.

Phil Jackson was an unusual RSM for the Scots Guards. He was a Geordie from Newcastle and an imposing man, well over six foot tall. I had known him for some time, and we had served together in the Falklands War, where he had done a very good job as a platoon sergeant. He was a likeable man, very well respected in the battalion, and had the useful knack for any RSM in the Foot Guards of getting on very well with the officers and particularly with me, the CO. He also ran a well-organised and disciplined sergeants' mess and he had the measure of the Guardsmen.

There was no nonsense with him. He took part in everything and he was equally at home in the field, on patrol, on the drill square or in the sergeants' mess. He was particularly good in Northern Ireland, where he accompanied me everywhere. We were out on patrol together on most days, for four or six hours at a time, and he organised the CO's Group of two Land-Rovers and six to eight Guardsmen. Phil was a good man to have at your side in any tight spot.

This training, which is spread over six months, is constantly monitored by the Northern Ireland training experts and we passed with flying colours. However, the important part of that monitoring is that the training teams are constantly giving you tips about the current state of play and any new IRA tactic that is currently being used, updating your intelligence and pointing out anything that might have started since your previous tour.

One of the devices which had just appeared was known as the Mark XV coffee-jar bomb. This, as the name suggests, consisted of a large coffee jar packed with a detonator and Semtex explosive, into which was crammed a selection of metal, nails and scrap iron, and which, when detonated, filled the air with blast and flying metal fragments – the heat of the explosion vaporised the glass. The Mark XV coffee-jar bomb was at worst lethal and at best extremely nasty, and more and more of them were being thrown at army and police patrols.

The other snag with the Mark XV coffee-jar bomb was that it was very difficult to identify as a weapon. It was normally thrown at mobile patrols from behind walls, which protected the thrower from the blast, and was usually carried about in a plastic shopping bag, the sort supplied by supermarket checkouts, which would then be used as a sling to add range to the throw. The bombs could cause havoc and the difficult question was how to counter them.

The final snag was that the IRA had also persuaded the younger element among their supporters, the yobbos, to throw coffee jars filled with paint at the patrols, to wind up the troops and get them to open fire. If they did so, this would create an incident that IRA propaganda could exploit. If not, it would probably get the troops used to the plastic-bag-and-paint-pot routine, so that they would not fire until it was too late when it was a real bomb.

The Mark XV was clearly an ideal terrorist weapon, one which could suck us into some really serious situations. We had a lot of discussions on how to handle this new threat within the context of the existing 'Yellow Card Rules' which govern all military action in Northern Ireland. My view – and one which follows the wording of the Yellow Card – is that if the soldier genuinely believes that his life or the lives of his comrades are under threat from something like a Mark XV, then even if it was not immediately obvious one was being thrown he could open fire.

We went over this problem time and time again and had a presentation in front of the whole battalion at the Sennelager training area, during which the military police and I gave them a demonstration of the Mark XV and told them that if they thought they were going to be killed, they could open fire, but if they could avoid injury in some way, by taking cover or diving into a doorway, they shouldn't open fire. Ultimately, it is the responsibility of the individual soldier, but he must know the rules and if he follows them the system must support him.

But the decision is still his, and this is the problem in Northern Ireland. An awful lot of responsibility is placed on the young soldier. You can train the soldier until he is blue in the face, set up situations and tell him how to react in individual cases, but in the end the decision on the ground as to whether he should open fire or not has to be his – and he has to make that decision quickly, at best within seconds. It might be the responsibility of the platoon commander, but he might be looking another way, or on the radio, or otherwise busy when the threat comes in. If lives are at risk, the soldier has to make a decision. And on this tour, exactly this sort of situation arose with two of my soldiers, Guardsmen Fisher and Wright.

When we got to West Belfast we were deployed in various company locations around the city. Battalion HQ and 'B' Company were in the North Howard Street Mill, an old Victorian linen mill off the Falls Road. It was virtually a fortress but I liked it. Right Flank were in the Girdwood Park Barracks covering the Ardoyne; this was a little more civilised, being a proper barracks with football pitches and so on, built long before the present round of Troubles. It was quite comfortable but very vulnerable.

Left Flank were at White Rock near Turf Lodge, and we also had under command a company of 1 Para, who were at Woodburn Police Station, where I had been based on my first-ever trip to Northern Ireland. Because of the level of enemy activity, we also had the patrol company of 1 Para under command, plus any other troops I could get my hands on, including, from time to time, the Maze Prison guard force or some of the RAF Regiment from Aldergrove airport, who quite liked a break from guarding. At times I had up to two and a half battalions under my command. The Brigade HQ was at Lisburn, where I went for 'O' (Orders) Groups at least once a week.

Otherwise we were very much on our own, although I had established a very good relationship with our brigade commander, who was a very good brigadier, and spoke to him on the radio or telephone at least once a day. He gave me his directives, and provided I let him know what I was doing, he let me get on with it. Our duties were very much in support of the police and we tried hard not to tread on the RUC's toes, keeping in close touch with them at local level and making ourselves useful. I was in daily, sometimes hourly contact with the Chief Superintendent.

One of my main tasks was to convince the police that we should try some new tactics. We inherited a system of semi-static vehicle check points (VCPs) which ringed Belfast, and the main purpose of these VCPs was to stop car bombs being brought into the city centre and causing a lot of damage and casualties. This might seem a good idea, but there were snags. First of all, the check points were static and prone to targeting by the IRA. I was worried that my men operating these VCPs would be shot at, for there are only so many positions a soldier can take up at a static post and after four hours on duty they got careless. Also, the VCPs caused traffic jams to private cars, school buses and delivery vans, and this constant irritation did nothing to help our 'hearts and minds' efforts with the general public. However good the justification, we were annoying a lot of innocent people every day.

I wanted this changed for a mobile system, where the VCPs appeared at different places and for varying amounts of time, so that the opposition did not know when or where they might be stopped and had no time to organise a sniper. If these mobile VCPs were matched up with the four static OPs, it would be a very effective screen; the OP might spot a van coming into the city from the Falls and could radio to a mobile patrol which could stop and search it. We tried this on our own and eventually, towards the end of our tour, we persuaded the police to try it – and the first night out we stopped a car carrying a 500lb bomb.

Right from the start of the tour we had a hard time. This was the last real, all-out burst of IRA campaigning and there was an increased level of activity, with the hard men constantly having a go. We had to cope with that, but we had also been charged with developing 'peace and reconciliation groups', working behind the scenes with community leaders, including members of Sinn Fein, some of whom were almost certainly in touch with the IRA. This was an attempt to do just what the name implied: achieve peace and reconciliation, and ease the tension between the troops and the local community. I had lots of local groups into my HQ for coffee and sandwiches, trying to open a dialogue about issues of mutual concern, explaining the role and the duties of the army. We are not talking about the Good Friday Agreement here, but perhaps this work helped to sow the seeds. Some of these people were very wary about coming into our barracks and the police were not happy about it either, but we persevered. Up to a point, it worked, and we all got on well enough.

Out on the streets it was a different matter. We were constantly under attack and during that six-month tour I had one man killed and fifty-five wounded – and by wounded I do not mean falling over and twisting ankles, I mean wounded by IRA activity or rioting. We had some corking riots too. In a way, it was almost back to the level of activity of ten years before, but on the other hand we scored some definite successes against the IRA.

To give one example, Ben Wallace, one of our platoon commanders, was returning on foot with his platoon to the White Rock base up the Mona bypass. This bypass leads to a roundabout which is set in a very narrow cutting, the ideal spot for an ambush. However, you do develop a sixth sense for trouble after a while and somehow, on approaching this spot, Ben felt that all was not well. He therefore decided to stage a double envelopment of the cutting, a classic flanking movement up either side, while giving the impression, right until the last moment, that he intended to take his patrol right through the middle.

As a result, the patrol picked up a four-man IRA team preparing a 'sweetie-jar bomb', one of those big, screw-topped display bottles found in confectionery shops and a larger version of the Mark XV coffee-jar bomb. This one had been filled with explosives and scrap metal and was due to be thrown into the cutting as the patrol went through. Ben got the men and the bomb – and he had the wit to pick up lots of forensic evidence at the same time, so the terrorists went to prison for a good spell.

Another successful catch involved one of our NCOs, Sergeant Goodman, a man who had once served in the Rhodesian Army and was a very good operator. On the day in question he was leading a combined mobile police and army patrol consisting of two police and two army Land-Rovers and they were going through the Beechmount Estate, one which has a grid-style pattern of parallel streets, rather like a chess board.

As well as basic weapons like rifles and pistols and homemade bombs, the IRA also has the capacity to create some sophisticated devices, and one of these consisted of an anti-tank rocket built into the side of a car. They could fire the rocket from a nearby house using a camera flash-gun to initiate the charge, which is also pretty sophisticated. Goodman's four-vehicle patrol moved into the Beechmont Estate, always a tricky area, and for greater security they split into two groups, two vehicles in each, driving down adjoining streets – and then the IRA fired a rocket at one of the police Land-Rovers.

The rocket missed. It went across the bonnet and into a grass bank, where it exploded harmlessly. Sergeant Goodman was in a parallel street, but he heard the bang and realised what had happened. He also worked out where the firing point must have been positioned. He roared up to that spot, dismounted his men, spotted the terrorists running away and went after them, chasing them up the road and into a house. Sergeant Goodman got ahead of his patrol – some shots were fired at them during the pursuit – but he followed the terrorists into the house, chasing up the stairs after them to a top room, where he arrested two men single-handedly, just as they were getting their kit off and divesting themselves of their cameras and other evidence.

He also picked up a lot of forensic evidence, something else we had stressed in training. Forensic evidence was invaluable when you got these people into court, for unless you catch someone with a bomb or a gun in their hand it is often very difficult to prove that they had it. Goodman's men then came pounding up the stairs to truss these two men up; when I arrived shortly afterwards with a search dog, Goodman was standing over them with a grin on his face, asking what had kept me. Thanks to his fast thinking and initiative, the two men got ten years apiece.

Meanwhile, the Mark XV coffee-jar bomb had appeared on our patch with a vengeance. Within a few weeks we had had more than twenty coffee-jar incidents, with a number of people injured; Charles Page, the commander of Right Flank Company, was nearly killed by one in the Ardoyne. Not all the incidents involved real Mark XVs, but hardly a day went by without an incident involving a real one or a fake one and there was a growing risk that either we would shoot someone throwing one or they would kill or seriously injure one of us. That was the background to the tragedy surrounding two of my men, Guardsmen Fisher and Wright of Right Flank Company.

To set the scene, Right Flank were working in the Ardoyne, where, with tensions rising, we had already had some rioting. We had also had some shooting and a number of incidents involving coffee-jar bombs and it had all culminated in September 1992, when one of my men, Guardsman Shackleton, was hit by a sniper while acting as top cover sentry in a Land-Rover. I knew Shackleton well. He and I had served together before and he had been in my company on the previous tour to Crossmaglen. He was standing in the rear of the vehicle, half of him out through the roof hatch, and was shot as the vehicle was turning right at some traffic lights. This was always a vulnerable moment, but military vehicles had to obey traffic signs and were not, like police cars and ambulances, able to move through without stopping, even if the road was clear. A number of shots were fired, and although he was wearing a flak jacket, it did not save him as he was hit in the neck. They rushed him to hospital, but when I got there he was dead.

Events like that have a big impact on a battalion. The soldiers are torn between feeling depressed, wanting to go out and 'get the fuckers' who killed one of their mates and just getting out on the streets and causing mayhem. This is understandable in the circumstances, but you cannot allow that feeling to persist. It was necessary to get the battalion by the scruff of the neck and underline the fact that we were professional soldiers.

We had been there, on the streets of West Belfast, taking a lot of stick, for four or five months, and doing all the right things. Now this had happened and they wanted to sort it out, and such a reaction was only human. Even so, there is no room for revenge in the British Army, so I visited all the companies, gave them a pep talk, told them what had happened and underlined the fact that any overreaction simply played into the hands of the IRA. The soldiers appreciated that fact, but it is not easy to have one of your soldiers killed, and in a place like Belfast – which is, after all, part of the United Kingdom – it is much worse.

That sets the scene for what happened some weeks later. My involvement in the Fisher and Wright affair began at about ten o'clock one morning, when I was attending the Brigadier's weekly 'O' Group at Lisburn. This meeting was proceeding much as usual when the Brigadier's chief-of-staff came in and said, 'It looks as though the Scots Guards have shot a gunman.'

I knew we had a major sweep for coffee-jar bombs on that morning but I did not really believe we had shot a gunman, though I would have been delighted if we had. I knew that Right Flank Company had had reports that coffee-jar bombs were circulating in the area and they were out on the streets that morning, trying to pick them up in transit. First reports are rarely accurate anyway, so I decided to stay at the 'O' Group and await further news. I had my Land-Rover outside, fully kitted up with a radio on the battalion net. The sergeant-major was in it with the rest of the Rover Group, my own, eight-man patrol, and he would receive any information that came over the air; if we had indeed shot a gunman, he would come in and tell me. The Brigadier did ask me if I wanted to get back to the battalion but for the moment I said no and stayed on. The next solid piece of information was that no weapon had been found – at which point I started to worry.

I left the 'O' Group and returned to battalion HQ while asking over the radio for 'sitreps' (situation reports) from the commander of Right Flank, Charles Page, in an attempt to find out what had actually happened. It appeared that two of his men, Guardsmen Fisher and Wright, were part of a four-man 'team' – a small patrol – commanded by Sergeant Swift of the Irish Guards, who had been attached to the battalion. They had stopped a young man, Mr McBride, who was carrying a white plastic bag containing some items, and Swift was asking him some questions while the others gave cover. Suddenly, for no apparent reason, Mr McBride took to his heels and ran off, jumping over a low wall and sprinting away, still carrying this white plastic bag which appeared to contain a cylindrical object.

The soldiers did not open fire. Sergeant Swift shouted out 'Stop him!' and Guardsmen Fisher and Wright ran after McBride, who was now racing away down the street. Then, for some reason, McBride stopped running and ducked down between two cars. Fisher and Wright therefore also took cover and challenged McBride three times before they opened fire, each man firing two aimed rounds. Mr McBride was hit and staggered off through a house and into an alleyway – an 'entry', as they are called in Northern Ireland – and although the soldiers came running up and tried to save him, he died there . . . and that was it.

So far, this had been an all-too-typical Irish tragedy. If McBride had not run off, and if he had not taken cover among the cars and led the soldiers to believe that he was taking cover before throwing a bomb at them, none of this would have happened. The problems that would affect Fisher and Wright began to appear, especially when a search failed to find the white plastic bag Mr McBride had been carrying – a point I will return to. There are standard follow-up procedures for this kind of event and among them is an immediate search for the weapon or supporting evidence, in this case the plastic shopping bag.

Two points. No one, at the time or later, for the defence or the prosecution, denies that Mr McBride was carrying a white plastic shopping bag when he was stopped and was still carrying it when he ran off. The prosecution alleged that it contained a packet of crisps and a wet swimming costume. The soldiers stated it contained something heavier, and round. So, the second point, if what was in the bag was only a swimming costume and a packet of crisps, why was the bag not found?

Perhaps, as had happened at other incidents, it had been spirited away by the IRA or their supporters, who often carried away weapons or explosives in order to support an allegation that the army had shot an innocent man – but why do that in this case? If the bag only had a swimming costume and a packet of crisps, that was damning evidence against the soldiers. Finding the swimming costume and crisps would have proved that Mr McBride was totally innocent of bomb carrying – though it would not have explained why he ran off or took cover, two actions that clearly contributed to the shooting. The only reasonable conclusion is that, whatever the bag contained, the contents were somewhat less innocent than the prosecution subsequently maintained.

When I got back to battalion HQ and heard the story, my immediate reaction was to get the two soldiers back on the street. Both of them were very upset and in a state of shock, and it was simple common sense to get them back out there, doing their jobs, just as you get straight back on a horse after you have been thrown off. These men were professional soldiers and they had to accept this sort of thing, but it was anyway the standard procedure. I also visited the local police station to find out what the police knew, and spoke to the Brigadier and the Commander Land Forces. I then went to see the two Guardsmen, who were now back in barracks. Their own weapons had been taken away for forensic tests but we had spares and the sensible step was to rearm them and send them out again. But I was not allowed to do this.

When I was talking to the General, he asked me what I intended to do with the two soldiers. I told him that as soon as they had recovered, they would go back on the street. He told me that that was not to happen, that the shooting was going to be investigated by the RUC and that the men would very probably be arrested. I thought this was very, very premature.

I then went to interview the men myself. I was with them within two hours of the shooting and this interview was attended by the RSM, our doctor and the company commander. I asked these three to attend the interview with me and gauge the men's response, because they knew them better than I did and I thought that between us we could reach a pretty balanced judgement on what had happened.

It was immediately clear to me that both men were in a state of shock. They were both young, just nineteen and twenty-one, and had not been in this sort of situation before. They recounted their story to me and their story never changed – not later, not during endless police interrogation, not to their lawyers, not during the trial, never. They told the same tale, the story given above, every time, without any deviation.

Both men believed that the plastic bag contained a coffee-jar bomb. Bombs were what they were looking for, the bombs were carried about and thrown in plastic bags, there had been constant incidents involving just such bombs and bags, the man ran off and then took cover. All of this contributed to their state of mind in the split second they had to decide whether to open fire or not. I believed them at the time and I believe them to this day. I believe they were telling the absolute truth.

At a swift meeting outside afterwards, the doctor, the RSM and their company commander all agreed that Fisher and Wright were telling the truth, 100 per cent. We were all pretty experienced in gauging whether soldiers were telling the truth or not and we had to have the truth if we were to help them. I believe the truth is what we got. And there was still the question of the bag. If it had been found, complete with crisps and so on, it would have made the case for the defence very dodgy, but it would still have supported no more serious a charge than a tragic accident – which is what it was. I do not see how the evidence ever supported the charge of murder that was eventually brought against these two men.

They should never have been charged with murder, let alone convicted of it. No one suggests that they went out intending to kill Mr McBride or anyone else. They believed, and the evidence suggests they had good reason to believe, that they were about to come under attack. They fired because they believed they were facing a threat, and the absence of the plastic bag supports that belief rather than detracts from it. At the subsequent trial, these facts and the context of the shooting were simply ignored. The whole question of the 'Yellow Card Rules', the support of the system for the troops on the street, any recognition of the situation these soldiers were placed in, was either completely dismissed by the court or handled badly by the barristers. As a result, there was a terrible, disgraceful miscarriage of justice in the treatment, trial and conviction of Guardsmen Fisher and Wright.

Soon after I saw them, I was told they were going to be arrested, taken to an RUC centre outside Belfast and questioned. I went out there later, in the middle of the night, to see them and was most unhappy about the way they were being treated. They were questioned continuously throughout the night, denied sleep or any chance to relax, and although the Army Legal Service sent out a representative, the whole affair escalated very quickly into a circus, with the clear aim of charging these two young soldiers with murder in order to calm the situation in Belfast. These soldiers were sacrificed in the cause of political expediency. This was a weak decision, taken for political reasons without any attempt to consider the full facts or place the matter in context. I have always felt that the speed with which it was all settled was unseemly. The prosecution's story, about them deliberately deciding to shoot McBride, was believed and the evidence presented by the soldiers was rejected out of hand. The whole affair was an absolute disgrace to the state of justice in the United Kingdom.

The tour finished with a continuing level of violence. Fisher and Wright were transferred to the 2nd Battalion in Scotland, where they were kept under close arrest. I had asked for military bail when they first appeared in court, requesting that they be released into my custody by the magistrates' court, but they were still in custody, awaiting trial, when the tour ended.

TEN

A MISSION TO BOSNIA

'There are no good guys in Yugoslavia.'

On leaving Northern Ireland the battalion returned to Germany, where we went on leave. Six months in Belfast is a very long time and we really needed a break, for everyone was tired. I know I was exhausted, and we still had some six months left to serve in Germany before we returned to the UK and took up the round of public duties at Windsor. When we returned to Hohne to rejoin the 7th Armoured Brigade, we found ourselves armoured infantry without armour; our Warrior APCs had been taken away and we became foot soldiers yet again.

Our awards for the Northern Ireland tour arrived later, when we returned to Windsor, and although we did not get all we had put in for, we did pretty well. The procedure is that towards the end of the tour, a battalion CO is asked to recommend a number of men for awards, while the Brigadier is asked to brood on the merits of the CO. The task of singling out some men over others is very difficult and it is best to think of the awards as a compliment to the battalion as a whole. I finally put up about twenty-five men for awards.

We had two company commanders who, both having done well, deserved recognition, so I put in for two MBEs but we only got one; the other company commander got a Mention-in-Despatches. I put that very good Rhodesian NCO Sergeant Goodman up for the Military Medal but he got a Queen's Gallantry Medal, and his sidekick, whom I put up for a QGM, got a Mention-in-Despatches. We got a good number of Mentions-in-Despatches and Queen's Commendations – and I got the OBE, which means the battalion did bloody well.

Garrison life is never very stimulating but another problem was looming, this time in the Balkans following the break-up of the former Yugoslavia, and it seemed likely that some elements of Rhine Army would soon be redeployed there as part of some UN peace-keeping initiative. Indeed, one battalion of the Cheshire Regiment, a Warrior battalion stationed at Fallingbostel, just down the road from us, had already been sent there and others were standing by, so the possibility of going there certainly existed.

Our Brigadier, John Kiszley, did not want the soldiers getting bored, so we decided to lay on an exercise to test our capabilities for a possible Balkan deployment. This took place in the Saarland, a region of hills, lakes and forests in central Germany which was not the usual, rather boring military training area and not unlike the terrain in central Bosnia.

The Territorial SAS were recruited to act as the enemy and we laid on an ambitious, three-week exercise on the theme of different ethnic factions fighting each other and supported by external power from across the border. This was a 'limited war' exercise, on foot, starting with a full deployment into the operational area, partly by helicopter, and ending with a thirty-mile night infiltration exercise leading up to a night attack by the battalion on an airfield. We played it as realistically as possible and fortunately the weather was appalling; it snowed at the start and got steadily worse.

This was valuable training and rounded out our time in Germany before we returned to Windsor and moved into the newly built Victoria Barracks, which always contained the garrison for Windsor Castle. There had been a Guards barracks on the site since Georgian times, but only one of the old buildings remained. The rest, while comfortable and functional, were described by one of the officers as 'a cross between a prison and Tesco's supermarket' – very ugly, but totally modern and well designed.

Our main function here was to mount the Guard at Windsor Castle as well as public duties in London, and somehow maintain our fitness and operational ability. That apart, we provided patrols around Heathrow Airport against some perceived terrorist threat, we deployed one company to Cyprus and we kept up the shooting and fitness training, but our main outlet was adventure training, which is valuable because it not only tests the soldiers' initiative and courage, it is also good fun. This training focused on a summer-long exercise, 'Alp 4,000', an attempt to climb every peak in the Alps over 4,000 metres in one season and raise money for the cot death charity. The attempt was led by Mark Whitcombe from 22 SAS and Captain Douglas Glenn from the battalion, plus a mixed group of SAS instructors and Scots Guards climbers, and the idea was to rotate as many as possible of the battalion out there during the season, with so much sponsorship for each peak climbed.

Halfway through, I took HRH the Duke of Kent, the Regimental Colonel of the Scots Guards, out to the Alps to see how they were getting on, and I went out again with my thirteen-year-old stepson Ben, when we joined the rest to climb Mont Blanc. This proved a bit of a trial, since everyone else had been out there for weeks and they were all very fit. To get an early start we spent the night before the climb in a snow hole and started out for the top at 1 a.m.; getting to the top took ten long hours and we were both exhausted but very pleased to have done it.

During this time we still had the trial of Fisher and Wright hanging over us. I appeared at the trial and gave evidence on their behalf. After they were convicted I appeared again at the appeal and when they were found guilty of murder and sentenced to life imprisonment we were all outraged. This was when I began to doubt the validity of a system that puts young soldiers in these situations, expects them to perform in a restrained way under any provocation and then fails to support them when they do what appears to be the right thing. I was particularly incensed because I had trained these men and had them under command and I knew, as they knew, the difficulties we were working under.

It seemed so unjust. There was no suggestion that they had left barracks intending to shoot Mr McBride or anyone else. I believed then and I believe still that they were perfectly right to open fire and what happened was, at worst, a tragic accident. I also believe that the system treated them appallingly. They went to prison and it took a five-year campaign by the former officers of the Scots Guards – the Fisher and Wright Release Group – and others to get them out. Mo Mowlam, the Secretary of State for Northern Ireland, finally released them on licence in 1998 after a lot of pressure. Quite rightly, they then returned to duty in the army and are currently seeking to have their sentences quashed.

I could not play as large a part as I wanted in the Release Group campaign because by the time it got going I was out of the army and working with Sandline in Papua New Guinea. A 'former CO of Fisher and Wright runs mercenary operation' line would have been a propaganda gift to the IRA and the people opposing their release, so, having discussed it with John Kiszely, who was then the Regimental Colonel, we decided that I should keep a low profile.

And so my time in command of the 1st Battalion, Scots Guards, came to an end, and the question now was what to do next. I had been a lieutenant-colonel for four years and had various hopes, either to go on the higher command and staff course and get promoted, or to go to the MOD on some good staff job, preferably in intelligence, operations or plans.

There were all sorts of reasons for this, not least the question of my family. I had been moving about constantly over the past two years. I had not taken my family to Germany or Ireland and, having a house in London, I liked the idea of living there for a while, giving my family more of my time and attention and getting some balance in my life. It was also a fact that working at the MOD was something I ought to do, if only to add that experience to my list of qualifications. One thing I wanted to avoid at this stage in my career was yet another training post, but in the event I was posted to run the commanding officers' designate course at the School of Infantry – or Combined Arms Training Centre, as it has since become – at Warminster in Wiltshire.

I have to say this posting did not go down very well. It was sold to me as a place I could be hauled out of on promotion or to go to the higher command staff course, but I did not find that convincing. To begin with, I thought the COD course a total waste of time. It is supposed to teach potential commanding officers the basics of commanding a battalion but, frankly, if they do not know how to command a battalion, they have no business being considered for that appointment anyway. You either had the necessary skill or not.

Anyway, if training was needed, the COD course would not provide it, for it only consisted of two weeks of lectures and discussions. I had attended a couple of days of this course and had not found it valuable. There were only two COD courses a year, so what I had been offered was four weeks' work a year; for the rest of the time I would presumably kick my heels. Frankly, I thought I was worth something better than that.

Reviewing my career, I could not see how me spending a couple of years hanging about at Warminster would benefit anyone. I had done nothing wrong, I had done a lot of courses, seen a wide variety of service and just been awarded a military OBE for my work in Northern Ireland, and now I was being shunted into this siding in Wiltshire. With all due modesty, I did not see this posting being anything other than a total waste of my time and talents, but I went there anyway. Orders are orders and in the army, at any level, when you have made your point, you do as you are told. So I got on with it, but I was not happy at all. One of the few high spots was a trip to Fort Leavenworth – the US Staff College – to look at training methods. It was on this visit that I met Bernie McCabe, a US Special Forces officer, who became a great friend and one of the mainstays of Sandline.

Looking back, I suppose that posting was simply a reflection of what was happening in the British Army at the time. The Empire had long gone, the Cold War was over and the army was shrinking. The promotion ladder narrows at the top and there were a lot of good officers around, all competing for the same, steadily shrinking number of posts. A good many of them were taking redundancy and leaving the army, a move coupled by an extremely expensive army advertising campaign to recruit more soldiers – and officers – to fill out the shrinking ranks of our already overstretched battalions.

I decided to leave my family in London rather than move them into a 'quarter' at Warminster and, commuting to and fro, I had time to think about where I was going and what to do about my career. I was now forty-two, and if I was going to make a change I could not wait much longer. That apart, I really needed to make some money to provide for my growing family. Nobody joins the army for money, and although the army is very good with allowances for the education of children and so on, army life is essentially a vocation. There is certainly no fortune in it.

The outcome was that I had lunch with an old friend of mine, David Juster, who had been in the Gulf Bunker at High Wycombe. I told him that I was pretty fed up and that if the right opportunity came along I was ready to leave the army. David had become a head-hunter in the City and had a wide range of contacts, so he promised to look around.

His response was extremely rapid. I was driving back to Warminster after lunch when my mobile phone rang. It was David, suggesting I should contact Jamie Ogilvy, a former Scots Guards officer who was now chief executive of Foreign and Colonial, a well-established City investment company that was interested in expanding into the Middle East and might find my contacts there useful.

Matters then proceeded rapidly. I had an interview with two people at Foreign and Colonial, Fred Packard and Jonathan Lubron, and that went well. Although they considered me a bit of a risk, since I had no City experience, the upshot was that they offered me the job. We then had further meetings to agree terms and, having agreed to leave the army and join them as soon as possible, I returned home that day to find that the MOD had been on the telephone with an urgent message: 'Where the hell have you been? Mike Rose wants you in Bosnia – tomorrow.'

This was a tricky one. I had already decided to resign and, having thought it all through carefully, had realised this was the right decision. I had also just accepted a very good job, but the army still had me and this post in the Balkans, where the Serbs were on the rampage around Sarajevo, sounded both interesting and exciting. In the end, after several telephone conversations with the military secretary's department, Mike Rose, the School of Infantry and Foreign and Colonial, we struck a deal. Foreign and Colonial would keep the job open for some months while I went to Bosnia, and when that task was over the army would raise no objections and expedite my departure to civilian life. With that much agreed, I took off for Sarajevo to do a four-month tour for Mike Rose. This deal was done in about twenty-four hours and everyone was happy, especially me, with an operational tour working with Mike Rose to round off my service career.

Michael Rose is a very impressive individual. He has had a well-documented and adventurous military career, starting off in the Coldstream Guards but then joining the SAS, which he commanded in the Falklands and during the Iranian Embassy siege. He then went on to be the Director, Special Forces, before commanding a brigade in Northern Ireland and the 2nd Infantry Division. I knew him from the time he had been in the Coldstream Guards and when he was commanding 22 SAS, but I did not know him very well before I went to work for him in Bosnia.

Mike Rose looks the part. He is the ideal of a modern general, and a very striking person when you first meet him. He came up through the Special Forces system, is very fit, looks much younger than he is and has very piercing, fierce eyes which he fixes on you when you are talking to him. They seem to bore right into you so that he not only hears what you are saying, he also knows what you are thinking. He had a reputation for being a hard taskmaster but I did not find him particularly intimidating as I liked his style, which largely consists of getting on with the job and standing no nonsense from anyone around him, be they his superiors, juniors or civilians. This particularly applies to those civilians in the UN.

He was the sort of commander I enjoy working for; if he trusts you, you are allowed to get on with the job with the minimum of supervision, but if you let him down or fail to measure up, you are out. I thoroughly enjoyed working for him in Bosnia and his single-minded determination to carry the job through and do what he thought was right was very refreshing, especially after coming across a number of rather wishy-washy people in the army.

Rose was accompanied everywhere in Bosnia by an SAS staff-sergeant known as 'Goose' Cryer, who was another product of the SAS system and a very affable, genial, relaxed individual who could switch from inactivity to furious and aggressive activity in a split second. He was a perfect support to the general, and the ideal bodyguard – he could be very unobtrusive most of the time but very obtrusive if the situation required it. There are a number of accounts of him dealing out very swift justice to some of the thugs that appeared on the scene in Sarajevo.

I always found Goose very easy to deal with. He tended to take care of those around the General, though this never distracted him from his primary role of looking after the boss. He was very knowledgeable, very good with weapons, a very good driver and a thoroughly good sort who developed a friendly relationship with most people. He had a particular talent for establishing solid relations with his opposite numbers, the bodyguards among the warring factions we went to talk with. He would chat them up and thereby glean a lot of useful information about the various leaders.

The background to the Balkan wars of the 1990s is well known. The conflict is a form of internecine civil war involving a high level of atrocities, massacres and murders, many under the heading of 'ethnic cleansing'. This is the fashionable term for genocide, one of the Balkan 'tribes', a more accurate term than 'nations' – the Serbs, Croats, Slovenes, Montenegrins, Albanians – attempting to drive out one or more of the other tribes, encouraging them to leave by bombing their homes, burning their farms and slaughtering their young men. These conflicts are aggravated by religious divides between Christians and Muslims. That this should happen in supposedly civilised countries on the fringes of Western Europe in the last decade of the twentieth century is tragic – and amazing.

In an attempt to limit the slaughter, the UN had put in a protection force

Expedition to southern Jordan to find T.E. Lawrence, 1993.
Left to right: David J, Douglas Glen, Colour-Sergeant Ali, Tim Spicer

With the Jordanian Army, 1993

With Michael Rose in Bosnia, 1994

Bosnia, 1994

MI-24

MI-17 with ECOMOG troops, Sierra Leone

With Defence Minister Matthias Ijape, Central Highlands,
Papua New Guinea, 1997

The Sandline helicopter at Zimmi, Kamajor
operational base, Sierra Leone, 1998

Sandline helicopter on operations

RUF rebels on Kenema Road

Sierra Leone

Kamajors, Bo, Sierra Leone

called UNPROFOR, composed of troops from half a dozen nations. Mike Rose was currently the commander of UNPROFOR and was having some problems with the media – 'a press nightmare', as he put it. I had met him when I had taken the SAS selection course many years ago, and now he wanted me to get a grip on the press and public-relations side of UNPROFOR. Since I had no knowledge of working with the media other than a five-day course for battalion PR officers in the days of my youth, this was a risk for both of us and a considerable challenge for me.

Basically, Mike wanted someone who could not only understand the military situation facing UNPROFOR, which called for a military man, but could also put this over to the media in simple, understandable terms, without equivocation. I had always been interested in the power of the media, but I arrived in Bosnia to find the most God-awful PR mess.

The first point that we had to get across was that UNPROFOR was not tasked or equipped in any way to take on the Serbs – the vector of the current Balkan conflict around Sarajevo – or anyone else. The press felt that we should be undertaking offensive operations against the Serbs and were plugging that point hard. As a result Mike Rose was losing the PR battle and needed someone to put his story across.

Just to complicate the situation further, public relations was supposed to be the remit of the UN civilian side rather than the military, and they were supposed to lead on it. There was a civilian PR set up but it was not working; it was not winning the war of minds. It was therefore clear to Rose and me that we had to take over control from the civilian side and explain to the media – and the world at large – the realities of life in Bosnia at that time. This caused a lot of friction but it was clearly the right thing to do: the situation in Sarajevo was a military situation and the UN troops were the central organisation.

UNPROFOR's mandate was to protect the safe havens and escort food convoys, not to wage war on the Serbs; in short, peace-keeping, not peace-making – and even peace-keeping was hard enough given our shortage of manpower and equipment, the lack of a clear-minded doctrine and the relentless antagonism of the Serbs and their Bosnian Muslim opponents. We had a very mixed bag of troops – British armoured infantry, French paratroopers, Bangladeshi infantry (very poorly equipped), a Dutch battalion, Ukrainians – and even if these could be handled as a united force, there were distinct limits to our rules of engagement. Lacking force and authority, with no artillery, no mortars and no common doctrine, it followed that much of the work, which amounted to holding the ring and keeping the factions apart, depended on personal contacts, persuasion and will-power. It was also very important to keep the media informed and, if possible, on side.

Mike Rose was not in Sarajevo when I arrived and did not arrive for another two days. The city was closely besieged by the Serbs, who had snipers on the lower slopes and artillery in the surrounding hills and kept the citizens under sporadic attack. The only thing that prevented them from coming into the town and slaughtering the Muslim population was that if they did so, the UN troops, British and French would certainly have fought back with everything they had, and called in air power – a fact that Mike Rose had already impressed on the Serb commander, the notorious General Mladic.

While waiting for Mike to come back and brief me, I found my way around and made contact with the media and the people at his headquarters. Many of the media seemed to have become closely involved with the war and were featuring the Serbs as the bad guys. There was a lot of truth in this but, as the days went by, I began to realise that in the Balkans they are all as bad as each other; the Croats and Muslims were not above a spot of 'ethnic cleansing' if the opportunity presented itself. In fact, most Yugoslavs would kill each other, given half the chance.

One incident that occurred just before I arrived was the tragic 'bomb in the marketplace' incident when many Muslims were killed, but when all the evidence was collected and examined, there appeared to be at least some substance in the allegation that the Muslims had mortared their own people in order to accuse the Serbs of a further atrocity and keep the Muslims' predicament in the public eye. How this incident was presented to the world depended on the point of view taken, and there was also a lot of hostility between UNPROFOR and the media. Finally, to complicate matters still further, the official UN line was that, in spite of all the evidence, Sarajevo was not under siege.

Being a simple soldier, I found that position hard to maintain. Sarajevo was under fire from artillery, mortars and snipers; people were being killed every day. Granted, some convoys were allowed in and out, but on Serb sufferance, and any Muslim found in one of those convoys was in danger of execution. The city's water and electricity supplies were in the hands of the Serbs, who cut them off whenever they felt like it. Every building was pockmarked with bullet holes and no one inside the city was in any doubt that we were under siege.

Mike's HQ was run by his military assistant, a Greenjacket officer, Colonel Jamie Daniel, who had already established a good rapport with the media and with the UK media in particular. Jamie ran the General's private office, where we all worked, and handled the day-to-day business of being personal staff officer to a general. He had an extremely difficult job in Sarajevo, for not only did he have to look after the interests of his boss, he also had to deal on a minute-by-minute basis with the warring factions, NATO, the UK headquarters in Wilton, the MOD in London, the UN headquarters in Zagreb, the Americans, the press and just about anyone else who made up the cast of characters in Sarajevo at that time.

Jamie worked long hours and handled the complexities of dealing with all those different agencies and organisations, all with their various agendas, extremely well. He was also very helpful to me and quickly showed me the ropes, took me into his confidence and did not feel threatened by having another experienced and senior British officer on the team. In fact, sharing the duties with him proved the ideal combination, given the complexities of the situation and the long hours involved.

Then, apart from the usual HQ personnel, signallers and drivers, there were the JCOs, the joint commission observers, mostly SAS, commanded by Jamie Lowther-Pinkerton. These men were invaluable in finding out what was really going on and I formed a very close relationship with them. Major Jamie Lowther-Pinkerton was an old friend, someone I had known for some time, and he and I arrived in Sarajevo on the same aircraft. He was an Irish Guardsman – people might be forgiven for thinking that Rose's headquarters were rapidly becoming a base for the Foot Guards Mafia – and a delightful individual, a bit of a wild Irish boy but a very capable soldier, an enthusiastic party animal and great fun to have around in trying circumstances. He and I formed a very good working partnership and he ran his team very well, using his unusual mind to come up with some good ideas. In this he was ably supported by Geordie Sim, his No. 2, who was very effective in steering his way through the rock-strewn waters that the JCOs were required to cover.

The final member of the headquarters team that has to be mentioned is Mike Stanley, or Milos Stancovich, who was a Serb by descent and spoke the language fluently. Mike probably had the most difficult job of all, not only acting as Mike Rose's interpreter but trying to get into the mind of the Bosnian Serbs. He had been in Bosnia almost from the start, he was very mercurial, he had seen a lot of awful things – and it showed. He naturally had an affinity for the place and an understanding of the culture and language of the people, but the trying circumstances he found himself in all the time – and he had been there for two years – were starting to take their toll, as they would have done on anybody. Nevertheless he did a very good job and I enjoyed working with him, although occasionally, due to his flashes of temper, he did not do much to ingratiate himself with some of the others. My task was to work with these people and then present the media with what we hoped was an accurate picture of the situation each day.

The main forum for this was the daily briefing, when we gave an update on what had happened during the previous twenty-four hours, but this was complemented by regular private briefings both on the record and off the record. There were about fifty or sixty journalists in the city, all with sharp pencils and all asking very sharp questions. These included some very good people like Kurt Shork of Reuters, Jackie Shymanski of CNN, Malcolm Brabant and Jim Muir of the BBC, Joel Brand of *The Times* and *Newsweek*, Emma Daley of *The Independent* and two very good French journalists, Ariane Quentier and Reny Ourdun. I became very fond of the media community. I thought some of them were completely biased and very difficult and nothing would change their minds, but the better ones were open to discussion and prepared to accept something that was open and logical and clearly honest.

So, having taken control of the PR department, I put together a military team including a very capable and amusing French officer named Herve Gommilon who was clearly working on an agenda emanating from Paris, a Dutch officer and a number of civilian assistants who acted as subordinates, including a delightful Burmese, Thant Mint-U, who was a nephew of U Thant, sometime Secretary-General of the UN.

The situation in Sarajevo, working with the UN and interposed between two warring parties who hated each other, is somewhat hard to describe and best illustrated by a few short examples. There were one or two other incidents during my four months in Bosnia that are worth recording, incidents that illustrate what a curious life we led there at that time, under constant pressure, especially from the Muslims and the Americans, to be more pro-active against the Serbs. To achieve this end, various stratagems were common.

The Muslims were holding a section of the perimeter around Sarajevo and on one occasion, in spite of the cease-fire negotiated with the Serbs by Mike Rose, they attacked out of the city, in order to precipitate a Serb counter-attack and then claim they had been attacked. We could hear the start of this business from our headquarters, a massive amount of firing from up near the old castle that dominates the city. We could hear it even before the reports came in, so we went out and piled into vehicles. Mike and Jamie got into one and I got into another, and off we went to find out what the hell was going on, since first reports indicated that the Serbs were coming in to overrun the city.

There was quite a lot of incoming fire, and Mike and Jamie got up to a British position near the castle, a Cymbeline mortar-locating post, which was invaluable in deciding who had started it and who was actually doing the firing now. I used their information a lot later, as the media had an obsession with cease-fire violations and who had started them, and we needed evidence to prove to the journalists the violations were not entirely one-sided.

Mike and Jamie were watching this fight when a burst of fire hit the wall nearby and nearly killed Jamie – Mike had to drag him to safety in one of the armoured vehicles. There was a lot more firing, but we went back to headquarters and gradually it died down, though later that night a French armoured car was hit by a rocket-propelled grenade when it was trying to interpose itself between the warring factions. No one on board was hurt but that sort of thing was what we had to put up with on an almost daily basis.

To give another example, we all tried to keep ourselves fit and to this end Mike would take his headquarters staff out for runs, uphill and back, about a mile and a half each way, perhaps half a dozen of us, trotting up the road. We were always under observation by both sides, Serb and Muslim, and occasionally there would be the crack of a round passing over us as someone got off a shot at us. There was no one else on the road, so these shots were clearly designed to worry us. Mike Rose started this daily run to try and restore an air of normality; he also used to go riding on the city trams, talking to the locals, and he got the band of the Coldstream Guards to come out and play in the football stadium – anything to restore at least some semblance of normality and give the people a little hope. To this end, going for a run was an indication that we were not going to be intimidated by either the Serbs or the Muslims.

War and peace in Bosnia largely depended on where you were. On another occasion we had to go up to Zagreb for a conference with Mr Akashi, the UN representative. I think Mike Rose wanted to thump the table a bit about the lack of support from the civilian PR apparatus; in fact, far from being supported, Mike felt we were actually being undermined. We flew up there in a clapped-out Russian aircraft flown by a crew of former Spetsnaz, Russian Special Forces, and we piled out on to the tarmac at Zagreb, all in combat gear and carrying rifles – only to be met by a limousine and whisked off to the luxurious Intercontinental Hotel.

This was typical of the incongruity of the entire situation. Sarajevo was an historic city, a university town, once the site for the Winter Olympic Games, and now it looked like Stalingrad in the Second World War, with buildings in ruins or marked with shell and bullet holes – while in Zagreb, an hour away, normal life went on.

When we flew back to Sarajevo, the passengers included Mike Rose's group, some Russian generals and a lot of nuns – quite bizarre. And when we got back, we could not land at once as the airfield was under fire. We circled round and round for some time, watching tracer flying about below, but the most startling moment was when one of the crew suddenly ran up the aisle to the front of the aircraft, pulled up a panel in the floor and bashed something with a hammer. It transpired that the delay in landing was not due to the firing but was because the landing gear would not go down until he gave it a clout with a hammer – which did nothing to restore my confidence in some of the aircraft we were expected to fly in.

The press tended to live in the Holiday Inn, which was right on the front line. In fact, you could not live in one side of the hotel, a bullet-scarred building often under fire, but they all had rooms there and kept their cars in the basement car park. Getting out of the car park was quite risky, especially at night. The press tend to assume that they are on the sidelines in a war, though quite a few journalists were killed in Sarajevo and they were definitely not popular with the Serbs. One day, in the late afternoon, I was sitting in the office and the telephone rang. It was Joel Brand of *The Times*, saying, 'We are under attack at the Holiday Inn.' I could hear the noise of firing and breaking glass over the phone. I said, 'Don't panic, I will come down and see what is going on.'

I grabbed some of the JCOs and off we went. The hotel was indeed under fire; in fact, there was a hell of a gun battle going on. The front of the building, facing the Serb lines, was not occupied and everyone was cowering in the centre of the hotel, but I wanted to take a look out towards the Serb positions and see what was going on. This was a trifle tricky, but with some of the JCOs I crept up the stairs.

By now it was dark outside. All the corridor lights were on and we needed to have these off, so that we could get into one of the rooms and take a peek through the windows without being detected. We managed that and saw that there was sporadic fire coming towards the hotel. We were trying to spot where it was coming from and see whether it was the Serbs or the Muslims having a go – it could have been either – but just as we were getting settled down to observe through our night-vision glasses, the hotel janitor came in through the door and put all the lights on! We threw him out but, even so, we thought we ought to move, so we changed rooms and this time we locked the door.

Unfortunately, our new position must have been spotted because the opposition let rip at this room with just about everything they had, really hosing it with fire, and something very powerful, a rocket-propelled grenade round or something similar, struck the lintel of the window. We decided to leave pronto – only to find that we could not get the bloody door open.

Eventually we managed and piled out, slammed the door shut, ending up in a heap on the carpet, and looked up to find an ABC film crew in the corridor, filming the whole incident. I told them that we had been trying to find out what had been going on and gave them a quick soundbite interview on the spot before I went outside. Then the French started to bring up armoured cars, and I was standing there talking to Jim Muir of the BBC when there was a great burst of machine-gun fire down the road before us. The French returned fire, the JCOs returned fire and a big gun battle started again. We never really got to the bottom of it but I suspect that the Serbs knew the media were in the Holiday Inn and, there being no love lost between them, decided to get a bit of their own back. Crazy, perhaps, and not the way to get the press on side – but that was what life was like in Sarajevo.

For the first couple of days I went to the daily press conference as an observer and said nothing and then Mike Rose came back and we sat down and thrashed the whole thing out. He said that I had to be right in his pocket and know the reason for and background to every decision, so in effect I became his second military assistant and often shared that work with Jamie Daniel. We opened the doors to the press, gave them information, gave them tip-offs and tried to be as transparent as we could, but at the same time being forceful in the statement of the UNPROFOR position.

The fighting around Sarajevo had calmed down, but the Serbs had a stranglehold on the city. It was almost impossible to get into Sarajevo – the airport was the only real lifeline – and the Serbs were conducting military operations against the city. The Muslims needed to keep themselves in the eye of the international community as the injured parties in this affair and they were not too fussy how they did it, even creating incidents that put them in a good light.

We then got into the situation where it was proposed to deter the Serbs with air strikes. The Serbs promptly retaliated by taking hostages and chaining them to high-value targets, stopping aid convoys and carrying out even more ethnic cleansing. During the time I was there we had a British battalion defending the safe area at Gorazde and doing a brilliant job in very difficult circumstances, and I went in there on a number of occasions. On one occasion I went in with a number of the JCOs, tasked to bring out the first of the medical convoys through Serb territory. This convoy consisted of sick people who needed to go to hospital.

We flew into Gorazde by helicopter, taking some of the Muslim leaders with us, but on the way we had to put down at a Serb position to get clearance for the convoy and there we were searched and done over by the Bosnian Serbs. They went through the Muslim leaders' personal items and gave them a very hard time. It began to look nasty until I collared the senior Serb officer present, General Tollemir, and said to him that these people were under my care and that General Rose had agreed this mission with General Mladic and Radovan Karadjic and we did not expect any problems. Tollemir seemed to accept this and very soon we went on our way.

I think this incident provides a clue to the Serb character. If you do not back down in the face of their bullying attitude, they will ease off and leave you alone. We flew on into Gorazde and spent the day getting the convoy together, mostly old and sick people and some children, in order to evacuate them to Sarajevo.

Gorazde was in an almost medieval state of siege. Nothing moved on the streets by day, transport was either on foot or horse-drawn, there were stacks of logs and timber in front of the buildings. The bare necessities were all that mattered: food, water, shelter, heat. Many of the buildings had been badly damaged, the hospital was covered in sandbags, British and Ukrainian troops were everywhere and the entire place was closely invested by the Serbs. I remember a small child coming up to me; all his teeth were rotten, but he was otherwise a beautiful child, except for the dead look in his eyes. He wanted food, and that was the classic dilemma, for our stocks were limited and who did you give it to? Fortunately I had some sweets, so I distributed these among the children and slipped this one a tin of tuna fish as well; he ran off with that, probably to take it back to his family.

There were a number of problems with the Serbs surrounding Gorazde, who were a very aggressive bunch, and we insisted that since we had to drive through the Serb lines most of the way back, we must be accompanied by a Serb officer in a Serb army jeep who could pass us through the check points. It took about six hours to drive back to Sarajevo but we delivered the convoy safely and I count that as a worthwhile and successful operation. We could not get the young men out as the Serbs would not have let them pass, thinking they would then go and join the Muslim forces. This was useful experience but it also enabled me to give the press corps an accurate account of the operation and chalk up an UNPROFOR success.

Gorazde was still under siege and there were a number of instances where the British battalion there actually engaged the Serbs to protect the Muslim population. The CO himself got involved and a great deal of ammunition was shot off to keep the Serbs back, but the British troops stood firm and the Serbs did not come in. This is not what happened at Srebrenica, not far from Gorazde, where a Dutch battalion allowed the Serbs to overrun the town. Once in possession they went on the rampage and massacred some 6,000 people. If there had been a British battalion there, they would have put up a fight. It is easy to be wise after the event but, had it been me and my battalion, I would rather have put up a fight, whatever the outcome, than put my hands up and then stood by and watched a massacre. There was a ghastly photograph afterwards of the poor Dutch commanding officer being forced to have a drink with General Mladic, after the Serbs had taken over the town – a complete and utter disgrace.

I met Mladic several times. He is a typical intransigent Serb bully-boy, very cunning, very patriotic, a thoroughly malignant piece of work. In Serb terms he was a good soldier but we found, as with the other Serbs, that if you stood up to him and did not give in to his bully-boy tactics – and showed him that you meant it – he would back down. There was a lot of toing and froing between Mike Rose's HQ, Mladic's base at Jarharina and that of the Bosnian Serb President Radovan Karadich at Pale, where the whole Bosnian Serb gang was assembled, as we tried to negotiate the evacuation of civilians and the passage of food convoys. I think that had there been a properly constituted and equipped UN force, we could have negotiated from strength and forced Mladic and Karadjic into a proper kind of behaviour, and a lot of innocent lives would have been saved.

We used to see a lot of the Serbs and the Muslims. Sometimes we would see one lot separately and sometimes the other and sometimes we would be there when they were both negotiating. These negotiations would go on for hours and hours and hours, starting, in the case of the Muslims, with a long harangue about how the UN were doing nothing. Deputy Prime Minister Ganic was particularly vitriolic about what Michael Rose was or was not doing, and Mike was brilliant, not least in that he did not succumb to the temptation to get up and punch Ganic on the nose.

Ganic was another thoroughly unpleasant piece of work and it was quite clear to anyone who was present in the negotiations with these people – a situation the journalists unfortunately could not see – that the Serbs and Muslims were just as unpleasant as each other, just as devious and just as ruthless.

The Bosnian Serb gang were very difficult, very tough, but in some ways less devious than the Muslims; what you saw was what you got, and you had to chip away at it. Our secret weapon was Major Mike Stanley, an extremely valuable member of the team, but the Serbs and Muslims knew his Serb background and detested him. The Muslims thought he was an enemy and the Serbs thought he was a traitor.

What happened in Bosnia came back to haunt Mike a year or so later, when he was back at the Staff College in England. He was detained and questioned by the MOD police for allegedly passing NATO secrets to the Serbs. He was never arrested and charged, just detained and questioned, and it is noticeable that it was the MOD police who were doing this rather than, say, the Special Branch, who would normally handle such a serious matter. I thought that these accusations were complete rubbish; anyone who has ever had the pleasure of serving with Mike Stanley would know he was an absolutely loyal, capable soldier and an indispensable member of the Sarajevo team. These accusations were probably orchestrated by some of the enemies he had made among the UN hierarchy, and in my view he had absolutely no case to answer.

However, back in Bosnia, my time with the UN, my four-month tour with Mike Rose, was coming to an end. When my time was up, Mike was away, but I had clearly made some kind of contribution because we had been visited by General Sir John Wilsey, Commander UK Land Forces, who wanted me to stay on in the army and even stay on in Bosnia after Mike left, becoming military assistant to the new UNPROFOR commander, General Rupert Smith of the Parachute Regiment, since Jamie Daniel was also due to leave.

General Wilsey and I had a long chat about this, standing on the steps outside the HQ in Sarajevo, but in the end I had to ask what was in it for me. We knew each other well, since he had been GOC (General Officer Commanding) in Northern Ireland when I had been there commanding my battalion, so we could talk frankly. I had made my decision to leave the army, I had a good job waiting, and although I had enjoyed my army career and this work in Bosnia, I had to look ahead. I had to say that staying on in Bosnia was very tempting, but unless he had something positive to offer after that, in the shape of an interesting job and the certainty of promotion in the longer term, it was time to move on. He was very nice about it but had nothing concrete to offer, so we had to leave it.

Leaving was still a problem because Mike Rose and Jamie Daniel were away and I seemed to be holding the fort at headquarters, where I had been acting as Mike's second military assistant, quite apart from my role with the media. There was talk of the UK Rapid Deployment Force coming in with Rupert Smith as a stop-gap measure by UNPROFOR, which had almost exhausted its credibility by this time – through no fault of Michael Rose.

Mike was always in an untenable position, given the activities of the warring factions and the pressure of the international community. It was clear that there was a need for a more properly constructed military force, one with the capacity and authority to do something against any warring faction – and the muscle to back it up if need be. That was the transition between UNPROFOR and IFOR, the present, full-blown NATO deployment. We were also having problems in the Bihac pocket, where the situation was deteriorating, and Rose had gone home for some consultations and to have a break, which he clearly needed after a year in that environment.

I was deputed to speak on Rose's behalf and to liaise with the deputy commander of UNPROFOR, a highly professional French parachute officer, General Gobillard, who was also responsible for Sector Sarajevo and in charge while Rose was away. Most of the French contingent in Sector Sarajevo were from parachute units, who were in regular contact with the Serbs and stood no nonsense, having a very tough approach and not being averse to using force when necessary. My remit from Rose was to support Gobillard while Rose was away but to ensure that his policies were still applied and that we maintained the campaign direction.

This is one of the problems with a multi-national force, with all the vested national interests involved and the different ways of doing things. There is a UN chain of command, and that works up to a point, but you have to accept that national governments will get involved and communicate with their own troops over the heads of the UN commanders. The British and the French were the major contributors but we also had a Dutch battalion, plus Ukrainians, Danes, a Pakistani battalion and some Bangladeshis and Jordanians, so the situation was always complicated.

Keeping the show on the road was not easy, for there were other pressures. There was friction between UNPROFOR and NATO, largely because UNPROFOR had been badly mandated. To give one example, in order to call in an air strike, Rose had to go to the senior UN diplomat in Zagreb to get the authority to call in NATO air power and then go right though the NATO chain of command to get the thing in the air, and by the time the aircraft was overhead it was probably far too late.

NATO had the view that they were there to back the UN, to provide the muscle that UNPROFOR did not have, but because NATO command was dominated by Americans, who were strongly anti Serb – for good reasons – I believe the American media had the idea that we should be acting against the Serbs, which was not, repeat not, the UNPROFOR mandate. The UNPROFOR mandate was to separate the warring factions, negotiate, keep open the food-supply lines, protect the safe areas and not to attack the Serbs. It did not have the force to do that but it did have the ability to call on NATO. NATO, being a well-equipped and well-structured military organisation, could see that the time had come to whack the Serbs, but we still had to go through this complicated UN structure before we could get to NATO and ask them for help, and so the problems continued.

Anyway, all that would be someone else's problem – it was time for Spicer to get back to the UK and leave the army. Eventually I got in touch with Mike Rose and he said I could go. He even added, very kindly, that if I got myself to Split, since the Sarajevo airport was not reliable, he would lend me his private aircraft to fly me home. So I went up to Split, spent the night there and, still in my full combat clothing and equipment, including rifle, flew back to Heathrow in Mike's aircraft, where I was met on the tarmac by an old friend, George Dryden, who had been picking me up and driving me about for years.

George was somewhat surprised at being allowed to drive his car out on to the airport ramp at Heathrow and even more surprised when I came down the aircraft steps in full combat kit. This was at the time when the IRA were active in London, planting bombs, and army officers living in London were well advised to keep a low profile. Years before, when George had asked me what I did for a living, I had told him that I was in the map-making business. George drove me home, where the guests at a family lunch party were still sitting over the debris, and they were equally surprised when I walked in in combat kit and invited them to leave.

That was on Sunday. On the following day I drove down to Warminster and started to go through the procedures for leaving the army: handing in my kit, sorting out the pay and allowances, signing the Official Secrets Act. The final act was to hand over my identity card and, that done, suddenly, after eighteen years, I was a civilian.

The sensation is rather hard to describe. It felt lonely; the sensation is rather like finally leaving school. I was now directly and personally responsible for everything; for the last eighteen years, whatever the risks of the job, I had known that the pay cheque would be in the bank at the end of the month and that food and shelter would eventually be provided. The army offers risks and dangers, but it also provides a safety net and now that net was gone.

On the other hand, it was exciting. I had got my life back in good time to make a fresh start and see what I would make of it in the future. Mixed in with this were other emotions: a loss of comradeship, doubts over whether I really wanted to be a 'civvy' or, as we say in the Guards, an 'idle civvy', all civilians being essentially idle. So, wondering about the future, not yet missing the past, I drove back to London and a new life.

ELEVEN

AN 'IDLE CIVVY'

'Every man thinks meanly of himself for not having been a soldier.'
DR JOHNSON, 1778

My job title at Foreign and Colonial was Middle East Marketing Director. My task was to develop business with institutions and private investors throughout the Gulf, and to sell the benefits of Foreign and Colonial's financial-management services to interested parties in the Arab world. Foreign and Colonial was a City institution, very British, quite traditional, very well respected, similar in outlook to a merchant bank like Robert Fleming. It had been that way for over two hundred years, and now it wanted to expand its business, especially into the Middle East, a region it had not traded in before. I had been taken on as part of a new effort to sell the company's products and services to emerging markets throughout the Third World.

The chairman was a former Scots Guards officer, Jamie Ogilvy, a delightful fellow who was well regarded in the City. The directors were a very good crowd who gave me a great deal of encouragement and support, which was especially valuable as I had never worked in the City and had no real experience of civilian life. Knowing the Middle East as I did, I had to warn the board that we were in for the long haul, that matters did not happen overnight in Arab states and that they would have to be patient in awaiting results, which they fully understood.

Having said that, I was always conscious of the commercial imperative, the need in the City to produce results within a reasonable time – or you were out. Like everyone else I was on a one-year contract, which might or might not be renewed. It was a good lesson for me later in starting Sandline, the knowledge that the Queen was not going to pay the bills, that the business had to succeed and there was no safety net. The success of the business would be determined by my efforts.

So I went to work, ascending a steep learning curve, learning to talk to large investors and doing a great deal of travelling, mostly in two-week stints, to Saudi Arabia, the Oman, the Emirates, Jordan, Kuwait and the Lebanon. The work consisted of meeting institutions that needed to invest funds, organisations like the Kuwaiti Investment Authority or the Abu Dhabi Investment Authority or local banks, as well as high net-worth individuals. Our aim was to offer a better rate of return than they currently enjoyed and to provide access to an expanding range of investment opportunities all over the world.

Basically, if an individual or an institution had money to invest, we wanted them to invest it with us. We would then invest it on their behalf, based on their personal preferences, low risk or high risk, depending on the rate of return they wanted, in order to provide them with a dividend income and growth of assets outside their own country. We wanted to unlock their funds and put them to use, rather than have the cash sitting in a bank vault or under a bed. That was my task, and I think we did quite well. The Arabs are understandably cautious and you have to earn their trust before you get a whiff of their money, but once you have their trust and have put their money to good use, you will have a friend and a client for life.

After a few months I felt I could make a go of this life. I could see the way to make a career in this business and was establishing a bit of a reputation as a competent person, but I was not entirely happy. I was still linked in to the military world; the Fisher and Wright affair was still going on, with the trial and the subsequent appeal, and I had to go to Northern Ireland on a number of occasions. I also kept in touch with what was going on in Bosnia and met my former army colleagues regularly, and in the marketing team I was working with a former Greenjacket officer, who had previously been employed by Robert Fleming. He and I often used to talk about military matters.

As a result, I began to feel that my real vocation in life lay in the military or in the security business. At the same time, I did not want to go back to the army. I had done all that and it was over. What really interested me was matters military, and I felt that some activity which would keep me in touch with that world would be more in line with what I wanted.

A number of ideas flowed through my mind. One idea was to become a war correspondent. I had plenty of media contacts from my time in Bosnia, I liked the media ambience and the work interested me. I had even been co-opted from time to time by the BBC to make broadcasts on Bosnia as things happened out there. I was also in touch socially with two old friends, Richard Bethell and Alastair Morrison, both of whom had been in the Scots Guards. Both were also ex-SAS, and they now ran a company called Defence Systems Limited, or DSL, a commercial security and training company. There were mutterings from them from time to time along the lines of 'Why not come and join us?', and Alastair and I would have lunch and talk about it.

In October 1995 I went stalking in Scotland, and when I got back to the house there was a message asking me to ring Simon Mann, another former Scots

Guardsman, whom I had co-opted into Peter de la Billiere's team after the Gulf War. So I rang Simon and he said he would very much like to meet me for a drink and a general catch-up on our lives to date.

Simon was another old friend, with a military and sporting background. His father, George Mann, had been a highly decorated officer in the Scots Guards during the Second World War and was a famous cricketer. Simon has always been a good mate, and he and I have had some amusing times together. He is a great sailor and skier and a thoroughly good sport, and I always looked forward to meeting him.

I also knew that Simon, along with a friend of his, Tony Buckingham, had been involved in organising some form of military training operation in Angola. I knew about that because Simon had contacted me when I was working for the Director, Special Forces, before taking command of my battalion, and had asked me if I was interested in leaving the army and taking up some form of military contract in Angola. I thought carefully about this, for it sounded interesting, but it also sounded a bit fly-by-night and I wanted to know a lot more about it – and about Tony Buckingham – before I took any drastic step. The story he told me was interesting.

It transpired that Simon had been working with Tony on a number of entrepreneurial-type ventures, primarily in the oil industry. Tony had been representing an oil company who had had a quantity of valuable drilling equipment captured by UNITA, the Angolan rebels, in the town of Soyo, equipment which was on hire to the oil company and costing them a fortune in fees. He had therefore contacted UNITA and requested their permission to get this equipment back, explaining that they wanted no part in the war and just needed to get the kit out, but UNITA said no.

Tony Buckingham thought long and hard about that and decided that, since he had to get the kit back – it was costing some $20,000 a day in lease charges – it might be a good idea to suggest to the Angolan government that they recapture the entire town of Soyo, which is a key component of the national oil sector. He suggested to the government that he could introduce them to an outfit who could do the job alongside an Angolan army (FAA) force. The government was very attracted to the concept and, as a result, Tony introduced them to the fledgling Executive Outcomes (EO) of South Africa and a deal was struck. The attack duly went ahead, Soyo was retaken, Tony got his oil company's kit back, EO got paid and the government had its first major victory in its war with UNITA. So that was supposed to be it – end of story.

However, a week later, the telephone went in Tony's London office. The Angolan Embassy in London were on the line saying that President de Santos would very much like to meet him for a chat. Tony was looking in his diary and was about to suggest a date for the following week when it transpired that the presidential jet was even then at Stansted Airport waiting for him, and President de Santos wanted to see him in Angola – tomorrow.

This suggestion was so intriguing that Tony and Simon duly flew to Luanda and met the President, who, it appeared, was so impressed with the EO operation in Soyo that he wanted them to broker a deal between the Angolan government and EO for a comprehensive programme to improve and update the military capability of the Angolan Army, specifically in the area of training. Simon had rung me because the Angolan government needed an experienced senior officer, someone capable of training or commanding a battle group, to become involved in this training project and create a battle-group-sized unit for the Angolan government – and he thought of me.

This, I repeat, was in 1993, when I was working for the Director, Special Forces. Simon gave me a rough idea of the requirement and asked what it would take to make me leave the army and take this on. I thought it over and talked to my wife Caroline. She thought that if I were to do it, it had to be worth my while. It would mean giving up my next slot, commanding the 1st Battalion, Scots Guards, a great honour for any officer and one I was reluctant to abandon. Any offer would have had to have been really good to make me forego that chance and, to be honest, I deliberately set my demands too high, saying that it would require a great deal of money to make me give up command of the battalion. Actually, I was not too fussed about going to Angola – but filed away in the back of my mind was the thought that I had skills, military skills, for which governments were prepared to pay serious money and that there was potential in this idea.

The scene now moves forward to October 1995, when I got another telephone call from Simon, saying that Tony Buckingham would like to meet me. I had not met him, but he was an entrepreneur and former soldier, a man with his fingers in many pies, especially in the oil industry, and a man who has an insight into the military mind. We met for lunch, at Alvaro's excellent La Famiglia restaurant in Chelsea. We hit it off at once and he told me what was on his mind. What that was eventually became Sandline International, a private military company.

Tony Buckingham looks every inch the entrepreneur. He is a solidly built individual, usually sporting a suntan, always with a twinkle in his eye, often chomping on a huge Havana cigar. He has a penchant for matters military and adventures generally and has been described as a pirate, but I would describe him as more of a buccaneer; buccaneers tend to be on the side of the good guys, rather than the free-booting, taking-on-all-comers attitude more often found in pirates. He has an extraordinarily sharp mind, he is very good with people, he makes friends easily and he is adept at talking to heads of state and other important players. He also has a wide range of interests, from fine wines, fast cars and paintings, to sporting interests of the more adventurous kind, such as diving, skiing and stalking.

He has also had a wide range of occupations, ranging from North Sea oil diver to university lecturer, and has made a large fortune through his business acumen. He is great company, a very loyal individual, and once he becomes your friend he will always stand by you, especially in a tight corner – and I cannot think of anyone I would rather be in a tight corner with.

Before our meeting I had a drink with Simon, who brought me up to date with what Executive Outcomes had been doing in Angola and, more recently, in Sierra Leone. As a result, even before I met Tony, I began to think that there might be something for me here, something that would get me back into the military arena. This would involve working only for legitimate governments, helping them solve internal conflicts; it would not be mercenary activity, but a properly organised, professional company marketing military skills as a commercial operation. It transpired that this was more or less what Simon and Tony had in mind also.

This project might have been taken up by EO but by this time it was becoming clear that EO, however well established, carried a lot of political baggage. Most of those involved in the company were former members of the South African Defence Forces, dating back to the apartheid regime. I still believe and would still maintain that they did good work in Angola and Sierra Leone and they were certainly not a rag-tag outfit full of would-be Rambos, but Tony and Simon felt that it would be better to make a fresh start. All this came out in the course of conversation with Simon, but I was not exactly clear what they had in mind or what was on offer. I said as much to Simon in the pub, and that meeting was followed by the lunch with Tony Buckingham.

Tony asked me if I would be interested in setting up the sort of organisation that has now become known as a private military company, though that phrase was not in existence at the time. If I would be interested in developing business in this field, he thought I could do it. He also thought it was a marketable idea and that there was clearly a market for military skills. What did I think? Was I interested?

I said that I was. I thought it was a good idea, although there were, of course, a thousand questions to be answered. We left it like that and I went away to think about it. Matters then went quiet for a while, though I did get confirmation from Simon that Tony was quite serious and proposed backing this idea as a business venture.

Although the idea was rarely out of my mind from then on, I did not commit my thoughts or ideas to paper, or start working up the concept into the kind of outline proposals that might form a contract with a potential client. Tony is brilliant at spotting a commercial idea and developing it; that is what he had done here, and the nuts and bolts would come later. Our meeting did, however, unlock a lot of those ideas I had been filing away in my mind, consciously or unconsciously, over the years. It made me consider them as viable options for a private military company and useful in the rather complex international stage we all found ourselves on after the Cold War.

I could see that the world stage had a slot for people who are prepared to go where governments fear to tread in order to prevent further mayhem and further conflicts. There were plenty of people around with the necessary military skills at almost every level, and now there was an international businessman who thought marketing military expertise was a good idea and who was prepared to back it. It was the perfect combination, if I could put it together.

Discussions went ahead slowly, not least because I was still working for Foreign and Colonial and travelling a great deal. By the end of the year, with Simon liaising between Tony and myself, we had made some progress and were now talking figures. However, these things never come singly, and in mid-December I met Alastair Morrison for one of our periodic lunches and matters there suddenly got serious. He said that he and Richard Bethell wanted me to join them at Defence Systems Ltd (DSL) and made me a firm offer.

This was just before Christmas 1995 and we agreed that I would meet him and Richard after the New Year to discuss the details of what they wanted me to do and what the return would be. I had heard nothing concrete from Tony and Simon but I had decided that, one way or another, I would leave Foreign and Colonial. It was not that I had become disillusioned with the company or the work, but I had decided that my vocation lay in the military field. That was the area where I would be both happy and successful; I believe that you cannot have one without the other and, that being the case, I wanted to find a way back to the military world.

My year in the City was still very useful. I had got out of the army, away from the safety net; I had found my feet and I had learned a great deal. I knew how to prepare a business plan and how to read a balance sheet and I understood the commercial imperatives. Working in the City was not me, but I shall never regret doing it.

I went to see DSL after Christmas and they made me a formal offer, a complete package. I said that I would like to think about it, but in principle I liked the idea. In the interim, Simon had come back from his Christmas holiday, and when he rang me I said that we had been talking about this PMC project for some time, going round and round, and I now had another offer from DSL which I had to consider seriously. Therefore I needed a decision. I had to get out of Foreign and Colonial and Richard and Alastair were old friends and I did not want to muck them about. That ultimatum did the trick. Within three days Simon rang back, asking me to come into Tony's office as they wanted to make me an offer.

I duly went in, and there I met Michael Grunberg, Tony Buckingham's commercial adviser, who has since become another good friend. Michael has no military background whatsoever. He trained as an accountant, became a senior partner in a large City accountancy practice and developed further skills as a management consultant. As a result, he is not only an expert at crunching numbers, he is also very adept at picking up the fine details of any business – and he is nobody's fool.

When I first met Michael, I found him the odd man out in this team, the one member with no military experience. It did not take me long, however, to realise that he was remarkably astute. He was a real financial expert and could give very sound commercial advice, as well as being terribly hard-working – the general opinion is that he works far too hard and when not at his computer or on his phone is simply snatching a few hours' sleep. Having said all that, Michael is good company and great fun, but his primary focus is on making money. We talked the whole matter over once again and struck a deal whereby they would back me for a year. So I had a backer and a very embryonic idea which I now needed to develop.

It is easier to describe what I had in mind by explaining what I had decided not to do. The word 'mercenary' was not a dirty word to me, except when those involved were technically incompetent or criminally inclined. My ideal role models when it came to the 'mercenary soldier' concept were the people who went 'on contract' to serve in Dhofar; yes, there were the drunks and incompetents and those who were running away from their debts or their wives, rather as the Foreign Legion has such people, but most of them were very good soldiers.

The units in the war in Dhofar were commanded by seconded officers, mostly British, and a combination of Omani and 'contract officers' – i.e. mercenaries – who were fighting a valid war for the Omani government and fighting alongside British units, SAS, Royal Engineers, Artillery and RAF pilots. This was what PMCs were all about, a way of formalising that 'contract officer' concept that had been used successfully in Dhofar. That was the basic idea, but the concept was much looser than that. I had no intention of getting involved with the head-banded 'Dogs of War' image. What I had in mind, at its simplest, was a commercial way of deploying military skills to help governments in difficulty.

As a keen observer of the international stage, and having been in Germany when the Berlin Wall came down, I had first-hand experience of how the world suddenly changed when the Cold War ended. One day I was in charge of the brigade war plan, how we were to deploy our tanks and armoured infantry into the German countryside and fight the Russians; the next day that plan was dead, finished, over, because the Berlin Wall had come down and the Soviet Union had collapsed. I can remember traffic jams on the *autobahn*, cars going one way to look at East Germany and cars coming the other way to sample the West. It was amazing.

Suddenly, our war plans were no longer valid. There was no need for them, as the frontiers had moved east, beyond Poland. And then there was a shrinking of the services and the so-called 'peace dividend' – which was simply an excuse to spend even less money on the armed forces – and the world I had grown up in had changed. Later on, we discovered that the Russian military capabilities were not as great as we thought they were, but the lid they had kept on their regional friends had come off and let a lot of demons out.

And then I found myself in Bosnia. That was almost next door; I had been on holiday with my family to the Dalmatian coast, to stay in Fitzroy McLean's house on Korcola, and now the people there were killing each other in a bloody great war. That would never have happened during the Cold War, because those in charge would not have allowed it to happen. Times had changed.

Mike Rose, who has a very good line in catchphrases, said about his time in Bosnia, 'I will not be drawn across the Mogadishu Line,' recalling that time when the UN sent a force to solve the problems in Somalia and got into a complete muddle because the locals did not want them. The upshot was that American families, sitting at home watching television, saw their soldiers – and in some cases their sons – being killed by the people they had been sent in to help.

This was the next contributory factor in developing the Sandline concept which is as follows: (1) increased conflict in the world arena; (2) reluctance of the superpowers to get involved; (3) reduced capability of the traditional policemen. Added to this is the 'CNN Factor', the manipulation of public opinion by instantaneous reporting and a resulting reluctance to commit national forces for fear of casualties and bad publicity. Now, if all those factors are true, and I believe they are, then there is a market for those who can and will go in and help these governments – in other words, the private military companies.

I now had the opportunity to develop a basic concept, a rational ethos to meet the demands and opportunities of this new situation, but it was, in the beginning, pretty loose. We now had to come up with some practical marketing ideas, something to sell to prospective clients. I discussed all this with Tony, who had now become the patron of Sandline. He is very well connected all over the world, and contacts would be the basic requirement in selling our services. When you are starting out on your own it is very useful to have people like Tony and Michael Grunberg to bounce your ideas off, people who are commercially very knowledgeable and astute. So we kicked the ideas around and put them on paper, trying to get an ethos that would lead to a concept, in order to arrive at the best course of action.

There was also the now-familiar commercial imperative to get the show on the road, but the first thing I had to do was clear the decks with my friends at DSL. I went to see them and told them, quite simply, that I had had a more appealing offer which I had decided to accept. They saw my point, wished me every success and we remain friends.

At Foreign and Colonial I was equally frank. I told them that I had tried it and given it a good shot but had found it was not for me. I thanked them for taking me on and said I hoped it had proved worth their time but my heart was simply not in it. I think they were a little bit peeved but, interestingly enough, Robert Fleming had already tried to head-hunt me to join them. I was not hungry enough to make the switch, although there were a lot of former soldiers at Robert Fleming and the atmosphere there might have been more to my taste.

Anyway, I parted amicably from Foreign and Colonial, made one last trip around the Middle East to introduce my contacts to my successor Mike Robertson and, in the middle of February 1996, I started work in London.

Sandline International did not even have a name at this point. I had a desk, an idea and a bookful of contacts. I had decided that I needed some help and it was at this point that I found out that my friend Bernie McCabe had left the US Army. He was quickly brought on board. I also had a week's holiday planned in March, skiing at Meribel in the French Alps, and since I was the boss I decided to take it. The weather was good, the skiing was excellent, and I was skiing along somewhere between Meribel and Courchevel, having a great time, when my cell phone rang. Alastair Morrison from DSL was on the line and he said, 'I have something that might interest you. We don't want to get involved but you might. Ring me back.' So I skied down the mountain and found a landline, and Alastair said, 'I have a friend who is the Defence Minister of Papua New Guinea . . . who would like to talk to you about helicopters.'

TWELVE

PAPUA NEW GUINEA, 1996

'Military action is important to the nation. It is the ground of death or life, the path of survival or destruction, so it is imperative to examine it.'

SUN TZU

To get a firm enquiry after just four weeks was a considerable boost and I was very grateful to Alastair Morrison for passing it on. I was aware that DSL had been handling a request from the government of Papua New Guinea, who wanted help in creating a Police Special Unit. This is why DSL knew the people there and it now appeared that Alastair had a friend in Matthias Ijape, the Defence Minister, who, said Alastair, was a very good sort and anxious to talk to me. He then passed on the relevant telephone numbers and left me to get on with it.

Immediately on my return to England I rang Ijape in Port Moresby, the capital of Papua New Guinea, to find out exactly what he wanted. Alastair had only mentioned helicopters, and although Sandline International is not essentially an arms dealer, these could certainly be supplied. Provided a country is not under a UN arms embargo and has a legitimate government, the process is fairly simple. You find out what they want, shop around for the right kit at the right price, arrange the appropriate 'end-user' certificates, which specify that the kit in question will not be shipped on to somewhere that is under an embargo (end-user certificates are vital in this business), despatch the kit and collect your money. We could do that, but this sort of work was not our main concern and, anyway, the process is rarely that simple.

First of all, what sort of helicopters did they want? Were the ones they had in mind suitable for the intended use? Did they want transport helicopters, or gunships, or surveillance machines? Were they for police or army use? What sort of ancillary equipment was needed? Did they have the trained pilots able to operate these machines by day and night and land in confined spaces? Did they have the essential training and servicing back-up? What about spare parts?

Helicopters can be bought 'off the shelf' but many other factors had to be studied first and, as a professional organisation, we needed to look closely at their actual requirements before we started shopping for machines.

Getting it right is always important, and if this was to be our first job, we wanted to make a particular success of it and demonstrate to any potential client what we could do and how we operated. In the process, we hoped to define in our own minds exactly what sort of company we intended to create. At this time, a scant month into the business, we were still working on the basic concept; even the term 'private military company' or 'PMC' had not yet been coined.

Many people suppose that we had the idea all worked out before we started, that we had formed a company, given it a name and were already going out to market it. It was not like that at all. We were at the stage where we had a good, sound, basic idea, but we still had to kick it around to try and focus on what we were doing. During that early period, Sandline was just me and some friends. Then, within a very short space of time, we had the first hint of a deal and the focus shifted rapidly to Papua New Guinea.

Matters can move fast in this business. Over Easter I had to fly out to Australia to meet Ijape and we still had not had time to develop anything resembling a clear corporate concept. Alastair had suggested I might be able to help him because he knew at least the broad outlines of what I had in mind. We had discussed it as friends and he knew that I wanted to develop the commercial aspects of private military companies – but even this is using terminology that did not exist then.

At least I knew what I did not want to do. I did not want to run a security company. Whatever Sandline International turned out to be, it would be something more than that. In Angola, Tony Buckingham had seen a legitimate government locked in a conflict situation, requiring expertise that was not forthcoming from other friendly governments or the UN, and EO had adapted what had previously been seen as mercenary work and put it in a formal package, which had never happened before.

Tony had seen EO at work and thought this method of applying military skills, formally, honestly and openly, for a legitimate government and for a worthwhile cause was a good, marketable idea that could be put in a corporate setting. That, in some way, was the path we intended to follow, but we had to develop the concept; in the beginning it was easier to see what we did not want to do. We did not want to go into commercial security; there are plenty of companies doing that, either well-known ones like Group 4 or specialist ones like DSL. Neither did we want to become a military training company, though training, of the basic kind as well as training in military affairs at the operational and tactical level, would certainly be one of the services we offered.

The template we had before us was the work of EO in Angola. I also had in mind the work of other companies, firms like KMS, which had worked in Sri Lanka and Nicaragua on 'operational support' activities, and, of course, David Stirling's company, the embryonic Watchguard. Finally, I had this concept of the 'contract officer' in Dhofar. What I had in mind for Sandline lay somewhere in those areas of expertise but the precise idea had yet to emerge. To clear the way therefore certain activities could already be rejected.

Guarding represents the 'passive' side of military operations. We wanted to go into something that was pro-active, to provide some service that helped governments, something approximating to the good side of mercenary work and the training element of the DSL kind of company – and to put it into one package, one that overlapped somewhat with the DSL concept but went on to be something where Sandline could develop its particular expertise and commercial reputation.

We would offer training, which is the basis of all military operations, but this would be training geared to the particular situation, in all its aspects. We would offer operational support, again in the broadest sense; we would prepare operational plans; we would fly the helicopters in the combat zone; we would put together the fire plans; and – in some cases – we would conduct Special Force operations in circumstances where they would make a significant strategic impact, hopefully by shortening or even ending the conflict.

Above all, we would work on the four areas of command, control, communications and intelligence, or 'C3 I', as it is called. The command and control element, the sound, professional commander's estimate, the creation of a viable plan, is implicit in what is now the Sandline concept, which was still being formulated when we went into Papua New Guinea. Having had that experience, I would say that our main value to a governmental client lies first in the assessment, planning and co-ordinating of the campaign and secondly in making the 'nuts and bolts' of the operation work, by effective campaign direction.

That is our value, far more than 'pulling the trigger'. Indeed, that is the true value of all good private military companies. They are about providing professional military expertise at the highest level, preparing the military plan and then making the plan work. PMCs do not put men into a country to do the work of the national armed forces. What we wanted to do was make these national forces do it themselves, but more effectively, and that is the Sandline ethos: 'Using the smallest force in the farthest place in the shortest time', always remembering – and reminding our clients of – Sun Tzu's dictum that 'The best general is he who wins a battle without firing a shot'.

None of this had been worked out when we started dealing with the Papua New Guinea government. On my return from Meribel, I rang Matthias Ijape, introduced myself and asked what he wanted. He said that he wanted to discuss the provision of helicopters to assist their operations in somewhere called

Bougainville, a part of Papua New Guinea that lay close to the Solomon Islands in the South Pacific. Somewhere in the back of my mind I knew there was a problem out there, a conflict of some kind in Bougainville, but I knew nothing substantial about it. I knew where Papua New Guinea was, but had no real idea of where Bougainville was.

This was early days, and although there were plenty of conflicts in the world, we had not yet scanned the likely trouble spots for possible clients or areas where we might have something to offer. Then again, there were areas where we did not want to get involved – in countries like Colombia, for example, which we shied away from, not least because we only wanted to work for legitimate governments and in places like Colombia it is hard to know who is who.

Clearly, the first thing I had to do before meeting Matthias Ijape was some reading up on Bougainville. It did not take me long to discover that there was a major conflict going on there and one which had been going on for some time. Before I got to that, I also needed to know how Papua New Guinea had come into existence and what sort of country it was, geographically and politically, before we got involved there.

Papua New Guinea (PNG) is a vast, tropical and composite country consisting of about half the island of New Guinea, which lies off the north coast of Australia, and a scattering of islands spread out across the Pacific Ocean to the north-east. One of these islands is Bougainville, which lies about 800 nautical miles from the mainland of PNG. After the Europeans came to the region in the late-eighteenth century, the territory which is now PNG was a European colony, split between the British, the Dutch and the Germans, until the First World War, when Britain asked the Australian government to take the German colony over. In 1920, the League of Nations, a forerunner of the UN, handed PNG over to the Australians to run it as a 'mandated territory', which it remained until 1964, when PNG gained internal self-government. PNG became independent in 1975, though much of the country's commerce and industry remains in the hands of the large expatriate Australian community.

The Australian influence is very strong. The two countries are both members of the Commonwealth and share a common defence agreement, which includes the provision of about fifty military advisers. The population of PNG is around four million, though only about 5 per cent of the population, say 250,000 people, are formally employed and the economy is dependent on large injections of Australian aid. The climate is hot and humid and the terrain mountainous, covered with jungle and generally inhospitable but ideal for guerrilla operations.

The main island, New Guinea, is shared with Irian Jaya, the former Dutch colony, which is part of Indonesia and plagued with unrest. However, the main problem affecting PNG in 1997 was an insurrection in Bougainville in the North Solomon group, the place which, until the conflict began in 1989, had provided

153

PNG with a great percentage – 45 per cent, according to some estimates – of its export earnings, most of it coming from the Panguna copper mine. In 1989 a secessionist movement had taken control in Bougainville and a guerrilla war between the BRA (the Bougainville Revolutionary Army) and the PNG Defence Force (PNGDF) had been raging ever since, with a steadily rising level of violence and brutality.

This was no small-scale bush war. Over 10,000 people had been killed, PNGDF losses had been considerable, millions of dollars had been spent, the Panguna mine had been forced to close, with a disastrous effect on the PNG economy, and there was no sign that the PNG government or its Defence Force were anywhere near getting a grip on the situation. As I read all this, it seemed to me that the problems of PNG were not going to be solved with the help of a few helicopters. I told Matthias Ijape we had to meet and agreed to do so in April 1996 in Cairns, Australia – just two weeks after I had had that phone call from Alastair.

I flew out to Australia with Tony Buckingham. This was to be Sandline's first assignment and I wanted him along, not least because it appeared that the PNG government were sending a high-powered delegation to meet us. This would consist of Defence Minister Matthias Ijape, Defence Secretary James Malagepa, the civil servant in charge of finance and defence procurement and Chief of the Defence Staff General Jerry Singirok.

Ijape was every inch what I imagined a Papua New Guinean would look like. He came from the mountains, the Central Highlands, and was a very squat, strong, tough-looking individual who had trained as a lawyer before entering politics and had been in and out of office and now held the top post at the Ministry of Defence. He has since become a good friend, and although he got into a certain amount of trouble during the Singirok affair (the mutiny of the PNGDF led by Singirok, who had been a whole-hearted supporter of the Sandline project but did an abrupt volte-face), I believe he will eventually bounce back and will remain a force in PNG politics. His military adviser, General Singirok, seemed to be a capable soldier but one who had been promoted above his ceiling. He was brave, but unscrupulous and a very tricky customer indeed. Behind his military appearance he was a weak individual, easily manipulated by some of the more devious PNG politicians.

The final member of the team, James Malagepa, was a pleasant individual, very affable and intelligent. He had a very difficult job, trying to balance the needs of the military with the rather limited funds, a largely incompetent administration and some outstandingly lazy civil servants. James was not given the backing due to him and was another casualty of the Singirok shenanigans, but he too became a good friend.

This was a high-level delegation, virtually the entire Defence Council of

PNG. Since this was a normal, legitimate, business meeting between a commercial concern and a sovereign government, it did not occur to me that holding such a meeting in Australia would be of interest to the Australian government, though in view of what happened later perhaps it should have done. After all, Australia had huge investments in PNG and the country contained a large expatriate Australian community closely involved in every level of PNG life – and then there was that bilateral defence agreement. If any government should have offered help to the beleaguered government of PNG in its decade-long problem in Bougainville, surely it was Australia, perhaps by offering training, or a squadron of the Australian SAS, or even some helicopters. But for some reason they had declined to offer any help at all – which is where we came in.

The meeting began with a general chat about the situation and the state of the PNG Defence Force. It was obvious that the Bougainville insurrection had developed into a nasty little war, an all-out guerrilla campaign fought out in terrible terrain, and at the moment the BRA appeared to be winning, or at least more than holding their own. The PNG Defence Forces were not large. The army consisted of two infantry battalions, organised on British or Australian lines, with an engineer regiment and an embryonic Special Force unit. The security forces had a number of armoured Land-Rovers for internal security work – not the most useful kit for fighting in a jungle and mountain terrain – and they also had some mortars, but no field artillery. The maritime arm consisted of a number of landing craft of various kinds, and they had some old ex-RAAF Huey helicopters and a chartered Russian MI-17 helicopter.

Tony and I introduced ourselves and explained what Sandline did. We had assumed that they wanted to talk about helicopters, but we did not really know what they wanted and, if the truth be told, neither did they. It transpired during our meeting that the Australian government had consistently refused to supply helicopter gunships or, indeed, any practical military assistance, and when I heard this I thought it was very strange indeed. Here was a large, powerful neighbouring country, in this case Australia, the former colonial power, which has a defence agreement with a friendly government, the government of a country where Australia has huge investments. Why was it that they were not helping these people win the war? The few helicopters they had supplied – those clapped-out Hueys – were supplied on the condition they were not to be armed or used in Bougainville at all, and that seemed very odd indeed. All this reinforced the views Tony and I already held, that there were legitimate governments that needed help and when friendly nations refused to supply it they would eventually turn in desperation to the private sector. What else could they do?

We asked them what they wanted us to do. They explained the situation in Bougainville, military and political, both of which seemed to centre on the

Panguna mine. They asked us what we could do, what we thought they needed, and in the course of conversation it gradually transpired that they wanted gunships, which they visualised as a war-winning weapon. However, to my mind, the problem already seemed to go much deeper than that, and the upshot was that I suggested we go away and put our thinking caps on before coming up with some far-ranging suggestions for actually ending the war, or at least creating a situation where the BRA would be willing to come to the conference table. This is the point at which the Sandline concept, as it now exists, first began to take shape; they thought they wanted helicopters but what they needed was a plan for ending the war.

It appeared that General Singirok would be in England some two weeks later and the meeting ended with the idea that we would meet him then and present him with our proposals. We also discussed the matter of money and that was that; the whole meeting was over in a few hours. They returned to PNG and, after a memorable day's fishing on the Barrier Reef, Tony and I flew back to London.

In the next two weeks I spent a lot of time examining their situation, talking it over with colleagues, measuring the problem in Bougainville and the capability of the PNG Defence Force to tackle it, thinking about ways to break the military deadlock and trying to decide what the PNG government really needed, rather than what they thought they wanted. Gradually, having decided on the aim – to end the war or bring the BRA to the conference table – an outline began to appear.

Our conclusion was that the first thing they needed was some form of electronic surveillance capability. With this they could gather intelligence and fix exactly where the BRA were by monitoring their radio transmissions, and so pinpoint the vital command centres deep in that mountainous, jungle-clad terrain. The PNGDF had tried the usual cordon-and-search and long-range-patrolling methods of rooting out the BRA for almost ten years and had got nowhere; what was needed now was a degree of applied technology. It was also necessary to get the local population firmly on side. There was a resistance movement in Bougainville rather like the Kit Carson Scouts the US used in Vietnam, a form of local militia which, rather surprisingly, was on the government's side rather than on the rebel side. But the PNGDF was not popular and was not getting anywhere or making any impact on the BRA. The situation was, at best, a stalemate.

At this point it should be explained that the BRA were not unsophisticated warriors. They were a well-equipped and fairly sophisticated guerrilla force which had been fighting for some time. They had a radio station, Radio Free Bougainville, they had satellite phones and they had radios, all of which were useful but which laid them open to the possibility of electronic surveillance. We thought that the most useful form of air support was a King Air fixed-wing aircraft to carry out this surveillance, plus two helicopter gunships and two transport helicopters to move troops into the jungle and close with the enemy if need be.

It all took a great deal of work in a very short space of time, but we had this proposal ready to present to General Singirok and were waiting for him in our office in London on the appointed day. General Singirok did not turn up, or telephone us. This was a surprise, but we eventually tracked him down to his hotel, the Royal Horse Guards near the MOD in Whitehall, and we went to see him there. We heard later that he was in London at the invitation of another defence supplier who was paying for the hotel, and it was subsequently revealed that he was getting under-the-counter payments from this supplier. This, however, was not known to us at the time.

I went to the meeting with Michael Grunberg. Although I was the one making the presentation of the military plan, Michael had done all the costings and he needed to be there to discuss them and answer questions on financial matters, the supply of end-user certificates for the military hardware and so on. If the PNG government accepted the basic idea, we wanted to get on with it as soon as possible and avoid any hold-ups over the technicalities, which we could iron out on the spot here in London.

General Singirok seemed to like the plan. I explained that it was not the kind of plan the Defence Committee had asked for in Cairns but we felt that this was the way to move forward and win the war, and he appreciated that. Singirok was an experienced soldier. He had had front-line experience in Bougainville, where he had been wounded rescuing one of his men under fire, and he had done very well on courses at the Australian Staff College. Singirok was not stupid; he had been personally selected by the Prime Minister, Julius Chan, to run the PNG Army and he could see the point of my proposals. Besides, since he was the officer directly responsible for fighting and winning the war in Bougainville, he was directly concerned with anything that might improve his chances of achieving that end – or so I thought.

He went off to present our plan to the PNG Defence Committee and a heavy silence fell over the situation. Weeks went by with no response. I periodically phoned Matthias Ijape to see what was going on, but nothing came back of any substance. Meanwhile, we were pressing on developing Sandline and I was travelling a great deal; as with any business we could not have all our eggs in one basket, or rely on the outcome of one proposal, and we had to look about for new business while the people in PNG decided whether they wanted to go ahead.

Most of my time was spent in Africa and it was at this time that I first met Ahmed Tejan Kabbah, the newly elected President of Sierra Leone. I had been to visit EO in Sierra Leone and had seen them preside over the transition from a military to an elected government. I had made friends with the political hierarchy in Sierra Leone, including Chief Sam Norman, the Deputy Defence Minister and Paramount Chief of the Kamajors (the Hunters), and a number of others in the new government, all of which came in very useful later. I had also run a small project for President Kabbah, separate from the EO deployment.

I was still monitoring events in PNG when, during the late summer of 1996, when I was in the Philippines, I heard about the Kangu Beach massacre, when a large number of PNGDF soldiers had been cornered on a beach by the BRA and cut to pieces in the course of an operation called High Speed II. Some of the PNGDF soldiers had been captured, but most of them had been killed. Clearly the war in Bougainville was taking a turn for the worse, and although we had had no response to our proposals, this silence from the potential client was not really a surprise. I had already learned that the 'hit-rate' for success in this business was about one in every ten proposals, so if our PNG proposal got nowhere, I would not be too surprised.

However, I rang Ijape, told him how sorry I was to hear about the Kangu massacre and asked him if matters were proceeding with the proposal. He said it was still difficult, there were problems over the money and Prime Minister Chan was very busy, and there were, inevitably, some unspecified administrative snags. I subsequently discovered that at this stage Chan knew very little about our proposals. The real snag was General Singirok, who, it later transpired, had other, more personally profitable irons in the fire. He had some other deal on the side, had at least partially contracted for some heavy-lift helicopters and was clearly dragging his feet over our proposal. While he did that, the whole business languished and the Bougainville war ground on.

Then I discovered that the Deputy Prime Minister of PNG, Chris Haiveta, was coming to London. Haiveta's visit was to promote the flotation of a PNG company and I was able to contact the people arranging his itinerary, saying that I would like to meet him, if only for an hour, for a discussion. I was in Kinshasa in the Congo at this time, October 1996, and the PNG business had now been going on for well over six months and, thanks to General Singirok, was getting nowhere.

I met Chris Haiveta in the boardroom at Sandline's London office. Chris is tall and very impressive, a gentle giant, single-minded and very intelligent. The meeting got off to a slightly strained start, as he seemed to think that I wanted to pitch for a contract to supply armoured vehicles. When I told him no, I wanted to talk about this helicopter requirement the PNG Defence Committee had been interested in earlier in the year and a subsequent proposal Sandline had made for ending the war in Bougainville, he became far more animated and I therefore told him the whole story in some detail. He said he was glad I was not interested in supplying armoured vehicles and that I agreed with his view that they were useless in PNG, adding that this proposal, which he had not known about until now, sounded much more interesting. He suggested that on his return to Port Moresby he would think about it and get back to me – and there we left it.

I went back to Kinshasa, where we had been asked to help President Mobutu, as Zaire was rapidly falling to bits. We were not over-keen on this idea but Mobutu was not then on any UN embargo and there was no reason not to talk to him – though he was certainly not the best of men. I spent a bit of time in Kinshasa trying to decide if there was anything we could do, but the situation was a complete mess. Mobutu was clearly going to lose, and although we were offered a great deal of money to help him, we decided not to touch it and pulled out – just as I got a phone call from Chris Haiveta asking me to fly to Port Moresby as soon as possible to discuss the whole project yet again.

I flew to Port Moresby in November 1996. The object of this visit was to discuss all the ways in which Sandline could help the PNG government with their problem in Bougainville, so the proposal had clearly moved on from the helicopter deal we had started out with. On this visit I saw a lot of senior people, including Singirok, Chris Haiveta and the commander of the PNG Special Force unit, Major Gilbert Toropo. We had endless meetings and we kicked a lot of ideas around, but we were still keeping the whole idea under wraps and it did not reach cabinet or government level for discussion.

Gradually, while working on the main proposal, we started to think about some other things we might do, perhaps involving the PNG Special Force unit, which was a pretty sketchy outfit at this time. The upshot was that Chris Haiveta asked Sandline to carry out a consultancy study, a proper, detailed, military 'commander's estimate', of what the Bougainville problems were, how they might be solved and how Sandline might help the PNG government with the Bougainville situation. For this study we would be paid a fee of US$250,000. This project also acquired a codename: Project Contravene.

This proposal was to be produced in a matter of weeks and be ready for presentation to the PNG cabinet in January 1997. I went to and fro between London and PNG on a number of occasions and wrote a very detailed commander's estimate, which I took to Port Moresby in January. There I met Tony Buckingham, who had been competing in the Sydney–Hobart yacht race and had flown to join me. He had been in at the start and now, hopefully, he would be there to see the end of these long-drawn-out consultations. Then we ran into a problem.

Tony and I were sitting outside the cabinet office in Government House, waiting to be called in to present our proposal to the cabinet, when General Singirok turned up. He asked what we were doing there and seemed annoyed to find us there, but when he discovered that we were waiting to present our proposals to the PNG cabinet he got extremely angry.

There, in the corridor outside the cabinet office, he started raging at us, shouting and demanding to know what we were doing there, talking over his head to the cabinet about a proposal he had not seen. If true, this last statement was another surprise, because on the previous day I had given Chris Haiveta a dozen copies of the proposal to circulate to the PNG cabinet, including Singirok, so that they would have a chance to study it and prepare questions before the presentation.

We did not see the cabinet that day, and Tony then left. I stayed on and had yet another meeting with a somewhat apologetic Matthias Ijape and Chris Haiveta, who were sorry that they had got us down there for this urgent consultation and still failed to get the proposal discussed by the cabinet. Haiveta said that if I would leave the matter with him he would present it to them and let me know the outcome. Feeling somewhat disillusioned, I flew home, fully expecting to hear no more from PNG – but two nights later the phone rang and it was Matthias Ijape, saying 'You're on'.

Matters then speeded up somewhat. I flew back to Port Moresby with Michael Grunberg and we did the deal, drew up the contract and agreed the fee for our work on the Bougainville crisis: US$36 million. We also got down to the really practical question of what we were going to do, step by step. In the new proposal, I had suggested that the Special Force unit should be trained as a strike force and that the 'force multipliers', the helicopters, should be used to get the Special Force unit to grips with the BRA – not to defeat them in detail in the field, which in that terrain was virtually impossible, but to put the government in a position of military strength and force the BRA to negotiate.

The Special Force unit needed to be expanded and trained – at the moment it was simply not good enough or large enough – and we agreed that we would have to bring in some of our own people for a while, perhaps some forty Sandline people to join with the PNG force, bringing it up to an establishment of some seventy to eighty men, ready for operations, and it was at this time that I met Prime Minister Sir Julius Chan for the first time.

Julius Chan is of Chinese origin and known in PNG politics as 'The Chinaman'. He is a very astute businessman with a very sharp brain and is a Machiavellian character, but a loyal PNG citizen through and through. His sole aim was to stop the war and continue to develop the social and economic infrastructure of Papua New Guinea. He was a thoroughly decent and capable politician and unfortunately the Singirok business, which I will cover shortly, forced him out of office, the worst thing that could have happened for Papua New Guinea.

It was a rather unusual first meeting. I was sitting outside the PM's office, waiting for Matthias Ijape to call me in, when Sir Julius Chan put his head round the door and invited me in. He was pretty terse and he asked a lot of probing questions. Could I guarantee success? What did I think the chances were? Could we capture some of these guys? Why should he employ us?

The situation in Bougainville had got even more tense recently because some of the prisoners taken on the Kangu Beach had been killed, while for their part the PNGDF had mortared a church on Bougainville, killing a number of the congregation. Clearly the PNGDF soldiers needed a grip taken on them, and I had put that in my proposals as well. This first meeting with Chan went very well and it concluded with him asking me to write a one-page memo stating simply why he should employ us. I got that done within the hour and he accepted it. At last we really were on; after more than a year of talk, the PNG operation was finally under way.

THIRTEEN

PREPARATIONS FOR BOUGAINVILLE

'Assess the advantages in taking advice, then structure your forces accordingly. Forces are to be structured strategically, based on what is advantageous.'

SUN TZU

Getting Prime Minister Chan's approval for our plan was only the start of a long process. We had, in effect, approval in outline, the basis for the contract, and we could commence to gather in the necessary equipment and forces, but there were still a lot of details to work out. As a first step I went back to see Chan again and we talked through the issues and timings in great detail, while he asked a number of probing questions, especially on how long it would take to get the operation off the ground.

I gave him a rough timetable, pointing out that the first task was to train up the PNG Special Force unit until they were capable of carrying out strategic operations against the command structure and propaganda organisation of the BRA in a very hostile environment. We were lucky here because most of the PNGDF had served in Bougainville at some time and knew what they were up against; they simply did not have the skills and expertise for Special Force operations.

We also needed at least two Russian transport helicopters to move the troops about and ensure that we were logistically self-supporting and had a casualty-evacuation facility available. This was very important to me given the nature of the terrain and the distance from any medical facilities. So we needed the transport helicopters and we needed the electronic intelligence-gathering package to pinpoint the command centres of the BRA and listen to what they were saying. Then, having gathered intelligence and the means to sustain ourselves, what else was required? Our role had clearly expanded a great deal since that first contact a year before and needed reassessment.

To go back to the first contact, the original request was for helicopters. Then it became clear that we would also have to supply suitably qualified pilots. In the course of discussion, it also became obvious that air power alone would not solve the problem in Bougainville. Therefore we had examined the entire problem again and developed a plan that would really clear the situation up. Now that plan had to be implemented. The end result had to be either victory in the field or the BRA at the conference table; given the situation on the ground, the latter was the more likely outcome. But once they were at the conference table, what then?

In talking to Chan, it became clear that there was no clear, high-level, all-embracing theory at either the strategic or the governmental level about how the Bougainville situation could be resolved once and for all, politically and socially as well as militarily. Beyond our military plan there was a vacuum. There was no grip, at any level, in Papua New Guinea. I put this to Chan quite bluntly, asking him what the deal was. How were we going to resolve this? As I observed to Chan at the time, if you don't have a plan, you can't change it. I fully understood his aim, to defeat the BRA and bring peace back to Bougainville, but what was the programme after that? How was he going to keep these people on side, kick-start the shattered Bougainville economy and deal with their political aspirations, not least the desire to secede from PNG and join the Solomon Islands?

I had already realised that it would be very difficult to go into Bougainville and defeat the BRA in the formal military way by taking them on in the field and rooting them out. What we really had to do was break their will to fight so that they would come to the negotiating table. That, in turn, would give the PNG government the ability to negotiate from a position of strength. Peace had to be negotiated. Otherwise the war would simply go on and there would always be guerrillas in the bush. The first step was to gather intelligence on where the BRA were, what they were doing, what their intentions were – everything we could find out would be useful. Then we would need to work on the psychology of these people.

The inhabitants of Bougainville are, in the main, a simple, uncomplicated people, not in the sense that they are stupid but in terms of their expectations, their beliefs and in the conduct of their daily lives. They are also attuned to the spiritual side of life. They have a belief in magic and the supernatural, and this was a side we could turn to our advantage. We decided that it would be better to attack the psychological side of their lives rather than the material and physical sides, but implicit in this had to be the implied use of force. We needed to demonstrate a level of attack the BRA had not seen before – and this was where the helicopter gunships would come in.

So, to sum up, the plan was to have the ability to go into the jungle after them and attack their bases using the Special Force unit (SFU). We would fly the gunships in parallel with all other operations, while the transport helicopters, the Air Wing, flying in the SFU, would be, in effect, the manoeuvre unit, spearheading the attack. The rest of the PNGDF would guard the other vital points on the island and secure the area for us to operate from. We would use the local, government-supporting militia as scouts, and I asked Chan to get some of them sent over to the main island for training in the scouting role with the SFU. This happened within a few days and it gave us something to start on while we waited for the kit to arrive.

The main element was the gunships. These would bring in a totally new dimension and the sight of them flying around Bougainville was sure to cause the BRA concern. I felt that simply having these helicopters there and occasionally giving a firepower demonstration on a piece of real estate would be very effective psychologically. There was a lot of talk later, in the first Commission of Inquiry, about the legality of all this, along with wild allegations that we intended to use the gunships to kill thousands of people, but that was never the intention.

The intention was to indicate to the BRA that the game had now changed. The last thing we wanted to do was to cause civilian casualties or shoot up fishing boats. We did intend to use the helicopters to intercept some of their sea routes and cut them off from the Solomon Islands, however. When you are in the middle of the ocean in a small canoe and a helicopter hovers close overhead, it is very frightening – and we might then fly off and fire a few bursts into the water, just to show what might happen and that this is serious. The word would get around and the BRA supply routes would soon be cut or much reduced.

Much the same process could be employed using our surveillance equipment. We could hook into their communications network, or just ring them up on their satellite phones and say, for example, 'Go and observe grid square 1234 at 1500hrs this afternoon and see what can happen to you' – both inviting them to see a helicopter firepower demonstration and indicating that their communications were no longer secure. That too would take their guerrilla war to a new dimension.

A further extension of psychological operations, or 'psy-ops', involved the use of 'Sky Shout', a Cessna aircraft rigged with a powerful loudspeaker that would fly over BRA jungle camps and local villages late at night broadcasting messages and information, telling the BRA that the game had indeed changed, that fighting on was unnecessary and that the government were willing to negotiate so why not come out and talk. Sky Shout could also be used to counter the BRA propaganda, and tell the people that there was no intention of foreigners grabbing the Panguna mine, and that there would be local participation and plenty of jobs and the prospect of prosperity. There would be land – land being a big issue – and there would be secure ownership of land. Any government solution could not rely solely on the stick, the implied use of force; we had to inject the carrot into it. All that apart, Sky Shout was a powerful 'juju' and would have a profound effect on BRA morale.

Later on, there was an allegation that Sandline was only in PNG to grab the Panguna mine, which is total nonsense. The mine was the crux of the entire

Bougainville problem, the reason the rebellion had broken out in the first place. Clearly, as part of the peace process, ownership of the mine had to be sorted out between the PNG government and the local people, and the latter had to have either participation or compensation, but the mine – which is owned by the Bougainville Copper Company, an Australian subsidiary of Rio Tinto Zinc – was vital to the PNG economy. Getting it back into production had to be part of the PNG government plan; attempting to seize it for our own ends was no part of the Sandline brief.

I talked all this over at length with Chan and we became extremely friendly, to the point where he installed me in the next office and allowed me to read all the security-related papers. I believe he came to regard me as a confidant, someone who was apart from local issues, had no political axe to grind, gave him good advice at the strategic level and simply wanted to do the job he had contracted us to do.

All this was very good and matters were proceeding well, but it later transpired that my growing intimacy with Sir Julius was getting up the nose of General Singirok. I was not aware of this, for Singirok was involved at every stage of the planning, saw all the papers and had open access to all our plans and proposals. Under our contract, we had been enrolled as special constables and Singirok was regarded as our superior officer and the overall commander of the operation. This, however, did not stop him getting the idea that I was, in some fashion, usurping his position.

I had no intention of doing that, but the problem was clearly not going to be solved by military methods alone. I told Chan that it would also be necessary to come up with a political and social package to sort the Bougainville problem out, and that alone put Singirok slightly in the shade. Yes, our prime function was to provide the military element, but I told Chan that if he wanted my advice on how to formulate some of the other elements in the mix, I would be happy to help – and he appreciated that.

Chan was not well served by his civil servants or his executive support, but I can see now that there was resentment at my friendship with the Prime Minister. I could not see it at the time because there were plenty of expatriate advisers about in PNG, we were all very busy and everyone was saying, 'This is fantastic – we believe you are really going to solve this problem.' I can see now that Singirok felt himself becoming isolated. I could wander into Chan's office whenever I wanted; Singirok had to make an appointment. I made a mistake there, but we learned from it and would never make it again.

There is a certain amount of background to all this. Chan had promoted Singirok over the heads of other, more senior officers long before we arrived on the scene and charged him with ending the war in Bougainville, which he had conspicuously failed to do. Then, in the nine months before we actually got our contract, Singirok had asked Chan for one more chance to show what he could do 'before the Defence Minister brought in these foreign advisers from Sandline'.

Unfortunately, his final attempt did not work either. His main offensive, Operation High Speed II, had been a complete disaster, culminating in the Kangu Beach massacre, and then the interim Minister on Bougainville had been murdered, allegedly by the PNGDF and allegedly at the instigation of General Singirok, who consistently refused to help the local police investigate the murder. It had also come to Chan's attention that some of the military funds allocated to High Speed II had been misappropriated, allegedly used for the refurbishing of army offices or for other purposes. The upshot was that Chan was totally fed up with Singirok and Singirok knew it.

We should have picked up on all that earlier on. We should have asked ourselves if we were muscling in too much, but we were all very busy developing the operational concept and the man in charge, the Prime Minister, wanted our input and was grateful for it.

To get back to the development of the Bougainville operation, it was now January 1997. We had a draft contract but we did not yet have the money. I went back to London, briefed everyone there on the proposal and started to put together the nuts and bolts of the operation, rounding up the equipment and the personnel. Michael Grunberg finished the fine details on the draft contract and I was in Singapore, on my way back to Port Moresby with the final draft, when I had a telephone call. It was Michael, and he told me there was a snag with the contract. He had just had an extraordinary letter from Singirok, asking us to drop the MI-17 helicopter element or consider co-opting, or building into the contract, the use of two Bell helicopters from the heavy-lift company at Mount Hagen in PNG.

This was impossible, for all sorts of technical reasons. The Bell helicopters were not big enough. It would also mean a mixed fleet – we would need different pilots with different qualifications, different mechanics and spares, and it would make a total hash of the plan. Apart from all that, I smelt a rat. It transpired that Singirok, on the quiet, had made a separate deal to use these Bell helicopters and had already paid a deposit on them. This needed sorting out at once, so I got on the phone to Matthias Ijape and asked him what was going on, pointing out that in spite of the fact that I had the Prime Minister's directive to get on with this operation, the minute I went to England and my back was turned, people started messing about with the plan. I added that I was already on my way back to get the final contract signed, so what was Singirok up to?

What was beginning to emerge was a pattern of obstruction, something that had been going on quietly ever since we had appeared on the scene at that meeting in Cairns a year before. On the surface Singirok was very affable and very interested in the plan. I had always been careful to point out that this was very much his 'show', that Sandline International wanted none of the glory when the concept paid off, that he was in complete command. He seemed enthusiastic, but every so often something popped up that interfered with the progress of the plan.

Anyway, we got the helicopter business sorted out and then we decided that we would have to bring in some manpower. After dragging out the process for almost a year, suddenly it was all systems go, mostly because the PNG elections were pending in April 1997 and Chan wanted to report the end of the Bougainville problem – or at least some significant improvements in the situation – before he went to the polls. We were therefore obliged to sub-contract the manpower element, not least because it was considered advisable to have as many black soldiers on the scene as possible so that it would not look as if a mass of white men were running the show. I therefore contacted Nic Van den Bergh, the chief operating officer of EO in South Africa, and he came on board as ground tactical commander in PNG. Nic's task was to work hand in glove with Singirok and his staff and make the thing work.

We had still not had the money, but we had elected to go ahead to demonstrate our good will and commitment. Administrative hiccups are inevitable, if very frustrating, and one of these arose when the advance party arrived in Singapore and attempted to board the Air New Guinea aircraft, only to be stopped by a booking clerk as they did not have the right visas. This did not matter because they were due to be met at Port Moresby by the chief of the SFU, who would get them through immigration, but the clerk was adamant; no visas, no flight. They phoned me and I phoned Chris Haiveta and it took a personal call from him, the Deputy Prime Minister of PNG, to the check-in desk at Singapore Airport before they were allowed on the flight.

There was another hiccup over the lack of funding. PNG did not have a 'secret vote' which could allocate funds for special purposes, the Central Bank seemed to be short of funds, and I eventually had to say that we were ready to proceed but we could not do so until the contract was signed and we had the first tranche of the money – $18 million. The clock was ticking, and it was up to them to come up with the goods. They did not want to sign the contract before they had made the money available, because the sum fell due on signature, so there was another delay.

Meanwhile, we started getting the show on the road, getting the kit in, briefing the staff and so on, but there were more delays on the contract and money fronts, culminating in whole days when Michael Grunberg and I sat around at the Bank of Papua New Guinea, waiting for things to be signed. Eventually they said they were going to go ahead. I was given two letters confirming that they were going to sign and, as a demonstration of good faith, they gave me a cheque to hold for the Kina (local currency) equivalent of $18 million, pending the arrival of funds. I then had to come back to Europe to sort out some of the details, leaving Nic Van den Bergh in charge with the documents, telling him to sign on our behalf. As soon as he had the money, we would get the helicopters and all the other kit *en route* to PNG.

At this time I had a holiday booked, two weeks in Mauritius with my wife Caroline and my son Sammy. The plan was for me to fly from London to Johannesburg, where I had to see some people, and then fly on from there to Mauritius, where Caroline and Sammy would already be at the hotel. I walked into the office in Johannesburg and they cried, 'Thank God you are here! Go back to PNG at once – there is a problem with the contract.' That afternoon I got on a plane for Singapore; within twenty-four hours I had flown from Port Moresby to Singapore, from Singapore to London, from London to Johannesburg and then from Johannesburg back to Singpore, *en route* for PNG. On the way I flew right over Mauritius, where my wife and son were already on the beach. I was, to be blunt, pretty annoyed about all this – though not half as annoyed as my wife.

I got back there and ironed out the problem, which was simply yet another bureaucratic blip, but Nic had become very worried about it. He pointed out that while he was holding the baby, he did not know all these people or have any real idea of how they operated and was running into brick walls. However, it was far from being a wasted journey. On that day we finally got the contract signed by Chris Haiveta and the money was transferred. I then got back on the plane, flew to Mauritius and had a few days' holiday with my family.

I then returned to PNG, where matters were at last reaching a climax. We had the first of four arms shipments in, the training team and Special Forces people were arriving and the SFU training was well under way. It was all looking good – and we were still only in January, with time in hand before the elections. We had now established an office at Jackson Airport, where most of our people were to be accommodated before they moved up to carry out advanced jungle training at Wewak, where we would stay with the local battalion of the PNGDF. The command and intelligence-gathering people, with their aircraft, would remain at Jackson.

This was before we moved over to Bougainville and set up an advance base for the entire force at Loloho, a perfect location on a former copper ore dock where there was a hangar to accommodate the men, a deep-water dock for landing craft and large areas to land helicopters, all surrounded by a blast-proof wall.

We had to make an operational plan with Singirok's staff while the training was going on, and we would do this at Jackson. While Nic and his people worked on this, the aircraft would be prepared at Jackson before going up to Wewak for training with the SFU. We flew in a shipment of arms and ammunition and we flew in the manpower, a total in all of about seventy, including sixteen pilots and ground crew, British, American and South African. The air operations officer was Mike Borlace, another old friend of mine who had been in the Fleet Air Arm and the Rhodesian Selous Scouts. Mike would eventually have a fleet of about eight aircraft to look after, including two MI24 attack helicopters (which in the event never arrived), transport helicopters, a Casa 212 and the Cessna with the Sky Shout system. We also used a massive Antonov 124 transport aircraft which flew in most of the stores and people.

Then the Australian government got wind of what was happening in PNG. That happened quite accidentally, when the eagle-eyed Australian Assistant Military Attaché in Port Moresby, Colonel Gary Hogan, spotted one of our aircraft unloading at Jackson Airport one Sunday morning and noticed that a PNGDF officer, Lt-Colonel Sasa, was in charge of the unloading operations on the ramp at the back of the aircraft. Hogan thought this strange. He asked a few questions, and reported his finding to Canberra. A report was leaked to an Australian journalist, Mary-Louise O'Callaghan, and on 7 February 1997 the story broke in the Australian newspapers and flashed around the world. Mary-Louise O'Callaghan covered this story in detail and in a thoroughly professional way. She was later awarded the title of Journalist of the Year for her coverage.

I met Gary Hogan later and we became good friends. At first sight Hogan looks like the typical rough-tough, hard-charging Aussie soldier, but behind all that there is a keen intelligence and an extremely good brain. Gary is a very cultured man, with a great deal of sophistication. He is also a superb cook, a great devotee of good Australian wines – and a very nice guy. He is also totally professional – he never let a developing friendship get in the way of his duty to his country. The story broke when I was in London and I decided that I had better get back down to PNG as soon as possible and do some damage limitation. I had always told Chan that the story was bound to get out and that he must have an explanation prepared and be quick off the mark with their side of the story. I rather wish we had prepared some statement, as PNG were not ready to handle the press and the story was poorly presented.

So this too had to be remedied and my first port of call after seeing Chan, who had no objection to my making the contact, was at the British High Commission, where I met the High Commissioner, Bob Lowe, for the first time. He struck me as a very competent, calm, level-headed sort of person. I rang him up, introduced myself and suggested I should come in and give him a full briefing on who we were and what we were up to. He was more than willing to see me so I did that, and he was very affable. The view of the British government, as I understood it, was that they were not in favour of internal disputes being settled by force – the usual Foreign Office patter – but it was a matter for the sovereign government of PNG.

I then asked him if he thought his Australian opposite number would also like to be briefed, and he said he was sure he would but how did I feel about it? I said I did not mind, as we were not doing anything illegal, in spite of what the over-excited press in Australia were currently saying. They claimed that we were destabilising the region and so on, which was, I believe, a plan deliberately designed to create such a furore in the area, among the countries neighbouring PNG, that Chan would be obliged to drop the idea. The Australians could not actually order Chan to stop the Bougainville operation, for PNG was a sovereign nation, but they could make their disapproval known. In doing so they underestimated Sir Julius Chan, who was very firm on this point.

So, again after clearing it with Chan, I went to see the Australian High Commissioner, David Irvine, a very reasonable, sensible guy. Present at the meeting was the Defence Attaché, another nice guy but not in Hogan's league, and when I got back to my hotel that night I found a note from Hogan under my door, asking me to lunch at his house. I went and we had a very good lunch, which Gary cooked. We sat across the table, two professional soldiers, summing each other up. He had got me there to find out what I was about, which was his job, and I understood that, but he was sensible enough to see what we were trying to do and, knowing he would have to report on this, I told him most of our plans.

There was no harm in this, and possibly some good, for, having seen the quality and accuracy of the reporting in the Australian press, I thought it could only help if the Australian government learned exactly what we were planning and knew that a bloodbath was no part of our intentions. I could not tell him any fine details but I did agree to keep him informed on matters as they developed. I think Gary Hogan did a thoroughly good job and provided the Australian government with a calm and reliable account of what was actually going on. When it was all over, the Australians should have promoted him and given him a medal, but there was some muttering that he had been too sympathetic in his reporting. There is nothing in this – Gary was always highly professional and, although friendly, never let his guard drop.

Technically, he was an adversary, for the Australian government were totally opposed to our plans. David Irvine could understand what we were doing but his government in Canberra got everything out of proportion and did not want the Bougainville operation to happen. I still don't know why. The only thing I can think of is that they had some reason for keeping the campaign going and sitting on the Papua New Guineans. The only other possible explanation is that they were embarrassed because they had failed to support a friendly nation in its hour of need and were now sulking because this nation had finally sought and found help elsewhere, and, even worse, private enterprise was now taking a hand. A similar thing happened later with the British government over Sierra Leone.

I do not know if Singirok was influenced by any of this. I do know that the

Australian government would have considered him a source, for he had been at the Australian Staff College, had been educated at their Military Academy and had many contacts in Australia. The Australians certainly did not want him to stage a coup; the one thing they were worried about was internal ructions in PNG. They had a brigade of troops on standby, to come in and protect Australian interests in PNG if trouble broke out.

However, all that apart, we now had an added complication to the project in that it was 'blown' – the BRA now knew what to expect, what the government had in mind, what was coming, which would make them think. We had to deal with the PR problem but, as I said to Chan, this could work to our advantage and perhaps it was no bad thing. However, I had to ask him again what he wanted us to do, and he said, 'Go ahead.'

He was under a lot of pressure from the Australian government, with whom relations became very strained. They invited him to Canberra to talk the matter over and he asked me what he should do. I said that it was entirely a matter for him, but PNG was a sovereign country and I could not see why the Australians should be permitted to interfere or dictate his policy. He was trying to do his best for PNG and I thought he should stick to his guns.

The project then went into overdrive, and we were rapidly reaching the point where the operation would commence. Singirok was always there, always in the office, but he delegated much of the work to his chief of operations, Colonel Walter Salamas. At some stage during this time Singirok went on a trip to the Philippines and Singapore, where we now know that some of the planning for his subsequent intervention was done. The press excitement calmed down gradually, the training continued, the operation order had been prepared and we were just waiting for the attack helicopters to come in before starting the final part of the pre-operational stage.

I came back to Port Moresby on Friday, 14 March, and did the rounds. I went to see Haiveta and went into the base at Jackson Airport and saw everyone there. I also had a call from Chan asking me to come in on Sunday afternoon, as he was having a meeting with a number of his Foreign Office officials over the question of relations with Australia and wanted to have a chat with me about that and how the operation was going. Everyone seemed to be happy when we met on the Sunday, but when I went in to see him we had a very serious discussion over whether he should break off diplomatic relations with Australia. My view was that this was a bit extreme and I did not think it was a good idea; it would be far better to keep talking but be robust, and he accepted that.

This was on the afternoon of Sunday, 16 March. At 7 p.m. that evening I had a meeting arranged with Singirok, who wanted to have a discussion with me, Nic Van den Bergh and Carl Deats, the intelligence officer, a final briefing on our plan for the operations in Bougainville. The meeting with Chan was at 5 p.m.

and it went on a bit. I had told Nic that I would meet him at Singirok's office and that he should go there first with all the relevant documentation, the operational plan and the logistic support plan, for Singirok and his principal staff officers to sign off; once all this had been agreed and signed, Singirok himself would sign the operational order.

I had my meeting with Chan, where we shared a rather good bottle of Australian wine which the Australian Foreign Minister had brought up on his recent visit, and at some point I looked at my watch, realised that I was running late and explained that I should be going to see Singirok. Chan's last words to me were 'Please give my compliments to the General. Ask him to bring the plan here and present it to me and my cabinet and I too will sign off on it.'

I then left. It was pouring with rain and it would take me about fifteen minutes to drive to Murray Barracks, the HQ of the PNGDF, in my red four-wheel drive. I had a cell phone with me and I tried to phone Nic Van den Bergh and Singirok to say that I was going to be late, but neither of them responded. I thought nothing of that, for the local system was pretty antique and prone to failure, especially in bad weather. I reached Murray Barracks and drove in through the gates without being stopped. I had been there many times, so I simply swept past the sentry and drove up to the HQ building.

I was slightly concerned that I was late for this meeting, for Singirok was a stickler for old-fashioned military protocol. I noticed that his car was not there, but there were other vehicles about, and as I stopped I saw that Colonel Walter Salamas was standing at the bottom of the steps, hovering about as if he was waiting for me. As I leapt out of the car and sprinted through the rain for the shelter of the veranda, the thought did pass through my mind that, if they were having a meeting, what was Salamas, the chief of operations, doing outside and missing it, but it was no more than a passing thought. I greeted Walter and we chatted about the weather as we climbed the three flights of stairs to Singirok's office. As we neared the top of the stairs, I noticed that Major Gilbert Toropo, the head of the SFU, was on the veranda outside the office and again I thought this was odd as, like Walter Salamas, he should have been in the meeting, which I assumed was now in progress. But I assumed that they were simply waiting for me to turn up, and taking a bit of fresh air.

We then went into Singirok's outer office, where Singirok's ADC usually sat, and the ADC was there, with a military policeman who was usually on guard outside the door. They were both in uniform. The ADC asked me to wait here in the outer office and I thought this was definitely odd, as normally, especially as I was late, I would be ushered straight into Singirok's sanctum. I had told Nic to go ahead with the briefing, which I still thought must be going on in the inner office. As a result, I got slightly shirty with the ADC, pushed past him and entered the inner office. Much to my surprise, it was empty.

I was standing in the door, taking all this in, when suddenly, from the back of the office behind Singirok's desk, where there was an alcove and another door leading to a shower, a number of armed men rushed out. They came charging round the desk towards me, all in plain clothes but brandishing a number of weapons, including 9mm pistols and M16 rifles . . . and then somebody shouted, 'You are under arrest – this is an officers' coup!'

FOURTEEN

KIDNAPPED!

'You have never lived until you have almost died, and for those that fight for them, life and freedom will have a flavour the protected never know.'

ANON

To say that I was surprised would be an understatement. My memory of what happened next is a little confused, as I was completely amazed by the whole performance, but I do recall thinking that this was a joke; at any moment, Singirok and Nic Van den Bergh would emerge from the back room laughing – a notion which seemed a good deal more plausible than what was actually going on at the time.

I can also recall that one of the officers was taller and more distinctive-looking than the rest. I subsequently discovered that this was Major Walter Enuma, the architect of this caper, Operation Rausim Quik, on behalf of Singirok, and Singirok's chief acolyte in all that followed. Other thoughts that went through my mind were that this could be a genuine coup, which prompted me to ask where the commander was, to which they replied, 'He has been taken care of.' This rang an alarm bell in my mind since that could mean anything, including that Singirok had been killed. But I also continued to think that this was all Singirok's little joke, designed to test my reactions, and at any moment he would pop out from the alcove and cry the equivalent of 'April Fool', or that Nic and the others would be ushered in and we would all enjoy a good laugh.

However, I quickly came to see that this was not a joke and that these people were in earnest. The ringleader, Walter Enuma, was very excited. He had wild, staring eyes, which made me wonder if he was on some kind of stimulant. He was brandishing a 9mm pistol and kept shouting 'Put down your briefcase!' and 'You are under arrest!' and 'Put your hands up!'. In fact, there was a lot of shouting going on and, if anything, they all seemed to be rather scared, half afraid of what they had started and where it was going to lead. They did not know what my reaction was going to be or whether I had a weapon on me or in my briefcase, and perhaps it was this that made them so nervous and excitable.

The PNGDF officers had been slightly in awe of us all along, probably

174

because of our different backgrounds and more extensive military experience. There was some sort of myth going around that we were supermen who could do all manner of amazing things – a notion confirmed to me later in conversation with some of my guards. Apparently they had all been briefed to be especially wary, as we had the ability to leap into the air, cross the room, bounce off the far wall and generally do some kind of Bruce Lee number on them before effecting an escape.

Such skills would have been useful, as things were now getting a bit testy. I was resisting their attempts to arrest me and they were hauling me about – and then Enuma stuck his pistol into the centre of my forehead and screamed, 'If you don't do what I say, I will kill you! I have killed before and I will do it again.' Strangely, I did not feel any particular fear. A number of things went through my mind but I knew somehow that he was bluffing. I knew he was not going to shoot me, there and then in Singirok's office, though he might do it later, so I told him to go ahead, as I was not going to play his game. At this a general fracas ensued, punches were thrown and I ended up worse off, following a number of kicks and blows to the head with various weapons. I was forced on to the floor while they took my briefcase away and carried out a rudimentary search of my pockets.

I was wearing a pair of khaki chinos, a blue denim shirt and a pair of slip-on shoes – not the best of clothing for going into captivity, more for lounging around in Port Moresby – but apart from a wallet with credit cards and all the usual items, I did have a small lock knife and quite a lot of money, together with one or two other useful items. I always carried a lot of cash; I believed that the two things one should always have on one's person are a knife and a lot of money. Having done the combat survival course at Hereford, I knew about the full range of survival kit – fishing lines and traps and all the items useful for surviving in the jungle – but in my business the best form of escape kit is a knife, a compass and a lot of money.

The lessons of the combat survival course were still very useful during what followed, once I fully grasped what was going on. I was conscious, for example, that I had made a fundamental mistake by not following procedure, in not co-operating with these people as far as possible and playing the 'grey man', while waiting for a chance to escape. I had done none of those things. My reaction had been aggressive and I had fronted up to Enuma – not in itself a bad thing, perhaps, as it gained us all a degree of respect, but it made things harder for me later. So I had made an initial mistake and now I was lying on the office floor, being searched.

The search missed the knife, the compass and the money. Afterwards I was hauled to my feet and hustled outside, my briefcase disappeared, and a number of armed men in plain clothes or mixed dress arrived. I remember one who was wearing a headband, a camouflage jacket, denim trousers and flip-flops. I noticed that Gilbert Toropo, the commander of the Special Force and supposedly our best friend, was also there and it struck me as odd that he had taken no part in the arrest, though he was clearly a party to it.

I was half dragged, half frogmarched to the back of the building, where a number of vehicles had been assembled, including Nic's four-wheel drive. I was put in the back of Nic's car, two guards crammed in with me and I was told not to try to escape – if I did I would be shot. At this stage, as we started to move, my thoughts turned to getting away. The golden rule of escaping is if you are going to go, go early; take the earliest opportunity to get away, while you still have most of your escape kit and your wits about you and the opposition are not yet fully geared up to detain you.

However, the car was now moving at some speed, and it is hard to escape from the back of a moving vehicle when two people are sitting on top of you. We left Murray Barracks and headed off into town along a well-known route towards the naval base. I tried to engage the guards in conversation, asking them where we were going, and got the expected response of 'You'll see'. We drove down through the business centre of Port Moresby and along the road that led towards the landing-craft base – or out of town towards the jungle. I did not feel particularly frightened, as I did not feel that I was being taken to some remote jungle spot for execution. I was far more curious about what was going on, and was racking my brains about who these guys holding me were. Apart from Toropo I had not seen any of them before, and although I was beginning to suspect that Singirok was behind it, I still had this lingering idea that it really was all a joke and would end in laughter and fun and games.

We drove into the landing-craft base and by now my intention was to try and escape, perhaps back to Chan's house, or to our own base – I was now becoming worried about the others – or perhaps to the British High Commission. The lights were on at the base and I could see quite a number of armed men, many in fighting order with helmets on, not like their usual, casual style. I began to think that there really was something going on here. We screeched to a halt by a large landing craft that was moored to the jetty, its gunnels just below the level of the jetty, and I was bundled out. The boat was clearly ready to sail – its engines were running, there were lights on, there were plenty of armed men on the decks. It was quite a large craft, capable of carrying at least a couple of tanks, with a ramp for'ard and a superstructure aft, and I was clearly expected to go on board. I refused, saying flatly that I was not going. I was starting to wonder, why a boat? Were they intending to take all the Sandline people to Bougainville, or where? Maybe part of the army had joined the BRA, and perhaps they intended to take us to face the wrath of the BRA. Anyway, once I was on the boat and out to sea, the chances of escape would be almost zero.

I demanded to see General Singirok or to confront whoever was in charge of this so-called officers' coup, but that too was a pretty futile gesture and provoked a violent response. I ended up with a few more kicks, thumps and bruises, including one particularly hard kick in the back that sent me flying on board the boat, where I was immediately grabbed by some members of the crew and taken into a cabin at the back of the ship. I think it was the Captain's cabin, for it had a shower and a lavatory and once I was inside the door was locked. I promptly started to poke about, looking for anything I could use to escape, but the door opened again and I was told to lie on the bed and stay there, not to move about and not to look out of the porthole.

My training was now starting to kick in thoroughly, so instead of obeying those orders I stuck my head out of the porthole and started to engage one of the guards in conversation. It was a man I recognised, one of the Special Force sergeants who had been very friendly towards me. I asked him what was going on and he was clearly deeply embarrassed, squirming under my questioning. I started chatting, asking him for a cigarette – not that I smoke cigarettes, but it is another good ploy for making friends, and might have been useful later.

However, before I could get very far with this, another very ugly customer came along, who said that he was in charge, I was not to talk to the guards and if I did he would happily kill me, miming with two fingers held to his head. I decided to front up to him as I had to Enuma, so I asked him who he was and what the hell he thought he was doing, threatening and incarcerating an officer of the PNG Defence Force.

This fellow let me know that his name was George, and he was clearly a member of the intelligence community, probably a civilian, very aggressive, with much longer hair than the soldiers. He also carried a big knife and made no bones about the fact that he would be prepared to use it. Throughout the week of my captivity he proved to be a particularly nasty piece of work, a man specially appointed by Singirok to keep an eye on me. I suspect that at about this time some consideration was being given to killing me, or all of us, or some of us. I therefore backed off, took my head in from the porthole and lay down on the bunk for a bit.

The craft was now moving out of the harbour, first out to sea and round a prominent headland; then it appeared that we were going to drop anchor. The engines slowed and I could hear the anchor chain going out. Although I thought this was strange, I was relieved that at least we did not appear to be going to Bougainville. I was still thinking about escape, because the porthole was large enough to get through and in the early hours of the morning the sentries would have relaxed a bit and I could go over the side, swim ashore and return to one of our safe havens.

While I was waiting for the guards to relax I thought I might get a bit of sleep, and I also asked if I could have something to eat. They brought me a cup of tea and from then on all ill-treatment ceased. My back was still agony from the kick I had received on the jetty, but apart from that and some bumps and bruises I thought I was in pretty good shape. Having done a little stock-taking, I found I had about $1,000 and some pounds, a knife, a compass and a pencil. I had not yet found anything of use in the cabin, but I was determined to make a fuller search of that later. In the meantime I would get a few hours' shut-eye.

I woke up with that horrible feeling of not knowing where you are for a moment before it all comes rushing back. I then decided to press on with my escape plan, and looked out of the porthole. I could see one sentry and sensed that there was another one around somewhere, just out of sight. I started to engage the nearest one in conversation and after a time he let slip that what had happened to me was part of a wider plan that had been cooked up for some time and that all the Special Force unit were involved in it. He thought that, while nothing bad would happen to us, this was the end of the Sandline contract. I had my doubts about part of that, given the treatment I had received on the jetty, and started to move on my escape plan.

While the sentry was still standing there, escaping would be a problem, but the porthole was quite large, more of a window, and I was just starting to ease myself out of it when the ugly George appeared again. Finding me leaning out of the porthole, he got very excited and doubled the guard on the walkway, which naturally increased my problems. There were now two guards just outside, both armed with M16 rifles. I had to get through the porthole and over the side into the water, which gave them plenty of time to open fire. If they killed me, so be it, but I was more concerned about being wounded. The waters around Port Moresby were notorious for sharks and salt-water crocodiles and I reckoned that if I was bleeding I would not last too long if I attempted to swim to the shore, which was a good mile away. Being attacked by sharks or crocodiles was not a particularly attractive proposition, so I decided to settle down in the cabin, get some more sleep and see what the morning would bring.

I was now pretty tired and I slept well. I woke with light streaming through the porthole, having had about five hours' sleep. I felt rested but I ached all over, particularly from that kick in my back. It was now Monday morning, and my first thought was to wonder about what was happening to the rest of my team. I therefore demanded to see the Captain, who was not only responsible for my safety while I was on his vessel but was also my means of communication with Singirok, who was obviously not on the boat. I wanted to remind Singirok that I held him responsible for the safety of the seventy-odd Sandline personnel on the island. However, the captain steadfastly refused to see me, although a very well-educated officer whom I took to be the first lieutenant did come and talk to me. I had found some paper in the cabin and I later wrote a very strong letter to

Singirok, stating that this whole business was outrageous and that I wanted to know what was going on.

Before that, though, I had been allowed out of the cabin and into the wardroom just across the companion-way. While there I heard the local radio, which put out a broadcast from Singirok and later another one from Sir Julius Chan, so I began to get a picture of what was going on. It was clear that Singirok had been the instigator of this coup and had condemned the Sandline operation and the Chan government, which he called on to resign, and it appeared that he was attempting a military takeover. I tried to discuss this business with George and at this stage I was feeling more frustrated than frightened; it is a very frustrating business, being held captive, unable to act and not knowing what is going on.

Later that morning I was sitting in the wardroom, passing the time by playing patience with a homemade pack of cards and looking over the forward deck of the landing craft, the tank deck, towards the ramp, which was down and level with the water, where various small boats were moving about. I do not know what time it was, since my watch had been taken away and they refused to return it, but at some stage I was told to go back into my cabin and not look out. It was not until later that I discovered that Nic Van den Bergh had been on the ship as well and was then being taken ashore in a small boat.

By then I had some inkling of what was happening ashore, not least that Chan had sacked Singirok, who was therefore no longer in charge of the PNGDF and had no status or government authority. I was able to play on this fact with the soldiers, telling them that if they were acting under Singirok's orders, they were doing so illegally. But, to be pragmatic about it, Singirok was still in effective charge.

On the boat time passed slowly, interspersed with meetings with the still-unpleasant George, who sometimes asked, 'What do you think is going to happen to you?' On the following afternoon, Tuesday, I was escorted out on to the tank deck, where it all looked pretty intimidating: a mass of soldiers, all heavily tooled up with full kit and rifles, were lining the superstructure and looking jittery, all of them covering me with their weapons.

There I was met by another officer, Captain Beldon Namah, who was dressed in running shoes and combat trousers with a pistol stuck in his belt, who asked me to hand over the letter I had written to Singirok. I refused, saying that the letter was to go to the Captain of the ship and then to its destination and nowhere else. I was then told to walk to the edge of the ramp, face out to the sea and not look back. At that moment I was pretty sure they were going to kill me. It seemed quite logical; they were going to shoot me in the back of the head and throw my body into the sea. Strangely, my main emotion was anger and frustration. I was angry with them and angry with myself, and frustrated that I was in this corner. I was also sorry that I would not see my wife again or see my son Sam grow up, but I was determined that I was not going to let them shoot me down without some kind of resistance.

However, the tension then eased, briefly, as there was a small boat at the edge of the ramp and I was told to get into it. I again refused and was told, 'Get in and do as you are told and you will be all right.' I therefore got in, my head was at once wrapped in a combat jacket and we moved off. I was made to lie in the bow and once again I thought that they would shoot me and toss me overboard. I was trying to see out, and thought that I could somehow grab one of the men on board, seize a pistol, turn and shoot, or at least give it a go and make a fight of it before diving over the side.

Frankly, it seemed surreal, like something that was happening and yet at the same time could not be happening, not to me, not here. It seemed that we were heading parallel with the coast and I realised that we were not alone, for I could hear the engine of another boat. At one point I was told to lie down in the bottom of the boat as a fishing boat came past and there was then a lot of shouting between Beldon Namah and the people in the other boat, plus some radio chatter.

However, it appeared that this shouting was not about orders to kill me but the report that Bob Lowe, the British High Commissioner, was now very active and was trying to find out where we were and what had happened to us. The tension suddenly eased considerably. My head was unwrapped, I was allowed to sit up and I was offered a cigarette; I think they were as relieved as I was. I was then told that I was being taken ashore to join the others at Tarama Barracks, where Carl Deats, who had been seized at our house in Boroko, was also being held. We eventually came into a beach, where one of our jeeps was waiting, and I had to get out of the boat and wade ashore.

The dreaded George, who had obviously gone ashore somewhere else, was also there and I was taken up to the barracks. I was put in the front of the truck with Namah and they started to question me again, asking if I had the keys to the safe at our house at Boroko. I said no, I did not. This was a rather half-hearted attempt at interrogation and they eventually asked me what they would find in the safe. I told them some money – actually quite a lot of money, about $400,000 – which I was a bit pissed off about the prospect of losing.

This was our operating fund, as we had been close to going on operations and since the PNGDF could not get any credit from local companies in Bougainville for items such as fuel, it would clearly have been useful to have cash on hand, perhaps to pay for aircraft or medical attention for our wounded, if any, in Queensland. We had already obtained a list of hospital and medical charges and knew that help would be provided if we could pay the money up front. That apart, the safe contained a pistol and some documents, and when I told them this it seemed to satisfy them.

I was then taken into the annexe of the officers' mess and put into a rather dilapidated officer's room with one of those large slatted-glass windows, rather like a venetian blind, with mosquito wire behind it. There was no furniture except for a bed, and after a chain was put on the door I was left alone for a while, though George appeared again, accompanied by another chap, another unpleasant-looking civilian, also armed with a large knife. They checked the door chain, satisfied themselves that I could not escape and went away. It was very quiet, although all the other Sandline officers, including Nic and Carl, were being held in other rooms in the same building.

I thought to myself, 'Right, now I'm getting out of here.' I knew where I was, not a million miles from the town, and although I had lost my shoes, I thought I could get out and get to the airport or the High Commission. I decided to make my bid at around 3 a.m., but I needed to make some prior preparations, so I got my knife out and started to cut away at the mosquito-wire netting over the slatted window, being very careful not to make a noise. That went well and, having cut a hole in the netting, I started to lift out the glass flaps, one at a time, very carefully. Peering out, I saw that the guards had gone from the corridor. It was early evening and I assumed they had gone for a meal, so I cut a bit more. Suddenly there was a terrible kerfuffle from the corridor, rushing feet, a rattle at the door and that bloody man George rushed in, shouting, 'What are you doing?'

By that time I was back lying on the bed, looking innocent, and, amazingly, he did not notice the cuts in the wire screen or the missing slats. He had been creeping around in the corridor and had heard a noise. I thought I had got away with it but two minutes later he was back, this time with Walter Enuma, Singirok's right-hand man. They started shouting, screaming and swearing at me, asking if I was trying to escape. I ignored all this and proceeded to ask Enuma what the hell was going on and what was going to happen. He said that we were not going to be killed but that we were going to be kicked out of the country, that they had had enough of us. He added that a plane was going to bring the rest of the Sandline people down from Wewak and we would all be deported in a matter of days, contract cancelled. The game was over.

I did not know whether to believe him or not, but he was very excited and I still decided to make a break for it as soon as things settled down. It got dark and suddenly I heard a vehicle draw up, my door was thrown open and armed guards came in, took me downstairs and stuffed me in a mini-bus. I thought they were either going to take me to see Singirok or going to take me somewhere quiet and shoot me.

They never found my knife, compass or the money. These guys were all in uniform, proper soldiers, none of this mixed-dress nonsense. They drove me around the barracks for a while in a rather pathetic attempt to disorientate me and then we stopped by a large building, the guardroom, and I was put into a proper nine-by-nine cell, where I was eaten alive by mosquitos.

It appeared that I was now in the custody of the regimental police, which was rather like being back in my own British battalion. Once the others had gone they were very decent, finding me a mosquito net, lending me a pillow and being extremely friendly. But I was still determined to escape. Although the walls were of breeze block, the roof was of wood, so I got my knife out when there was no one around and started hacking at the battens. While doing this I broke the tip of the blade off my knife.

The snag was that the guards kept stopping by for a chat, or to offer me food or cigarettes, so progress was limited. On the other hand, I could find out the current state of play. They told me there had been a military takeover, we were to be thrown out of the country but, not to worry, they would protect me from any funny business and their CO had ordered that I was not to be harmed. They let me out for a shower at about midnight, and they found me some books.

It was by now Wednesday, four days into the whole coup business, and I stayed in the guardroom all that night and the next day. I became friendly with one of the guards, a very nice guy, and I asked him if he could get a message to a friend of mine in Port Moresby. I had heard a rumour that 'a friend of mine' had arrived in Port Moresby and was trying to arrange our repatriation. This was almost certainly Michael Grunberg, and if it was he would be staying at the Travelodge, where he had stayed before. So I asked this man if he would smuggle a letter out and he took it; I gave him $50 and added a note saying that Michael should give him another $50 on receipt of my letter.

He returned after about an hour and told me that we were to be moved out in the morning, and that is what happened. At about 9 a.m. the jailers came up, unlocked the door and took me to the front of the building, where there was a convoy of vehicles. I got into a car driven by Walter Salamas, chief of operations, and I said, 'Walter, what is going on?' He said that it would all be sorted out and we were going now to the Defence Minister's office. I met Nic and Carl and the rest, everyone was fine, and we had a good laugh about being locked up,

We set off but when we got to the front gate we were suddenly surrounded by Enuma and George and all the hoods. They said, 'Get out of the car,' and Salamas said, 'What is going on? All this has been agreed.' But it was no go, we had to go back to jail. There was then a bit of a fight – or at least I put up a fight, and got a whack on the side of the head with a pistol for my pains. After that we were taken back to the officers' mess, where the CO of the regular battalion, Tokem Kanane, was standing, and a big argument developed between the regular officers of the battalion and the mutineers. I had met Kanane on my recce to Bougainville and so I marched up to him and asked, yet again, 'What is going on here?'

I told him that we should be kept together and treated like officers and that I had no intention of going back to jail, but he was in a very difficult position and the upshot was that the others went back to the officers' mess and I went back to my nine-by-nine cell in the guardroom with my old friends the regimental police. They were quite sorry to see me again and offered me tea and mangoes and another shower and so on; so there I stayed, until another night had passed. Later I heard that one of the concerns of the mutineers was that there seemed to have been a botched rescue attempt to get me out. Two men working for Sir Julius Chan's son's security company Network had been arrested carrying 9mm pistols near the perimeter of the camp.

On the Friday morning I was taken out and put into a Land-Rover with Nic and Carl and we were taken to the military side of Jackson Airport. There we were put into very decent rooms where the pilots messed, and though George was there, issuing orders and threats as usual, gradually the tensions eased again. The others went upstairs to join the pilots, we were offered showers and meals and I gradually eased my way in with the rest. Nobody objected, things started to look quite good and we were able to discuss what had happened to each of us. Then they told us that our kit was being brought back, including our personal belongings, and it duly appeared – or most of it did. I noticed that my briefcase and passport were missing, but when I asked for them I was told that we were going with or without the missing items, that flights had been arranged and that was that.

I then got a call in the middle of the night from Siale Diro, who had been our PNG intelligence liaison officer but had then joined the plotters. He said that I should stand by to go down to the airport office and take a call from the British High Commissioner, but this never happened. We spent the night at the airport and then on Friday morning things were starting to look good. We were packed and waiting and then, just as everyone was ready to go, a mini-bus drove up and two mutineers got out and said to me, 'Come with us.'

While all this was going on, the extraction/rescue options and details were being sorted out by Tony Buckingham, Michael Grunberg and Bernie McCabe, who had set up an advance base in Hong Kong.

I got my kit and they took me towards the civilian side of the airport. I thought I was heading for deportation but about halfway to the civilian side there was a radio message saying we had to go back to the office, so we returned to the military side. I was left in the vehicle while the two guys went inside for a long talk with someone, then they came out again and we drove off. I asked, for the umpteenth time, what was going on, and was told not to worry.

Our charter aircraft had arrived, arranged by Sir Julius Chan, working with our team in Hong Kong. Bob Lowe was at the airport, asking the others where Spicer was. Everyone else was being allowed to leave but Singirok had given the order to keep me back and I was driven back to the harbour, back on to the same ship and into the same cabin – and I thought this was not good at all. I saw our charter aircraft take off with all the other Sandline people on board and I was pretty hacked off about that. As it flew out of sight, we sailed out into the middle of the harbour and dropped anchor – and there I was, in a floating prison.

Luckily I still had my homemade cards to occupy me, but this time everyone was far more friendly. I was allowed on to the bridge and I met the Captain and was able to ask him, as I was asking everyone, what was going on. Behind the scenes, Bob Lowe was pretty furious about all this and was pulling strings, but he did not know where I was and the mutineers refused to tell him. We spent all that day in the middle of the harbour but the next day we went back in and I was told I would be handed over to the police. I saw this as a good sign; the police in PNG were pretty good and at least I would be away from these mutinous army jokers.

So there we waited, tied up to the jetty, from about 6 a.m. Nothing happened until about three in the afternoon, when a convoy of jeeps drove up and out got Namah and George and all the thugs. I was put into one of the vehicles, we drove off and I was then told that we were going to Boroko Police Station, where I was to be charged with illegal possession of a firearm and illegally importing money – the $400,000 from our safe. I started laughing, it was so ludicrous.

We got to Boroko Police Station, which was surrounded by thugs. The press were there and this was the time when the pictures were taken which made the TV screens and the newspapers. I was then taken inside, photographed and finger-printed, and this time I was told that I was to be charged with illegally possessing a firearm. I started to laugh again – after all, I had imported about fifty tons of firearms, with the full knowledge and approval of the elected PNG government. For them to get excited about one 9mm pistol seemed a little absurd.

I then insisted on seeing the British High Commissioner and the police inspector said, 'Look behind you.' I turned and there was the solid, Scots bulk of Bob Lowe – I don't think I have ever been so glad to see someone. I asked him what the score was and he said he intended to get me bailed into his custody. He was marvellous and did a most wonderful job and was also very brave. I was taken down to the cells, where I was not locked in but allowed to sit by the guard – Boroko cells are very dingy and there was a nutter in there singing his head off – until the army mutineers, realising they had made a mistake and that the police intended to bail me, burst in and demanded that I be handed back to them. At this stage Michael Grunberg called the police station. I was allowed to talk to him, opening the conversation – in spite of being very glad to hear his voice – with 'Where the fuck have you been?'.

The police sergeant refused to meet the mutineers' request, saying it was now a police matter and they could push off. While this confrontation was going on, Bob Lowe came back and fronted up to these thugs, in particular the leading thug, who was in the usual mixture of headband, combat trousers and flip-flops – and armed with an M16 rifle, which he stuck in Bob's chest. The thug said they were taking me back and Bob should mind his own business. Bob did not bat an eye. He told this thug he was threatening the British High Commissioner, that I was now in his custody and that he – the thug – could, in as many words, piss off. This took guts, for the mutineers were very excited and not in the mood for niceties.

I think Bob saved my bacon. The thugs backed down and left and I was taken back upstairs to the police office, where I found a high-powered police delegation. They told me that the matter was now in their hands, that they did not support the mutiny but that they had these charges to investigate. It was obvious to me that I could be released into Bob's custody, provided these charges were in place to stop me leaving the country. What I did not know was that Chan had agreed to hold a Commission of Inquiry into the whole affair, in which I would be a prime witness.

So, with a sigh of relief, I got into Bob's white High Commission Land-Rover with the Union flag fluttering on the bonnet and we left Boroko Police Station with what was left of my kit in the back. We drove directly to Bob's residence, where the first thing he did was press a very large glass of whisky into my hand. Bob and his wife Anita looked after me very well. I could go on forever singing the praises of Bob Lowe, his wife and his High Commission staff; there were only six of them and they were brilliant to me. One member I would like to single out is Brian Baldwin, whom I also stayed with; Brian and his wife took me out in their boat and looked after me extremely well.

I started going into the British High Commission every day, preparing myself for the Commission of Inquiry and dealing with the firearms charge, and the staff were wonderful to me and very supportive. Within fifteen minutes, Bob had given me a new passport, since I had lost my previous one. The Sandline team in Hong Kong were also superb; they were continuously working behind the scenes on every option to get me out and also sending excellent 'Red Cross' parcels and generally keeping my morale up. Bob Lowe gave me a cell phone so I could keep in touch with my family.

By this time Chan had stepped aside and the PNG government had appointed an interim Prime Minister and a judge, Judge Andrew, to conduct the inquiry. I had also acquired two local lawyers, Bill Frizell and Michael Wilson, and an outstanding Australian barrister, John Reeve, as my defence team. This legal team did a fine job, going out of their way not only to help professionally but to make life bearable as well.

On the following Monday I was charged at the local magistrate's court with possession of a firearm and ordered to appear in front of the Commission of Inquiry, where I was the first witness. There was then a pause and I had to wait from mid-March until sometime in April before I appeared in front of the Commission. I gave four days' evidence over a couple of weeks. The whole process was very tedious and very tiring. I was questioned continuously, by Ian Malloy, the barrister assisting Judge Andrew, by Chan's lawyers, by my own lawyer and by Singirok's lawyer, a particularly pedantic, stupid and irritating little man called Peter Donigi; by the end everyone was fed up with Donigi and his aggressive questions.

While all this was going on, Bob and my lawyers were working behind the scenes on the firearms charge which was eventually dropped, and finally Judge Andrew and the Commission decided they no longer needed me. This was at lunchtime and I was out of PNG by four in the afternoon, thanks to a lot of help from the local people. The Australian High Commissioner had got the agreement of the Australians that I could go into Brisbane for the night without needing a visa, and that was to be the first stop.

So, here was the end of it. I was smuggled on to the plane through the back door. The door closed, the steps went away and I sat back in my seat and thought, at last, freedom . . . and then the steps came back and the doors opened again.

When the door opened, everyone in the aircraft turned round and stared at me. It turned out that one of the ground crew was still on board, and it was nothing to do with me at all. There were quite a lot of questions asked at immigration in Brisbane, although I was only staying one night in a local hotel and was booked on a BA flight to London the next morning. Then I thought, did I really want to spend a night in Australia? I had an alternative plan, to fly home via Korea, and, having phoned my home and office to say that I was out of PNG, I caught the flight home.

Looking back, I can still only wonder at Singirok's motives. He was, for all his military appearance, a weak man, easily influenced by others and open to pressure, not least from Chan's political opponents. To this can be added his own financial interests. It later transpired that other military companies were seeking involvement in PNG and we had already discovered that Singirok's hotel bills during his visit to London had been paid by a private company. Self-interest clearly played a part in his actions, though he was careful to dress them up with some moral motivations, but he let his guard slip in a conversation repeated to me later by Michael Grunberg. 'I spoke with General Singirok and his wife during the five-day period when the Sandline team were incarcerated, and I clearly recall him saying, "The Sandline contract has given me the perfect opportunity to create a constitutional crisis,"' said Michael.

In addition, only a few months after these events took place, the true underlying motive for his behaviour was exposed by the Australian journalist Mary-Louise O'Callaghan, who had first revealed our presence in PNG. She revealed that Singirok had been paid £31,000, a fortune in PNG terms, which had been put into a secret bank account by a UK arms dealer called J. and S. Franklin. Singirok was the man who had orchestrated public anger over the Sandline contract by alleging that every member of the PNG government involved – except himself, of course – had received corrupt payments. Now it was revealed that the only person accepting such payments was himself. For a while he became an outcast, but in true PNG style, Singirok – though publicly exposed as a liar and a fraud – was recently reinstalled as commander of the PNGDF. Papua New Guinea has not earned its name 'The Land of the Unexpected' without good reason.

There had been a lot of press interest in our activities in PNG and I did not know what sort of reception I would get when I arrived back in the UK, so before I arrived Michael Grunberg got on to the police at Heathrow, who assured him that they would prevent me from being greeted by a mob. Therefore when I emerged from the aircraft, the first thing I saw was a number of armed, uniformed policemen, who were just standing around on the catwalk as you come out of the aircraft.

I was first off the plane and went through immigration with no trouble at all. I was then met by my trusty driver, George Dryden, and went to another location near the airport where I met up with the 'welcome home' committee, Tony and Michael, and we had a great laugh. Tony, Michael and Bernie had spent a lot of time and effort in supporting me and 'plotting' in case of trouble. I have a lot to thank them for. There was quite a crowd of press and TV people asking for statements at the airport, but we had already decided that nothing would be said until I gave a press conference a couple of days later. Having had a drink with Tony and Michael, I was whisked off to Blake's Hotel, where Caroline and Sam and the rest of my family were waiting. It had been decided not to go home in case the press had got hold of the address and were lying in wait. We had a great family reunion, with lots of champagne, and we stayed there for a couple of days until the first flurry of press interest died down.

One of the first people I met the next morning was Sara Pearson, who ran her own PR company called Sara Pearson Associates. Sara was known to Michael Grunberg, who had asked her to set up a press conference and handle all the press interest in Sandline, which was quite considerable. As Sara seemed to understand what was required, she got on with it, but I have to confess I got pretty testy about the press conference. I kept getting what seemed to be rather stupid instructions from one of her people who seemed to think that I had never given a press conference before, when in fact I had spent four months in Sarajevo giving one to the world's press every day.

We prepared a statement and arranged the format for the conference. I would be sitting on a stage with Sara and another individual who would help run the event. We held the conference one morning at the Hilton Hotel in Park Lane, with about fifty or sixty members of the press there. I read out the statement and they then asked questions for about forty-five minutes; I then had a photo call outside with Caroline and then we went home.

At that stage we decided that the press interest would tail off following reports in the paper on the following day and we planned a holiday in Antigua, where we went for two or three weeks. Getting back to my family having thought at one stage I might never see them again was highly emotional, and it took some time to get back to normal life – which did not last for long.

FIFTEEN

SANDLINE AND SIERRA LEONE

'The general rule for military operations is that the military leadership
receives the order from the civilian leadership. Let diplomatic relations
be established at borders.'

SUN TZU

I got home in April 1997 and started to pick up the pieces of the business again. Matters had not stood still in my absence and a large number of items needed attention. This included tidying up the PNG business. We were still owed the balance of the money due on our contract, $18 million, and, a point that particularly rankled with me, the return of the $400,000 of operating funds taken from our safe at Boroko.

Much of the work here was in the capable hands of Michael Grunberg and a team of lawyers from S.J. Berwin, headed by Richard Slowe. They subsequently brought a successful action against the government of PNG requiring a full payment of our account, securing a judgement in October 1998 after protracted litigation. While this was proceeding, I became involved in another interesting assignment, in the war-torn territory of Sierra Leone.

The situation leading to Sandline's involvement in Sierra Leone is complicated, and that involvement led directly to what later became known as 'The Sandline Affair', a three-act farce involving Customs and Excise and the Foreign and Commonwealth Office (FCO), with a cast ranging downwards from the Foreign Secretary Robin Cook to junior desk officers. It might be as well to start the story with a brief account of Sierra Leone and the situation of that tormented country in 1997.

Sierra Leone is one of the West African states. It lies on the Atlantic coast with Guinea to the north and Liberia to the south and was once a British colony. Freedom from British rule arrived in 1961, but although the country is rich in mineral deposits, notably diamonds and bauxite, the economy soon began to stagnate. By 1987 the annual inflation rate was 100 per cent – and political differences between the many tribes and factions led to the outbreak of civil war in 1990. By 1992 the UN had placed the four and a half million-strong population of Sierra Leone at the bottom of their 'quality of life' index and in

1992 a military coup overthrew the government and took control of the country.

The new leader of Sierra Leone, a twenty-seven-year-old army officer named Valentine Strasser, was sworn in in May 1992. In December of that year there was another coup, which failed, twenty-five of the conspirators later being executed by firing squad. It was at this time that the UK, the former colonial power, suspended all economic aid to Sierra Leone, where free elections and a return to civilian rule had been promised for 1995. Gradually, though, the initial stability promised by the new regime faded away, not least because of the ongoing campaign waged by the anti-government forces, now combined into the Revolutionary United Front or RUF.

These rebel groups do not seem to have been particularly interested in political control. Their main focus was on banditry, their principal aim being to control the interior of the country and the rich diamond fields it contains. This struggle, between the RUF and the government, went on for years, with each side gaining the upper hand for a while and then losing it again. During this time the interior became particularly dangerous for foreigners and expatriates working in the diamond and bauxite mines. Many of the companies running these fields and mines therefore engaged foreign security firms to guard their staff and their valuable installations.

Finally, on 29 March 1996, a democratic government was elected in Sierra Leone, headed by President Ahmed Tejan Kabbah. Just over a year later, on 25 May 1997, President Kabbah was overthrown by a military coup led by Major Johnny Koroma, after elements in the army had conspired with the RUF. President Kabbah and most of his government fled to Conakry, the capital of neighbouring Guinea, where Sandline's part in this story really begins.

As related briefly elsewhere in this book, I already knew Kabbah, and Sandline had already carried out one successful operation on his behalf. By the time his government was overthrown, we also had business interests in Sierra Leone, for although Sandline does not undertake security work, we have an associate company, Lifeguard, which undertakes commercial security tasks. In 1997 Lifeguard was guarding a number of industrial concerns in Sierra Leone, including a diamond mine, an industrial plant and the important Bumbuma Dam. The guards were armed and deployed in small parties numbering between half a dozen and thirty men, depending on the size of the operation and the location they had to protect.

These teams were prepared to put up a fight if their installations were attacked, and the RUF therefore tended to leave them alone; there were plenty of easier targets for the RUF to exploit in Sierra Leone, plants where there were no guards whatsoever, and they spent a considerable amount of time terrorising the native population, looting, raping and killing. To provide a rear link and to help the Lifeguard teams in case of serious trouble, Sandline had based a small team at Conakry in Guinea. We also had one person in Freetown looking after the Lifeguard personnel – but no one was helping the other British and American expatriates up-country when serious trouble broke out in 1997.

Kabbah's rise to power in 1996 had been greatly aided by Executive Outcomes, which had been working with the previous military junta against the rebel RUF and had helped considerably in the restoration of democratic government. However, one of the terms of the peace deal that brought Kabbah to power was that EO should be expelled. EO worked to a contract, and when Kabbah said they must leave they said, 'Of course we will go but, rest assured, in less than a hundred days the RUF will welsh on the deal.' In this EO were almost exactly right; the army/RUF coup that overthrew Kabbah took place on the ninety-fifth day after EO left.

Following Kabbah's overthrow the UN took a hand, issuing a Security Council Resolution (SCR 1132) on 8 October 1997, expressing support for the efforts of ECOWAS – the Economic Community of West African States – to restore Kabbah to power, condemning the coup and placing an injunction on the supply of arms or support to the rebel junta in Freetown. The coup was widely condemned by other countries, including the UK, and the task of expelling the junta was taken up by ECOMOG, a military force led by Nigeria and in effect the military arm of ECOWAS, which had an understandable interest in restoring and maintaining peace and stability in the region. ECOMOG met with only limited success and it was soon realised that military action would have to be supported by economic sanctions – again against the junta. At no time did any government or international body propose imposing sanctions of any kind against President Kabbah; since he was the man they were trying to return to power, this is hardly surprising.

This combined approach had a certain amount of success, or at least apparent success. In October 1997 a peace accord was signed in Guinea between ECOWAS and Johnny Koroma's Armed Forces Military Council (AFRC), an accord which contained proposals for the return to power of President Kabbah by April 1998. This accord did not hold, the AFRC used the time to import more arms from Liberia, paid for in diamonds stolen from local mines, and it took further fighting before ECOMOG forces finally retook Freetown in March 1998 and restored Kabbah to power – by force of arms.

During all this time Sierra Leone was in a pretty bad way, not least in Freetown, where the RUF were creating chaos and the junta were being very repressive. There was a US task force offshore, evacuating civilians, and by mid-1997 Sandline was operating a helicopter which was used to extract people from up-country, a large number from the Kono district, the mining area. Sandline and Lifeguard got a large number of people out – there was no one else to do it and our help was appreciated – but I might add that while we were happy to do it, we did so at our own risk and at considerable cost and none of the sums laid out in this work were ever repaid by the employers of the expatriates we rescued.

This help, the guarding and the operation of the Sandline helicopter, was not covert in any way. We were operating openly, as a legitimate business under contract to other legitimate businesses, and were in regular contact with both the US State Department and the Foreign Office. This was both via the High Commissioner to Sierra Leone, Peter Penfold, who was then with Kabbah's government-in-exile in Conakry, and in London, where our point of contact was John Everard at the Sierra Leone desk in the Foreign Office. We had to keep in touch with them, for they knew where the refugees were. They needed to know what we were doing to suggest where we might help; there was no 'secret agenda' here, no intention to 'involve them', as was later alleged. We were simply British citizens helping other British citizens, doing work the British government should have been doing. We were telling them what we were doing, whom we were pulling out, whether they were British nationals and so on. Lifeguard stayed on throughout the troubles, and we wanted to keep them there if possible, partly to protect the assets we had contracted to guard but also perhaps to provide a firm base for any further involvement in Sierra Leone, if that were deemed possible. Later on, though, we had to evacuate the group at Kono when the situation there became impossible.

So much for the background to Sandline's participation in Sierra Leone generally. Our contact with the exiled President Kabbah began quite casually in May 1997, a month after I returned from PNG and long before the issuing of SCR 1132. I rang President Kabbah in Conakry and said that if he needed us or thought there was anything we might do to help him or his government, the rightful government of Sierra Leone, we were on hand and willing to help.

We also offered to supply him with information on what was going on inside Sierra Leone, where, thanks to our work in evacuating civilians from the up-country areas and with Lifeguard groups in the country, we had a better idea of the situation on the ground than any other bodies then concerned in their various ways with the Sierra Leone situation – which is another reason why the US State Department and the Foreign Office were eager to keep in touch with us. We continued to supply the State Department, the Foreign Office and Kabbah with information, from May until December 1997.

However, our direct involvement in resolving President Kabbah's predicament arose in a rather curious way. In the early summer of 1997 we were approached by a businessman from Vancouver, one Rakesh Saxena, who asked us to undertake a study of ways in which Kabbah could be restored to power – a study for which he would pay. Apparently, Saxena had been in negotiations with the Kabbah government prior to the coup. They had been discussing mineral concessions – specifically diamonds and bauxite – and Saxena wanted Kabbah back in power so that he could capitalise on his initial investment.

This request put us in a mild dilemma. We only deal with legitimate governments and we are very clear and firm about that; it is a non-negotiable policy. Getting Saxena's concessions back was not our concern in any way. We could only intervene in Sierra Leone at all, at any level, if President Kabbah was happy about it, and that was the first thing we had to clear with him – even though, on the face of it, Saxena was offering practical help and, again according to Saxena, Kabbah and three of his senior ministers approved of his intention.

We duly contacted the President and he was content to let us go ahead. It has to be remembered that everyone, from the UN down and in particular the UK government, wanted Kabbah back in power. Clearly the best path back to power, the one preferred by the West and the UN, was through diplomacy, but this was obviously not going to happen, so there seemed to be no reason why we should not at least study military means to achieve that much-desired end.

In short, to revert to military parlance, we were prepared to carry out a 'commander's estimate' for Kabbah for an agreed fee which Saxena would pay – and we would only implement the proposals if Kabbah and his government approved of them. I then flew out to Conakry, met the three Sierra Leone ministers Saxena had referred to – including Sam Norman, chief of the Kamajors, guerrilla fighters loyal to Kabbah, a man I already knew – and got their approval. They wrote out a document specifying their requirements, a document which I still possess. The involvement of Sam Norman is particularly important, for it was his people, the Kamajors, that formed the bulk of the resistance forces fighting the RUF and any actions we took must involve them. We would clearly depend on their support.

All this took place in June 1997. Talks with the RUF military junta in Freetown were meanwhile going on at the official level but were getting nowhere. It was also becoming clear that the junta were flying in lots of weapons and military equipment and preparing to fight on; they were being supplied by Charles Taylor, the leader in the neighbouring state of Liberia, who was being paid in diamonds.

Shortly after we agreed to go ahead, two things happened. First of all, the story of our involvement broke in the Canadian press. It had been leaked from somewhere – and it has to be remembered that, following the publicity surrounding the PNG business, Sandline was in the news and hot copy for investigative journalists. The second thing was that during my time in Conakry I got the impression that Kabbah was not fully aware of what was going on *vis-à-vis* the three ministers and the intervention of Saxena. I was constantly in touch with him on the telephone and with nostrils attuned by the PNG affair I began to smell a rat, but I cleared the proposal for the commander's estimate with him and got his blessing.

This was in the autumn of 1997 when, among other events, President Kabbah was Prime Minister Tony Blair's personal guest at the Commonwealth Heads of Government Meeting in Edinburgh, a pretty public statement of British support. All this, I suggest, tends to indicate that helping Kabbah was regarded as a good thing and could be expected to gain widespread support in the higher echelons of the British government.

On 27 October, at the end of the CHOGM conference, the communiqué put out by the British government made direct reference to SCR 1132 as imposing 'weapons . . . sanctions on the military junta in Sierra Leone'. This was a clear statement which was to be repeated in an FCO bulletin in January 1998 and by Tony Lloyd, Minister for Africa, in the House of Commons in March that year.

We were still in periodic touch with John Everard at the Foreign Office, and meanwhile we continued to negotiate with Saxena over the work we had agreed to do. The problem, inevitably, was money – and not just our fee. We needed to be paid, but Saxena wanted to be sure he got his investment back and President Kabbah was concerned that his dealings with us or Saxena should not be interpreted as 'mortgaging his country' – Kabbah's words – to foreign investors or influence. This problem required analysis and was eventually resolved by regarding the mineral assets of Sierra Leone as a potential cash crop – which is exactly what they are.

In normal times, a Third World country with mineral assets allows foreign companies with the necessary funds and expertise to come in and develop these assets, on terms. A deal is struck whereby the foreign company is granted a concession limited in area and time, say to a mine in a given area for a specific period of time. It then exploits the concession at its own cost, which is often substantial, searching, say, for diamonds or oil. If the search proves fruitless and the company's investment is lost, hard luck. If the search is successful, however, a further deal is struck whereby the initial investment is recouped and the subsequent profits are split between the company and the national government on an agreed and equitable basis. In normal times, that process would have been followed by Saxena and the Sierra Leone government; the only current complication was the war. To explore ways of ending the war and getting back to power, Kabbah had to get the money from Saxena to fund our involvement – for we could not work for Saxena directly. Saxena could pay, but we had to work for Kabbah. This is not semantics; this is the way of ensuring political control over what happens.

The eventual deal was that Saxena would fund the commander's estimate and some subsequent action and recoup his money by exploiting mineral concessions which would be granted by Kabbah on his return to power. This represented an enhanced risk for Saxena, but risks are inevitable and the initial sums involved were not large.

The procedure having been agreed, the work went ahead. Our eventual plan, the basis of the contract between Saxena and the government, would involve a command and control (C&C) group to work with the Kamajor guerrilla fighters, liaison with ECOMOG (the UN-approved Nigerian forces), the provision of helicopter support as a 'force enhancer', a shipment of small arms for ECOMOG to arm the Kamajors, and perhaps a Special Force unit. The total cost of implementation would be in the region of US$10 million.

Through our work helping in the evacuation of the refugees, we had already done a lot of the spadework for free, and at this stage we can return to another participant in this story, Peter Penfold, the British High Commissioner in Sierra Leone before the coup. As mentioned before, he had withdrawn to Conakry with Kabbah in May 1997, was a man we already knew well, and Kabbah had discussed our involvement in Sierra Leone with him before agreeing to the deal.

The British government are well served by their overseas officials and Peter Penfold is a first-class diplomat and a pragmatist. Before taking up his appointment in Sierra Leone in January 1997, he had visited our offices in London – at the suggestion of the Foreign Office – and we had been able to brief him on the state of play in Sierra Leone at that time, and we have been in regular contact with him ever since. We had also been able to help him discharge his duty of protecting British expatriates when the trouble broke out. We were in regular contact with Peter in Conakry and were able to help him with information for the reports he was filing to the Sierra Leone desk at the Foreign Office in London. We were simply one of his contacts and a useful source, nothing more, but he knew what was going on.

Keeping in touch with legitimate government authority – as we had done with the UK and Australian High Commissioners in PNG – was normal Sandline practice. Less normal were our troubles with Saxena, for it was beginning to appear that Mr Saxena had a somewhat questionable track record in some of his dealings with national governments. This came to light one day in the summer of 1997, when I was visiting him in Vancouver. We were driving about the city when he stopped the car at a Royal Canadian Mounted Police station in order to 'check in'. It transpired that the Thai government were trying to extradite him from Canada to face charges of embezzlement, and while the deportation order was pending he had had to surrender his passport and had to check in with the local police every day.

This information did not enhance my confidence, but we pressed on. You meet a lot of strange people in this business, Saxena was not a proven villain and as yet the Canadian government had not deported him. In my view, people are innocent until proven guilty – and since our dealings would be strictly on terms of money up front, there would be no chance of President Kabbah's plan being thwarted or collapsing as a result of any inaction by Saxena.

All this took time. The next significant day in this developing story was 23 December 1997. Draft contracts were then being faxed to and fro between the Sandline office in London, Kabbah in Conakry and Saxena in Vancouver. On the morning of 23 December I got a phone call from Kabbah saying he wanted to do the deal. There was then a flurry of faxes and phone calls between the Attorney General of Sierra Leone, who would draft the contract, Kabbah, Saxena and me.

The final contract was between Saxena and the Sierra Leone government, not with us, but there was a 'military annexe' to the contract stating that the funds supplied to Kabbah were on the understanding that Sandline did the work. The final draft went off to Saxena on the morning of 23 December and later on Peter Penfold, who had returned to London for Christmas, came into our office for a briefing and lunch with Tony Buckingham and myself. At that lunch I showed Peter Penfold the draft of the contract we had brokered between Saxena and Kabbah. When we returned to the office after lunch, I gave Peter a copy, which he folded up and put in his pocket.

We agreed that we would be in touch and would keep him informed, if not directly then through his second-in-command in Conakry, Colin Glass, while Peter was on holiday in Canada, or via John Everard at the Sierra Leone desk at the Foreign Office – though John Everard was due to leave that post on 5 January 1998 and would be replaced by a Mr Craig Murray. Over the last few months, when we had had conversations about the evacuation of Western nationals from Sierra Leone, I must have spoken to John Everard twenty or thirty times, but I had never met him, so I suggested to Peter that we might speak to someone at the Foreign Office face to face. He thought that would be a good idea. A meeting was eventually arranged for the New Year and took place at the Foreign Office on 19 January 1998 – another significant date, as we shall see.

When we returned from lunch on 23 December we had the signed contract from Kabbah and could therefore proceed; this was the military annexe section, for Vancouver is eight hours behind GMT and we could not yet get hold of Saxena to sign the main agreement. With Kabbah's signature on the deal, we now got fully geared up for action and among other moves ordered thirty-five tons of weapons for shipment to the Lungi International Airport in Sierra Leone, which was still in the hands of ECOMOG forces and the only place where we could land a big cargo jet.

Kabbah was desperate for us to get on with the job, but Saxena had still not come up with the money. By January 1998, we had deployed fifteen people and a MI-17 helicopter, the latter being an aircraft that was in-country anyway. We had previously owned it and had tried to sell it to an American businessman, but he had not paid us for it so in January 1998 we took it back.

It was being flown under the Sandline flag by a very capable bunch of pilots including Juba Joubert and Neil Ellis, both South Africans, and a wonderful ex-SAS Fijian, Fred Marafono, who were all doing sterling work flying with ECOMOG. The Sandline team was commanded by Bernie McCabe, director of our American operation, who had done a great job liaising with the Kamajors and was well liked by President Kabbah; he had even accompanied Kabbah on a trip to the UN the previous October and had spent a lot of time with the Kamajors 'behind enemy lines'.

Matters then went awry, for Saxena was arrested in Vancouver, having at that time only paid some of the funds he had committed to. He had been picked up with a false passport in his pocket and, fearing that he was preparing to flee the country, the Canadians put him in jail. We also had problems with the weapons, not in obtaining them but in finding carriers willing to fly them into a war zone. However, PNG had taught us that these matters never go exactly to plan and we were not discouraged or dismayed.

We had deployed and paid for the first consignment of kit, the infamous thirty-five tons of weapons that the Foreign Office would soon get so excited about, weapons which we would hand over to ECOMOG for distribution to the Kamajors. The UN embargo referred to supplying the rebel junta, not Kabbah, and ECOMOG was the legitimate agency, recognised by the UN, for restoring Kabbah to power, so it would not have mattered if we had supplied the Kamajors direct – and the UN Legal Department subsequently publicly agreed with us on this point.

The mechanics of the situation were that command of the anti-junta operations was vested in ECOMOG, and we had to land the arms shipments at Lungi International Airport, the only place that could take a big plane. We were going to land the kit there and hand it over to ECOMOG for onward distribution to the Kamajors; it was all perfectly straightforward. We only had a limited amount of money to do this, about $1.5 million, but we had a committed programme and we had promised Kabbah $10 million worth of work – and then Saxena went to jail and the money dried up. Saxena had, in effect, reneged on the contract.

Nevertheless, we persevered; we helped ECOMOG, and we supplied the Kamajors, some 8,000 strong, via ECOMOG, the way agreed with Kabbah. That was why we had a liaison man with the ECOMOG forces at Lungi Airport, from where we flew scores of missions with our helicopter. During these ECOMOG missions the helicopter was being continually shot at by the RUF, and a price was put on the crew's head – dead or alive.

At this time we were supplying logistic support for the Kamajors and for ECOMOG, using the helicopter. Bernie McCabe was acting as our liaison officer at Lungi and assisting the commander of ECOMOG, a very good Nigerian officer called Colonel Max Khobe, with the supply of food to the Kamajors. All this was useful, but the planned expansion of our operation into the military sphere – Project Python – was seriously inhibited by the lack of funds.

We had intended to buy more helicopters and put in teams of advisers to support the Kamajors, each advisory team being supported by its own helicopter. The teams would help the Kamajors plan operations and supply fire support, while the helicopters would provide logistical support and casualty-evacuation facilities; the entire operation would be based at Lungi, the ECOMOG base. We had also intended to form a Special Force unit to strike at the opposition's supply lines; the opposition had an MI-24 gunship helicopter and we wanted to take that out. To do that we needed to form a strategic operations team to help ECOMOG, but lack of funds prevented us from doing this.

Then Kabbah got seriously annoyed with Saxena. He was not cross with us, for he realised that we could not operate without funds and had already done a great deal of work on his behalf, much of it unpaid. However, on the very day our kit arrived – those thirty-five tons of arms – he cancelled the contract with Saxena. This was in early February, and ECOMOG had just launched the offensive that eventually recaptured Freetown.

Now, in view of what happened later, this is the time to point out that all these actions – including the arrival of the arms shipment – were known to the Foreign Office, whatever they chose to deny later. They knew quite specifically what we were going to do regarding arms shipments and military intervention, for at that meeting on 19 January 1998 – the one arranged after Peter Penfold's visit to our offices on 23 December 1997, where we had shown him the draft contract – we had briefed them fully on what we were about to do – and they had said 'fine'.

They did not want a long and bloody campaign – because then there might be questions in the House to embarrass ministers – and they said so, but they made no attempt to stop us or warn us about the UN embargo – Security Council Resolution 1132 – or the British Order-in-Council, which misinterpreted that resolution. The nub of the later dispute – the entire 'Sandline Affair' – hangs around that resolution and that meeting at the Foreign Office on 19 January 1998, and since it is so crucial and happened some months before the Sandline Affair broke, it would be as well to go into it in detail now.

These are the events as I recall them. To check my memory of the facts, I have referred to the account I gave later, under caution, to the investigating officers of Customs and Excise at an interview on 12 May 1998 – only a few months after the FCO meeting. Other versions of this meeting come in the next chapter; the reader can decide which to believe.

This meeting was with the new man at the Sierra Leone desk, Craig Murray, and his assistant, Tim Andrews. The meeting was perfectly friendly and I began by telling Murray that I was there to brief him on what was going on in Sierra

Leone and what we were about to do, adding that we were not going to do anything that would cut across the policy of Her Majesty's Government and I did not want to go treading on anyone's toes. Murray said something like 'By helping Kabbah you or your company will not be at contravention with the Foreign Office', or words to that effect, which I took to be an endorsement of what we had arranged to do.

We then discussed the Kabbah contract – not in great detail, but we certainly discussed it, and he knew it involved the supply of arms. We actually discussed weapons. Another point he did make was that 'a long-drawn-out military campaign would not go down too well' – because, I gathered, there would then be outside involvement, human-rights groups would be concerned, the press would start poking around, questions would be asked in the House and ministers would get twitchy. But at no time, there or anywhere else, did anyone say anything to contradict what I then believed, that is that helping Kabbah was perfectly legal.

It was a fairly general briefing and included some talk about the export from the UK of a mini-gun, which is a powerful gun for use in helicopters. Murray and Andrews told me about the need to get an export licence from the Department of Trade and Industry. I knew about that, but they added that the application for a licence would come back to them, a procedure that might take some time. We did not have much time, however, and in the event never ordered the gun.

We discussed the UN embargo but only in general terms. They certainly did not go through it 'line by line', and the Order-in-Council, by which UN embargoes are given force in British law, was not discussed at all. Orders-in-Council are not debated in Parliament – the 'Council' is the Privy Council – and therefore are not covered in Hansard, the Parliamentary record. Unless someone makes specific reference to them, they do not enter the public domain at all. I was unaware that an Order-in-Council even existed, let alone that it varied the terms of the UN embargo.

Mr Andrews did not take any notes during this meeting and did not go out of the room and come back with a copy of the embargo, as was later suggested. Murray had it on his desk, and while he referred to it, he did not indicate at any time that what we were doing – supplying arms and training to Kabbah's supporters and ECOMOG – was in any way illegal. Had he done so, and we had verified this, we would not have proceeded. These were the only two Foreign Office officials I met and I had no contact with their superior, Ms Ann Grant, who headed the entire West Africa Department.

Before I left we agreed to keep in touch and Murray walked me out, back down the corridor and across the courtyard. I never saw Murray again but I did speak to him periodically on the telephone, as I had spoken to Everard. What I was really glad about was that we had established that they knew what we were doing. From that point on, I was rather more concerned about keeping in contact with Peter Penfold, the man on the spot, but the telephone bill reveals subsequent conversations with the FCO, to both Andrews' and Murray's direct lines. These conversations could only have been about Kabbah and what we were doing for him, because we had nothing else to talk about.

This meeting caused a lot of debate later. The Foreign Affairs Select Committee report concluded, 'The principal difficulty of arriving at any definite conclusion about what transpired at the 19 January meeting arises because of the gross inadequacy of the official record.' The detail of a meeting lasting forty minutes is contained in less than two hundred words. Mr Murray describes the note as 'accurate but not full' and the report then continues (point thirty-five), 'In the absence of any record to the contrary, we cannot conclude with absolute certainty that Mr Spicer was clearly informed on 19 January that arms supplies to President Kabbah would be illegal.' Point fifty-two of the report concludes that, 'Whatever problems or excuses there may have been in relaying information earlier, Mr Penfold had, by 2 February, clearly and unequivocally informed management at the FCO that Sandline had a contract to supply arms to President Kabbah.'

I had no contact or telephone conversations with anyone else at the Foreign Office, including juniors like Ms Lynda St Cooke, whose name was brought up by Customs and Excise at my interview with them on 12 May. However, I did have a further meeting with Peter Penfold in London on 29 January 1998, ten days after that meeting at the Foreign Office.

Peter came to our office at about 2.30 p.m. He had been on holiday in Canada and was now on his way back to Conakry; he was a bit late and he had been at the Foreign Office that morning. Basically he wanted an update, and we gave him a full briefing on all that had gone on in Sierra Leone in his absence, including our various difficulties with the money and with getting the kit in, plus a detailed account of the talks I had had with Kabbah. I also gave him a copy of our operational ideas, the concept of operations. We photocopied it for him and he took it away.

So, to sum up, from May 1997 we had been in regular contact with John Everard at the Foreign Office and Peter Penfold, the British High Commissioner to Sierra Leone, though currently in Conakry with President Kabbah and the exiled government. On 23 December 1997 we had given Peter Penfold a photocopy of our contract with President Kabbah. On 19 January 1998 I had had a meeting with Everard's replacement at the Foreign Office, Craig Murray, and his assistant, Tim Andrews. On 28 January I had had a further meeting with Peter Penfold, and apart from a full up-to-date briefing on what we were doing, I also gave him a photocopy of our operational plan. Given all this – and the meetings and phone calls are not denied – how can the Foreign Office seriously maintain that they knew nothing about what we were doing? To put it bluntly, pull the other one!

The Foreign Affairs Select Committee agrees with this, both in the point made above, point fifty-two, and by concluding in its report, 'We believe that it would have been reasonable for Mr Spicer to conclude that he had the tacit approval of the British goverment from Mr Penfold for his deal with President Kabbah.'

Incidentally, when Customs and Excise raided my family home, they took away the machine I have attached to my phone for recording telephone conversations. When they played it back, the first recording they heard was a conversation between Peter Penfold and myself in which I say, 'Hello, Peter, this is Tim. The kit has arrived,' and Peter replies, 'Fine.' The date of that phone call was confirmed later by the bill from British Telecom and by the Military Liaison Officer (MILO) in Conakry, Major – later Lt-Colonel – Peter Hicks. Any suggestion that that they did not know, or any allegation that we were 'conspiring behind the backs of the British government' or using these FCO contacts with Everard and Murray to develop a legal shield for our illegal activities, is therefore obviously untrue. No one thought – or had any reason to think – that we were doing anything wrong.

Though the whole matter of the Sandline Affair will be covered in the next chapter, it should be clear by now that we had been working all along with the legitimate government of Sierra Leone and that this work had been with the full knowledge and approval of the UK government. And this was my government, the government I had served for most of my adult life as a professional soldier.

As I have said before, we had been in regular contact with the Foreign Office and the US State Department and had always kept them fully informed. I would even venture to suggest they had found us useful, in briefing their officials, in providing them with information, in evacuating British citizens from a war zone and in assisting a friendly, legitimate government in regaining power. None of this counted later, when the Foreign Office found it more useful to deny these facts and reported us to the Customs and Excise department for allegedly breaking the UN arms embargo. But the UN embargo had been aimed at the junta, not at ECOMOG or the Kabbah government, so how were we doing wrong in supplying arms to Kabbah, the head of the government that the UN and the British government wanted to restore to power?

The Sandline Affair lay in the future, however, and in February 1998 ECOMOG commenced the campaign that retook Freetown. That was the extent of the ECOMOG advance and the troubles up-country continued. We would have liked to have helped there but we had no contractual basis to continue. Our helicopter stayed and almost flew itself into the ground supporting ECOMOG as the fighting continued, and the rebels made a bid to retake Freetown again a few months later. By that time the helicopter was almost unserviceable – although the mechanics on HMS *Cornwall* gave it a through service on occasion – and money to patch it up or buy a new one was not available. When the crew, Juba and Neil Ellis, offered to stay on their own account and continue flying it, we let them have it as a gift. They continued to fly it for ECOMOG and did great work. On 10 March, a significant day as we shall see, ECOMOG forces retook Freetown, Kabbah was restored to power and so our work in Sierra Leone ended.

Three weeks later, however, Michael Grunberg received a phone call in our London office from Andrew Breaden, an investigations officer for HM Customs and Excise. This call was regarding a report that Customs and Excise had received from the Foreign Office alleging that Sandline had breached the UN arms embargo on Sierra Leone, SCR 1132 – an embargo later ratified by the Order-in-Council issued by the British government.

This was a serious charge, a criminal matter, so a meeting was arranged that same day. At that meeting Mr Breaden met with full co-operation from all the Sandline people and the involvement of the Foreign Office and the High Commissioner in Sierra Leone at every stage of our involvement was fully explained. This seemed to satisfy him and I duly went off to France for a skiing holiday. I was in Meribel again, putting on my skis at around ten o'clock on the morning of Friday, 3 April 1998, when my mobile phone rang. It was Michael Grunberg, saying, 'You should know that four Customs and Excise officers have raided us and are now searching this office and your home for documents relating to Sierra Leone and an alleged breach of the arms embargo.'

SIXTEEN

THE SANDLINE AFFAIR, 1998

'Foreknowledge cannot be got from ghosts and spirits cannot be had by analogy, cannot be found out by calculation. It must be obtained from people, people who know the conditions of the enemy.'

SUN TZU

The previous chapter is concerned with what actually happened in Sierra Leone. It tells the full extent of Sandline's involvement in that unhappy country from start to finish, and that account is true, accurate and detailed, a precise record of a useful achievement.

This chapter is concerned with a far less edifying episode, the behind-the-scenes machinations of the Foreign Office during the later stages of the Sierra Leone operation. They were actions we did not know about at the time, and actions which led to the arrival of Customs and Excise officers at my home and office and, somewhat to the surprise of the resident mandarins, even at the Foreign Office itself. It will also cover the subsequent official inquiries, the Legg Inquiry and the House of Commons Foreign Affairs Select Committee Inquiry, searching investigations into what became known as 'The Sandline Affair'. There are a number of reports and newspaper articles referred to during this chapter; the full text of most of them can be found on the Sandline website at www.sandline.com.

To trace the development of the Sandline Affair we have to go back to 8 October 1997, when the UN Security Council passed Resolution 1132. This resolution covered 'the decisions on sanctions taken against the military junta in Sierra Leone'. On page two of the resolution (point six), it 'decides that all states shall prevent the sale or supply to Sierra Leone, by their nationals or from their territories or using their flag vessels or aircraft . . . of arms and related materiel of all types'. Point three on the same page expresses 'strong support for the efforts of ECOWAS'. The resolution makes it clear that the UN arms embargo was aimed squarely at the rebel junta.

ECOWAS was in no doubt about this point, for at their summit in Nigeria on 28/29 August 1997, before the UN embargo was issued, ECOWAS issued its own embargo and 'empowered ECOMOG [their military arm] to enforce the sanctions against the rebel regime', adding (article six), 'The embargo imposed by this decision shall not apply to arms, military equipment and military assistance for the exclusive use of the sub-regional forces, which shall be responsible for applying the measures contained in the final communiqué of the meeting of ECOWAS foreign ministers, issued on 26 July 1997.' This communiqué is referred to paragraph three, page one, of the preamble to the United Nations SCR 1132 of 8 October 1997, so the link is clear.

UNSCR 1132 is slightly flawed, for while it makes it clear on page one that the embargo is aimed at the junta – in line with the above-mentioned communiqué – the statement on page two (point six) simply refers to 'Sierra Leone' and does not refer to the parties, a fact that gave great comfort to the Foreign Office. To give Security Council Resolutions effect in the UK, they have to be embodied in British law, and on 14 October 1997 the Secretary of State for Trade and Industry made an order, 1997 No. 2464 Customs and Excise, stating that 'the export to any destination in Sierra Leone is prohibited of any goods specified in the schedule of this order', adding Sierra Leone to the list of countries 'to which arms in transit through the UK may not be exported without an export licence'.

Teeth were not given to this order until a meeting of the Privy Council on 30 October at which an Order-in-Council (1997 No. 2592, a Statutory Instrument) embodied this resolution into UK law, with one significant difference. It is clear that SCR 1132 refers to sanctions on the junta, but that fact had not penetrated to the Privy Council, who refer to 'the government of Sierra Leone' without making clear which one – the legal one or the illegal one. Nor was this matter cleared up in the House of Commons, as Orders-in-Council, though laid before the House – and this one was so laid by the Minister of State at the Foreign Office, Tony Lloyd, on 31 October – are not debated in Parliament or recorded in Hansard, the Parliamentary record, and therefore require some specific action before they become public knowledge. And so we see, through a combination of poor drafting and muddled thinking, the beginning of a completely unnecessary public scandal.

A Security Council Resolution has to be taken as a whole; it is not fair or accurate to pick out particular contradictory sections to bolster a subsequent allegation. It is clear that the UK's Order-in-Council was flawed and did not accurately reflect the words or intention of the original UNSCR on which it was based and from which it drew its authority. It was a matter of public knowledge that the UN had placed an embargo on the supply of arms to the RUF army junta in Freetown. It was necessary to read the fine print of the Order-in-Council to realise that it also prohibited the export of arms to anyone in Sierra Leone – which was not, in any case, the thrust of UNSCR 1132.

In their report on the Sandline Affair, the Foreign Affairs Select Committee stated, 'It is most regrettable but quite understandable that debate has arisen about the terms of the UN resolution. We therefore conclude that the UK should not agree to any Security Council Resolution . . . unless the terms are clear and unambiguous.'

Many people spotted this flaw in the resolution. Writing in the *Daily Telegraph*, political journalist Boris Johnson said, 'For some reason yet to be explained, the arms embargo against Sierra Leone, UNSCR 1132, was given a perverse interpretation when it was put into British law. The Foreign Office decided it should be a blanket ban, which amazed the Americans, and everyone else.'

The Foreign Affairs Select Committee report had more to say on this point later: 'It would still be reasonable to expect the FCO to give the Order-in-Council full publicity.' Instead, the territorial department involved was not even consulted in its drafting. This is something which Ms Grant called 'most unfortunate' and which the Foreign Secretary Robin Cook called 'an extraordinary working practice'. Nor was Mr Penfold, the High Commissioner in Sierra Leone, consulted. Furthermore, when the Order-in-Council was made, there was no public announcement and no attempt was made to notify the principal officials concerned.

The Legg Report, which preceded the Foreign Affairs Select Committee Inquiry, confirmed, 'Most of the main players had either no, or only a very vague and general, awareness of the existence of the Order,' and the Foreign Affairs Select Committee report comments, 'The cavalier attitude shown by the FCO in not making sure that the Order-in-Council was brought to Mr Penfold's attention is inexcusable.'

The Select Committee report goes on to conclude that these failures spread the problem up as well as down: 'There was an appalling failure in the briefing of ministers. It is on the basis of these briefings that ministers report to Parliament and it is of paramount importance that ministers give accurate and truthful information to Parliament.' How Sandline International was supposed to know about the existence or terms of the Order-in-Council in these circumstances is not explained.

Until the Foreign Office chose to take a different line in March 1998 – five months after the issuing of SCR 1132 – none of this mattered. Everyone was aware of the true meaning of the UN resolution and it is worth repeating that no one, at any time or from any official UK government source, though fully aware of what Sandline was doing and intended to do, including the supply of arms to ECOMOG for the Kamajors, ever advised me, or told me, or implied in any way that what we were doing was illegal. The British High Commissioner in Sierra Leone, Peter Penfold, thought the embargo only applied to the junta and so did

President Kabbah. He told me that had he thought otherwise or been informed that it applied to his forces, he would have taken immediate steps to get it changed. The problem lies not just with SCR 1132, but with its misinterpretation by the UK government.

If any body of officials should have been aware of the fine print of an Order-in-Council affecting one of their territories, it should have been the desk officers covering Sierra Leone and West African affairs at the Foreign Office. It was, after all, the Minister of State at the FCO, Tony Lloyd, who had laid the Order. Yet not one of these officials seems to have been aware of the Order-in-Council, or, if they were aware, thought that they should bring it to my attention, although Craig Murray and Peter Penfold had been informed of Sandline's contacts with Kabbah – and seemed to approve.

So the situation moved on until 5 February 1998, when a Liberal peer, Lord Avebury, wrote a letter to the Foreign Office alleging that Sandline had breached the UN sanctions by supplying arms to President Kabbah. On 9 February this letter was shown to Craig Murray at the Foreign Office. Nothing then happened for a full month, until 10 March – coincidentally, the day ECOMOG retook Freetown and Kabbah returned to power – when, on the instructions of Mr Murray, his assistant, Tim Andrews, sent Lord Avebury's letter to Customs and Excise.

This action by the FCO set in train a Customs investigation into an alleged offence under the Sierra Leone (United Nations Sanctions) Order, 1997, which led in turn to the visit to our office by Andrew Breaden of Customs on Monday, 30 March. At that meeting, Michael Grunberg told Andrew Breaden the full story, stating that the Foreign Office had known all along about our involvement in Sierra Leone and had been supportive of our efforts, and that contact between Sandline, Peter Penfold and the Foreign Office had been regular and friendly. He told him that we were therefore at a loss to know why they had now reported our actions to the Customs or why we were now the subject of an investigation.

However, we could hardly expect Customs and Excise to take our word for it. Though thoroughly efficient and pleasant, they clearly had a job to do and an allegation to investigate, and they would not stop until they got to the bottom of the entire affair. They needed verification of our story.

I therefore rang Craig Murray at the Foreign Office on his direct line and spoke to him for six minutes and six seconds (according to the British Telecom bill), asking him to confirm that knowledge of what we were doing had been communicated to the Foreign Office and to Peter Penfold on a regular basis. What he did is described below, but common sense would argue that unless he was able to confirm the truth of our story, there would have been no point in contacting him at all, nor would there have been any point in discussing the issue for over six minutes – he hardly cut me short.

It subsequently transpired that on 29 and 30 January 1998, there had been a number of meetings at the Foreign Office between Craig Murray, Peter Penfold and the head of the West African desk, Ann Grant, Murray's immediate superior, at which Ms Grant had instructed Peter Penfold to write her a full account of his dealings with Sandline. In particular, he was to record his knowledge of and involvement with the Sandline contract with President Kabbah for the supply of arms to Sierra Leone. Peter Penfold wrote that account on 2 February, and Craig Murray saw a copy on 23 February.

This account, which was quoted at the subsequent inquiries conducted by Sir Thomas Legg and the Foreign Affairs Select Committee, confirmed that Peter Penfold and I had had lunch in London on 23 December 1997, where he had seen the draft contract with Kabbah, and that he had advised Kabbah to sign it. Further, it also confirmed that on 28 January 1998 Penfold had come to our office, where I had shown him details of our plans – the concept of operations. Peter also confirmed that a copy of this document had been handed to Craig Murray's assistant, Tim Andrews, on 29 January and to Craig Murray himself on 30 January. It is reasonable to suppose that this document and Peter Penfold's meeting with me on 28 January prompted Ms Grant's request for a full account of Foreign Office/Sandline contacts on 30 January.

Therefore, long before Lord Avebury's letter reached the Foreign Office on 5 February, some of those there concerned with Sierra Leone affairs knew about the Foreign Office involvement – and some of them had known about it for a considerable time. However, when on 30 March 1998 Craig Murray spoke to Cedric Andrews of Customs and Excise, he stated that the Foreign Office had not been aware of any arms shipments to Sierra Leone and that Colonel Spicer had not told the Foreign Office about any such shipment.

This last statement is particularly interesting, as it was made one month after I had telephoned Peter Penfold in Conakry on 28 February and told him 'The kit is on the way' and he had said 'Fine' – a conversation that was still on my recording machine. Mr Murray might dispute what he knew but he could hardly dispute what Mr Penfold knew, and Mr Penfold was certainly obliged to report what he knew, especially interesting facts like these, in his regular reports to the Sierra Leone desk at the Foreign Office – which was manned by Murray and Andrews.

If Customs and Exise had been informed at that stage that the FCO knew of Sandline's contract with Kabbah, the matter would have been cleared up there and then. But because Murray had suggested that the FCO knew nothing about the supply of equipment by Sandline, Customs applied to the Chief Magistrate for search warrants. On 3 April, their officers descended on the Sandline office, my home and my wife's home, searched them thoroughly and took away a large quantity of documents, including computer files, my telephone recording machine and various business records. They also raided the Foreign Office – a matter which has not been widely publicised. The basis for obtaining these search warrants was Mr Murray's statement to Customs and the referral of Lord Avebury's letter to Customs and Excise by the Foreign Office.

It is also interesting that on 30 March, the day Mr Murray had that conversation with Customs and Excise, he wrote a minute to his superior, Mr Dales, about the conversation, a minute which contained the phrase 'We were not aware of any shipment of arms'. This minute was copied to the Permanent Under Secretary, Sir John Kerr, and eventually it came into the hands of the Foreign Affairs Select Committee. When called before the committee, Mr Murray stated that the phrase was accurate because 'The Department did not know that any arms had been shipped at that stage'. The committee had other information – from Major Hicks at the Military Liaison Office in Conakry, for example – and called Mr Murray's statement that the FCO were not aware of any arms shipments 'quite implausible and unacceptable'.

Being investigated on a criminal charge is not a pleasant experience, and when, in addition, you believe you are being 'stitched up' by some minor civil servants, the situation becomes positively alarming. The next significant step in this business was on Tuesday, 12 May 1998, when I was interviewed, under caution, by officers of the Customs Investigation Division. This interview took place in the curiously named Custody Suite at Customs House in Lower Thames Street in the City of London, a complex of interview rooms and cells.

The whole atmosphere in the Custody Suite is quite intimidating, probably deliberately so, and I was once again grateful for the time spent on that now long-ago combat survival course, where interrogation was part of the training. I attended the interview on a voluntary basis and was accompanied by Sandline's legal representatives, Ian Laurie and Andrea Hopley. The investigating officers, Atif Amin and Colin Tennant, were very professional and perfectly pleasant; they wanted to find out what had been going on and I was very anxious to tell them. Even so, it was not a pleasant experience. Had matters gone awry I had been told I was looking at criminal charges and a possible sentence of up to seven years in jail.

To show that this was serious, the interview began with a formal caution – 'You don't have to say anything but it may harm your defence if you do not mention when asked something which you later rely on in court. Anything you say may be given in evidence. Do you understand?' – to which I replied simply, 'Yes.'

The interview went on all day, with a short break for lunch, and lasted in all for over seven hours. On the following day, 13 May, Michael Grunberg and my ops officer were interviewed, also under caution and also for hours, and it is fair to say that by the end of those two days the Customs and Excise Investigation Division knew all there was to know about our involvement in Sierra Leone and the extent of our contacts with the Foreign Office.

The information they were given has been covered in detail in previous chapters. It included my background, my pre-Sandline military career, leaving the army, setting up Sandline, and all the events leading up to our involvement with Sierra Leone and what went on during that time. They were particularly eager to establish whether we knew anything about the Order-in-Council and whether anyone at the Foreign Office had at any time advised us that what we were doing was in any way illegal. I told them three times that I had been totally unaware of the existence of the Order-in-Council until the Customs and Excise officer, Andrew Breaden, turned up at the Sandline office on 28 March, and it subsequently transpired that there were some doubts whether Craig Murray or Peter Penfold had been aware of it either.

I pointed out that President Kabbah was supported by everyone, from the United Nations to Prime Minister Tony Blair, who had even invited him to be his personal guest at the recent Commonwealth Heads of Government Meeting in Edinburgh. I pointed out that the final communiqué of the CHOGM welcomed 'petroleum, weapons and travel sanctions on the military junta in Sierra Leone', which seems clear enough. And, finally, I pointed out that I could not understand why helping Kabbah was in any way illegal, when the entire political establishment of the Western world was vocal in his support and in no doubt that the sanctions were aimed at the junta.

In attempting to distance themselves from Sandline's activities, the Foreign Office was curiously inept. We had not kept a detailed log of our phone calls – we do now – but British Telecom do and provide it to their customers along with the quarterly bills. A study of those bills by Customs and Excise revealed a series of phone calls to the Foreign Office in London and Peter Penfold in Conakry. This fact tended to undermine Craig Murray's denials of knowledge – if we were not talking to him about Sierra Leone, his area of responsibility, and the matter about which he had reported us to Customs, then what were we talking to him about? Every household in the country gets such itemised bills, but this fact was apparently unknown to the mandarins at the Foreign Office. So, as a result of a few simple, incontestable pieces of evidence, and having heard the full truth, Customs and Excise were able to substantiate our story. The result was that on 18 May, a mere five days after the conclusion of our interviews with the investigators, and after consultations with the Attorney-General, they issued a statement:

> Even though offences may have been committed, the particular circumstances leading up to the supply of arms affect the fairness of the case to the extent that any prosecution could well fail and would certainly not be in the public interest.

This might well have ended the whole affair and, apart from commenting that whether offences had been committed or not was a matter for the courts and that the decision not to proceed with a fruitless case was made in the government's interest rather than the public interest, we might well have left it there. We had been vindicated, we had a business to run and we wanted to get back to it.

However, the ineptness and duplicity of the Foreign Office had not gone unnoticed by the press and the public and both were increasingly on our side. After all, this was not the first time a British government had been economical with the truth; the attempt to blacken Sandline International had disturbing similarities with the Matrix Churchill affair under the previous government. Our profile in the press was very high but our PR was expertly handled by Sara Pearson, whom we knew well from the post-PNG publicity.

The combination of Matrix Churchill and the Sandline Affair made a number of people in Britain wonder just what sort of country they were living in, where successive governments could behave in such a fashion. Nor was the Foreign Office's case helped by the actions of the officials involved or by the conduct of the Foreign Secretary, Mr Robin Cook, who alleged that he had known nothing of this business until he was alerted by a letter from our lawyers, S.J. Berwin and Co, on 24 April 1998 – though he admitted to the Foreign Affairs Select Committee that his right-hand man, Tony Lloyd, the Minister of State, should have known all about it on 12 March, six weeks previously. The public view of that excuse was that if Robin Cook did not know, he should have known. The Berwin letter landed on his desk six weeks after his officials had reported us to Customs and Excise – and in politics, six weeks is a very long time indeed. It should have been more than enough time to find out what was going on in his own department and to get his officials to come clean.

The Foreign Affairs Select Committee made a comment on this point:

> We understand why the government might have wanted to emphasise that the arms embargo was aimed at the junta while neglecting the fact that it applied equally to the democratically elected Kabbah government which the United Kingdom wished to see restored. Yet half-truths are a dangerous commodity in which to trade . . . The way policy was presented led to confusion within the FCO and without.

In the weeks during and after the Customs investigation, the Foreign Office came to resemble a basketball court rather than a Department of State, as the people involved – having failed to lay any blame on Sandline – ducked and dived and passed the blame for this fiasco about in an attempt to avoid any responsibility themselves. Looking back on this in March 1999, Nick Cohen of *The Observer* commented that the Sierra Leone affair 'reads like a script by Joseph Conrad, rewritten by Evelyn Waugh . . . the leaks, the narks, the spies, the contempt for accountability', before going on to recommend the regulation of private military companies, a move Sandline fully supports.

Had anyone at the Foreign Office had a morsel of common sense, the simplest solution on 10 March, the day ECOMOG entered Freetown, would have been for the Foreign Secretary to have gone to the House of Commons and hogged the credit. Rejoice! ECOMOG, the legitimate power, with the assistance of the Foreign Office, had restored democracy to Sierra Leone – and any awkward questions regarding Foreign Office involvement with Sandline could have been brushed aside in an orgy of self-congratulation and party-inspired euphoria; the good guys had triumphed and who but a member of the opposition could complain about that? Indeed, this is how Tony Blair sought to deal with the issue when he was forced to intervene personally in order to defend the growing attacks on Robin Cook.

After all, was this not a clear victory for Mr Cook's much-vaunted 'ethical foreign policy'? Perhaps it was; the problem now was the Foreign Office's policies at home, which seem to have had very little to do with ethics at all. Perhaps Foreign Office policies apply only to foreigners?

Besides, coming clean about their actions, let alone their mistakes, is not the way things are done in government. Governments like to have it both ways, especially governments operating 'ethical foreign policies'. Approving the actions of private military companies did not sit well with such a policy, and, with ECOMOG now in Freetown, the Foreign Office did not need Sandline any more; we had been useful but we were now expendable. Moreover, having brooded over Lord Avebury's letter and examined an article in *The Observer* which talked about 'mercenaries' in Sierra Leone, they spotted the possibility of trouble. To gain some distance from this potential problem rather than tell the truth, the whole truth and nothing but the truth, they sent Avebury's letter to Customs and Excise and sat back to bask in the warm glow of moral self-esteem.

Unfortunately, it did not work out like that. We had an excellent legal team at S.J. Berwin, led by Richard Slowe, and we fought back. We had excellent advice from some very eminent counsel: Sir Michael Burton QC, Clare Montgomery QC and Ian Laurie. Foreign Office attempts to distance themselves from Sandline and deny that they had full knowledge of what we were doing promptly fell apart when Customs and Excise discovered the full facts. The Attorney-General, also scenting disaster, swiftly decided that this was a can of worms best left unopened. So it might have been, but there are no limits to institutionalised stupidity.

In the face of this rising public disquiet and press comment and a growing furore in the House of Commons, Mr Cook, who had waxed eloquent over the Conservative government's deplorable conduct during the Matrix Churchill affair, decided on a pre-emptive strike. Unable to accept the Customs and Excise findings and sack a few people, on 18 May 1998 he commissioned Sir Thomas Legg to investigate the entire affair yet again. Whatever the aim was, the outcome was another miserable failure, for more Foreign Office failings were broadcast to Parliament and the public at large.

The Legg Report not only revealed glaring inefficiencies in Foreign Office procedures, highlighting a failure of the West African and Sierra Leone desk officers to properly brief ministers, including Tony Lloyd and the Foreign Office Minister in the House of Lords, Baroness Symons, it also uncovered more evasions and inconsistencies in the FCO's accounts of the matter. In addition, the creation of the Legg Inquiry annoyed the Foreign Affairs Select Committee in Parliament, who felt that they were being sidelined by its creation, a conclusion that was completely correct. Robin Cook's main aim in creating the Legg Inquiry was to keep the much more powerful Foreign Affairs Select Committee at bay.

Like all the other facets of this pathetic, ongoing shambles, this attempt to cover up failed. The Foreign Affairs Select Committee also had a go at the Sandline evidence and the result was that two investigatory bodies trawled through the growing body of evidence concerning the government's involvement in the Sandline Affair and the attempts of the people at the Foreign Office to shuffle the blame about.

As a witness for the Legg Committee, I wrote a complete account of all my dealings in Sierra Leone, concentrating on our extensive list of contacts with State Department officials in Washington and at the Foreign Office in London, as well as with their representatives on the ground in Conakry and Sierra Leone. When I had it down on paper, even I was surprised at how many there were. There was John Everard at the FCO, to whom we talked about diamond smuggling by the junta and their attempts to purchase surface-to-air missiles, as well as about our help for Kabbah. Both Bernie McCabe and I had visited the State Department in Washington and briefed senior people on the African Affairs desk.

Nor were Bernie and I the only ones keeping contact with these governments. On 10 December 1997, both Tony Buckingham and Rupert Bowen, our liaison officer in Conakry, had visited the Foreign Office. During their talks, which were carefully documented, they raised the issue of military action in support of Kabbah; this seemed to find favour at the Foreign Office, and there was no mention of any objection to this issue or any suggestion that it might be illegal, in spite of the Order-in-Council which had been issued two months before. Nor, incidentally, did it feature in conversation when Peter Penfold visited our office on 23 December. The only conclusion a reasonable person could draw from all this is that either some Foreign Office officials – and the High Commissioner in

Sierra Leone, HM Government's own representative – did not know about the Order-in-Council or they thought it irrelevant. It is worth adding at this point that Rupert Bowen had been in regular contact with Major Peter Hicks, the Military Liaison Officer in Conakry, who was fully aware of Sandline's involvement, including the matter of arms and equipment.

It would be possible to go on and on over this point, providing more examples, giving more names and quoting more contact dates and telephone conversations, but the point has surely been made. We had done nothing illegal – the UN resolution was concerned with supplying arms to the junta and everything we had done had been with the full knowledge of the UK government. Any arguments to the contrary are at best specious and at worst lies. The evidence extracted – dragged – from the Foreign Office officials in these two enquiries makes that abundantly clear – and it goes on for pages and fills several Stationery Office publications.

The Foreign Affairs Select Committee referred to the Sandline Affair as 'a political bombshell' and continued as follows:

> It is common ground that something went very wrong. Arms were delivered by a British company to Sierra Leone for use by President Kabbah's forces, in contravention of a UK arms embargo. This was a prima-facie offence, punishable by up to seven years' imprisonment. The facts that a contract to supply the arms had been agreed and then that the arms had been supplied were known to certain Foreign Office officials. There was undue delay in passing material information to the prosecuting authorities and an equally serious delay in informing ministers.
>
> A considerable number of mistakes were made. The crisis caused by the Sandline Affair at the heart of the FCO was palpable. Ministers were suspected of misleading Parliament and the Foreign Secretary has himself recently been quoted as saying that it took its toll of his standing as a minister.

The Foreign Office was fully aware of the situation, as the Select Committee confirmed in its report:

> Unless Mr Penfold was complicit with Mr Spicer in not passing on information (and we have absolutely no evidence of this), the only fair conclusion we can draw is that Mr Spicer had every reason to believe that the FCO was aware of the nature of his business with President Kabbah because of his dealings with Mr Penfold. It would have been entirely reasonable of him to assume that Mr Penfold was acting with the full authority of HMG.

> As Mr Spicer pointed out, the High Commissioner was the representative of
> Queen and government in Sierra Leone. If the FCO machine was working
> properly, once a matter had been reported to Mr Penfold, it had been
> reported to the government.

The Foreign Office must have realised that matters might not go entirely
according to plan soon after Customs moved in on the affair. Anxiety about the
outcome of the Customs investigation in the Foreign Office was confirmed when
I went to Freetown on 9 April 1998. I rang Peter Penfold soon after I arrived and
we spoke on the telephone for about twenty minutes. Although he was, as ever,
diplomatic and discreet, he was clearly desperately worried about the situation.
He told me he had been ordered to do nothing and say nothing, adding that he
thought he had been silenced because Ann Grant was away for Easter – Good
Friday was 10 April – and would not be back for another four days. He would
try to speak with her when she got back but in the meantime, because of his
position, it was impossible for us to meet. He also confirmed that he had not read
the relevant legislation but was keen to see it.

Peter Penfold was aghast when I told him that, if the Customs investigation
continued, we would have no option but to call in the lawyers, defend ourselves
in court and call on Foreign Office people, including himself, Murray and
perhaps even the Foreign Secretary, as witnesses. Over the next few days I had
meetings with a number of people in Freetown, including President Kabbah,
who was extremely friendly and said that the Customs and Excise investigation
was 'mad'.

I also met Colonel Khobe, the ECOMOG commander, who was also
surprised at this turn of events in London and added that ECOMOG had a
document which authorised them to procure whatever kit it needed to pursue its
stated objective of ousting the junta and restoring legitimate government to
Sierra Leone – and gave me a copy. In the country most closely concerned,
people at the highest level were grateful for what we had done and were unable
to see why we should be investigated, let along prosecuted, for doing it.

The Legg Inquiry took place at the end of June, and I gave my evidence on
the afternoon of 24 June. I was followed on 3 July by Michael Grunberg. Sir
Thomas Legg began by thanking me for coming along and told me that this was
an independent investigation and not an adversarial one and was mainly
concerned with the action of ministers, military officers and government
officials; as far as I was concerned, they wanted to know about my meetings with
Peter Penfold, with the Foreign Office and with Major – now Lt-Colonel – Hicks
and about our dealings with the British guardship of West Africa during the
recent troubles, which had helped repair the Sandline helicopter when it was
flying missions in support of ECOMOG.

There is no need to go over this meeting, for it was a rerun of the meeting with Customs and Excise. I repeated all that had gone on, giving dates and naming names, being as precise and detailed as possible. An interesting development was that at one point Sir Thomas put a scenario to me based on Craig Murray's and Tim Andrews' version of that meeting on 19 January 1998. At some point in our discussions they alleged that 'someone' had asked what would happen if anyone tried to import arms into Sierra Leone, in the first case to help the junta. At this point, allegedly, Tim Andrew left the room, returned with a copy of the Security Council Resolution and read out the operative passage which said there was an embargo on Sierra Leone; it was further alleged that I enquired what the scope of the resolution was and was told that it applied to all parties. According to Murray and Andrews, I then allegedly said that I disagreed with that scenario, that the UN embargo only applied to the junta . . . and that I had gone to the Foreign Office to make it clear that we were supplying arms to Kabbah.

If, on 19 January, Tim Andrews or Craig Murray had said we could not supply arms or would risk prosecution if we did so, why would we have gone on? I live in Britain, and flouting British law like this would not simply have been illegal, it would have been foolish – always accepting the argument that this exchange ever took place, which, of course, it did not. If the exchange had taken place on 19 January, why did they not tell their political masters or act to stop us for another two months?

Rather more to the point, if I had said I was supplying arms in January, how could Craig Murray tell HM Customs he knew nothing about it in March? These statements are contradictory, a fact that did not escape the notice of Sir John Stanley, who said, 'I do find it very difficult to reconcile two points you have made with equal clarity and firmness as far as your recollection is concerned. On the one hand, you have an extremely firm recollection that all Mr Spicer told you about the terms of the content of his agreement with President Kabbah was that he was going to provide logistic support – "non-lethal equipment", to use your phrase. And yet equally you are very clear that you had an extensive discussion about the arms embargo and potential breaching of the arms embargo, and I fail to understand how those two points can be reconciled.'

Coming back to the Legg Inquiry, it is worth making another point. One of the planks of the Sandline platform from our inception was that we would only work for legitimate governments. We had maintained that policy with Third World governments and made no secret of the fact that we would only operate in that way. This, it should be noted, had been our practice in dealing with Saxena and Kabbah over aid to Sierra Leone. Is it likely, therefore, that we would fail to inform the government of our own country or deliberately set out to break or circumvent its laws? Quite apart from the fact that there was no evidence we had done so, what motive would we have had for doing so? It would have flown in the face of our established practice and common sense, and as sensible people we would have realised well in advance that we faced prosecution.

The other points raised by the Legg Inquiry were quickly cleared up. HMS *Cornwall* had helped ECOMOG by servicing the Sandline helicopter flying missions to the Kamajors. Lt-Colonel Hicks had been informed about our work in Sierra Leone and, as MILO to Peter Penfold, would have been able to appreciate the importance of our work to the ECOMOG operation. Major Hicks – as he was then – was with Peter Penfold when I phoned him in Conakry on Saturday, 28 February 1998, regarding the arrival of the 'kit', the arms and ammunition for the Kamajors, and he made an immediate record of that conversation. Hicks's report was sent to the Ministry of Defence that same weekend and duly forwarded by the MOD to the Foreign Office. It then appeared that someone in the Foreign Office – believed by the resident clerk to be Craig Murray – telephoned the resident clerk at the Foreign Office Communications Centre and instructed him to destroy the report. This was given in evidence.

On 2 March, Major Hicks filed another report following a conversation he had had with a Lifeguard official, confirming that the arms had indeed arrived. This report was sent to the MOD, who faxed a copy to the Foreign Office, but again no record or receipt for that report now exists. It appears that both reports from Major Hicks informing the Foreign Office and the MOD about the arrival of the arms shipments have been destroyed.

So the sorry tale continued. Once again, I went over our many meetings and regular telephone conversations with Peter Penfold and the people at the Foreign Office, and the outcome of the Legg Inquiry was contained in the subsequent report, which included the following:

> Mr Cook, the Foreign Secretary, and Mr Lloyd, the Minister of State, have confirmed to us that they shared and approved the goal of drying up supplies to all parties in Sierra Leone. However, this aspect of the policy was not published abroad. This was partly because of sensitivities about the possible role of the UN-sponsored force, which, unlike HMG, had explicitly contemplated the use of force.

If that is 'partly' the reason, one might wonder what the other parts were. If HMG decided to have a separate policy from the rest of the world over arms to Sierra Leone, why did they not have the honesty to come out and say so? Why cloak their intentions behind a UN Security Council Resolution which stated something other than the Order-in-Council they created from it? Not only was this divergence kept from President Kabbah, it was kept from Peter Penfold, who thought he was supposed to restore Kabbah to power. Surely the truth is that the politicians were trying to have it both ways: using Sandline to help Kabbah when it suited them, then using us as a chance to parade their moral superiority when it all became public knowledge.

On the subject of public knowledge, the Legg Report continued, 'Government has a responsibility to give its citizens and its own officials reasonable publicity and explanation of the laws it makes under delegated powers, especially laws creating serious criminal offences.' The Legg Report placed most of the blame on the Permanent Under Secretary to the Foreign Office, Sir John Kerr, and his subordinates for failing to keep ministers fully informed, but, as a *Daily Telegraph* leader pointed out at the time:

> The catalogue of mistakes, ranging from the hopelessly inadequate briefing to gross failure to communicate, strains credulity. Were officials really so incompetent, or were they doing their best to execute a policy which pretended to be one thing and was in fact another? That suspicion switches the whole focus of criticism from civil servants to the Prime Minister and the Foreign Secretary . . . they presided over a policy whose implications were never explained.

Another interesting press comment comes from *The Times* on 8 May:

> Had President Kabbah not turned to the private sector he would still be in exile. He had universal verbal backing, but during and after last year's coup, the only force Western governments used was to evacuate their nationals; Nigerian troops had tried to overthrow the plotters and failed . . . Since the wrath of the international community had not the slightest impact on the regime, a rational observer might have expected the British government to be quietly pleased at the result. Instead, Sandline has been placed under criminal investigation and Robin Cook, the Foreign Secretary, has flatly condemned the operation.

By January 1999, Sam Kiley was writing in *The Times*:

> Whether or not Sandline was implementing British policy then, it is quite clear that it should be now . . . the deployment of mercenaries in this blighted nation would be an act of genuinely ethical foreign policy.

Comments from war correspondents and leader writers must take a measured tone. As the person accused of breaking sanctions, the man whose home was raided, the man who spent a day being interrogated in the Custody Suite of Customs and Excise, the man who, but for a body of impartial evidence to prove his case, could have been sent to jail, I might take a rather more robust view of this kind of conduct.

However, Mr Cook and Mr Lloyd, Sir John Kerr, Ann Grant and Craig Murray were not out of the woods yet. The House of Commons Foreign Affairs Select Committee also wanted to have a look at the Sandline evidence and they conducted yet another inquiry, running over October, November and December 1998. They duly published a report on 9 February 1999. The interest here switches not to the facts, which were public knowledge after the Legg Report, but to the attempted cover-up. The first FCO ploy, to distance themselves from Sandline and 'call in the law', had clearly failed; Customs and Excise dropped the case. Setting up the Legg Inquiry had not proved a clever move either, for Legg had flayed the Permanent Under Secretary and his staff. Now a senior and influential House of Commons Select Committee wanted a look at the evidence. Arrogance married to stupidity is a deadly combination, and the Foreign Office pressed on in denying responsibility, with their own man, Peter Penfold, next in the frame as the one responsible for all that had gone awry. The Foreign Office line now was that Peter Penfold had known what Sandline was up to but had not told them.

In her evidence to the Select Committee, Ms Grant began by denying that she had seen Peter Penfold's minutes on events in Sierra Leone before she had briefed her ministers. Since there were two of these minutes and she had asked for one of them personally, it was extremely surprising to hear that she had read neither. Craig Murray began by complaining that I had only mentioned the 'prospect' of a contract with Kabbah at our meeting on 19 January, when, he complained, the contract had actually been signed on 23 December. This again points the finger at Peter Penfold, who, it will be recalled, was lunching with us on 23 December, was shown the draft contract and took a photocopy of it away with him.

Murray then went on to deny everything I said about the meeting on 19 January, alleging that Tim Andrews had read out the relevant parts of the UN resolution and that he had explained to me that the scope of the resolution was geographic, i.e. it affected everyone in Sierra Leone, not just the junta. This discussion on the arms embargo, as Sir John Stanley was quick to notice, rather flew in the face of his other claim, that he knew nothing about the supply of arms. So what was the meeting for? Mr Murray claimed that he had wanted the meeting 'to look me in the eye, see if I was the sort of person he should have contact with or not . . . and found me extremely difficult to pin down and shifty'.

Ms Grant then chipped in to say that she had wanted Peter Penfold recalled but her boss, Richard Dales, had refused her request, though she was worried that

Peter Penfold 'was following a different policy from the official one'. Sir Peter Emery, a member of the committee, then queried Ms Grant's statement that she did not know about Sandline's involvement in Sierra Leone, specifically the supply of arms, saying, 'Ms Grant, that cannot be factually correct, because even if it was not on 30 December that the contract from Mr Penfold was supplied to the [Foreign] Office, it was certainly supplied by the meeting on 19 January. Whatever you may say about Mr Penfold, I cannot believe he was that inefficient.'

Ms Grant then told the committee, 'We did not get any report of that meeting [of 23 December] either orally or in writing. That is a meeting that Mr Penfold attended alone.' Sir Peter made it clear that he found that hard to believe and turned to Craig Murray again, asking, 'How is it that Mr Penfold had a copy of that contract and it had not reached you?'

Murray said that Penfold had denied having a copy of the contract and confirmed that he, Murray, had had no knowledge of the contract at our meeting on 19 January. Sir Peter then pointed out that Penfold, in his evidence, had confirmed, 'I told the officials [at the FCO] exactly what I had heard from President Kabbah, that he was contemplating an agreement with a company which, in return for mining concessions, was making $10 million available to a company called Sandline. All the evidence we have received is suggesting that any contract for $10 million must have been covering arms; it was not just going to be for tinned beans.'

Murray then stated that the 'officials' concerned, Tim Andrews and Ms Lynda St Cooke, 'are quite firm that nothing was told to them on 23 December about a contract between Sandline and Kabbah'. Sir Peter then asked Murray if he was accusing Penfold of lying. In fact, he had to ask the question twice, and Murray, without denying the implication of his remarks, said, 'He [Penfold] appears not to have a memory which conforms to that of the officials.'

Further critical remarks followed from Murray and Grant, notably that Mr Penfold had 'a tendency to freelance' and that, by encouraging President Kabbah to sign the Sandline contract, 'he was becoming implicated in a criminal offence' – which obliged the committee chairman to remark, 'It is not every day you hear the allegation that a High Commissioner may be involved in a criminal conspiracy.' Indeed, Peter Penfold was also interviewed under caution by Customs and Excise as a result of what his colleagues told them.

When Robin Cook, the Foreign Secretary, appeared before the committee on 16 December 1998, the chairman, Donald Anderson, referred to these allegations from Foreign Office officials – Craig Murray and Ann Grant – and pointed out (point 1982), 'It is not a question of preventing an arms supply. Here was a serious allegation relating to a criminal offence of one of our High Commissioners. Do you think that should have been brought to your attention immediately?' Mr Cook agreed that it should have been brought to his attention at some point after 30 March, when it was clear that a Customs and Excise investigation was proceeding, adding that he was 'in no way complacent about this episode and wanted recommendations on what might be done to put it right'. What was done to put it right remains obscure, but Ms Grant and Mr Murray were promoted shortly afterwards and moved to new posts.

The inefficiencies of the Foreign and Commonwealth Office are of no more concern to me than they are to any other British citizen. What is of direct and personal concern is when their functionaries act in a way that can put me in jail. Craig Murray's unwillingness or inability to confirm that the FCO knew all about our involvement in Sierra Leone set the whole affair in train, and his involvement needs more detailed analysis, especially of the six weeks before he sent the Avebury letter to Customs and Excise, when his role in the affair is crucial.

On 29 and 30 January 1998, Murray had meetings with Peter Penfold. On 30 January, Ann Grant, Murray's boss, instructed Penfold to write a full report of his dealings with Sandline, and in particular on his knowledge of the contract with Kabbah to supply arms to Sierra Leone. Penfold wrote that memo on 2 February and Murray read it on 23 February. Therefore, after two days of meetings with Penfold and the Penfold report, Murray knew that Penfold had met me for lunch on 23 December 1997 and been shown a copy of a contract with Kabbah for the supply of arms. In addition, Murray knew that Penfold had advised Kabbah to sign that contract and, further, that on 28 January 1998 Penfold had been to Sandline's London office and actually been given a copy of our planning document, our concept of operations. Penfold gave a copy of this document to Murray's assistant, Tim Andrews, on the following day, and to Murray himself on 29 January.

On 9 February, Murray saw the Avebury letter of 5 February alleging that Sandline had sold arms to Kabbah and was therefore in breach of UN sanctions, and a month later, on 10 March, Murray sent a copy of that letter to HM Customs and Excise. While doing so, Murray in evidence says he deliberately withheld relevant information regarding the FCO's knowledge of the arms supply because he thought that if he provided it he would be implicating a colleague, Peter Penfold, in something he believed to be illegal.

There is more. On 23 December 1997, Peter Penfold had seen the contract. On 5 January I had phoned Murray's predecessor, Everard, and told him Kabbah had signed the contract. Everard wrote a note to that effect and Murray must, or certainly should, have read that note when he took over Everard's post on 9 January, for going through the predecessor's paperwork and 'reading oneself in' is standard procedure. On 19 January, I met Murray at the FCO, as detailed above.

The two reports to the Foreign Office via the MOD concerning the delivery of arms to ECOMOG in Sierra Leone were not the only pieces of written evidence which allegedly went missing and, crucially, the missing evidence supported the Sandline story. For example, on 30 December, Penfold had written to Ann Grant, telling her, 'I have been in touch with Tim Spicer. Kabbah has signed the deal . . . for US$10 million of equipment and training for the civil defence militia. This will begin to flow in January.' This is another letter that cannot be found.

In early April, as already described, HM Customs obtained search warrants and executed them on 3 April, searching my home, my wife's home and the Sandline office. These search warrants were issued on the basis of the FCO's reference to Customs and Murray's statement to Cedric Andrews. Customs were entitled to a full and complete disclosure of all matters concerning the application for search warrants but the information laid before the magistrates considering the application was misleading, so the search warrants were fatally flawed. All these facts came to light when, as described above, Customs investigated the matter, considered the evidence – and dropped the investigation.

Had Customs been told the full facts at the outset, the investigation would not have been necessary; this belief is backed up by the fact that when they found out the full story of the Foreign Office involvement, the investigation was halted. Customs were left in ignorance of Sandline's openness with the Foreign Office regarding the intention to supply arms to Sierra Leone, a factor which was highly critical to the Customs decision as to whether it was appropriate or necessary to proceed with the search warrants or as to whether a prosecution would be fair or likely to succeed. By denying that I had ever informed the FCO about the intended supply of arms, let alone the fact that the supply had been tacitly approved, and by contradicting my account to Customs, Murray cast doubts on my integrity at a crucial stage in the Customs investigation and denied them the opportunity to consider whether Sandline had licence to proceed.

As a general point, the chairman of the Foreign Affairs Select Committee concluded, 'A mechanism [the Foreign Office] that prides itself on being a Rolls-Royce appeared more like an old banger.' The Permanent Under Secretary, Sir John Kerr, was castigated as someone who 'failed in his duty to ministers', not least because 'the Foreign Secretary was first informed about Sandline . . . more than four weeks after Sir John Kerr had first been told of the Sandline Affair, and three weeks after he had learned of the Customs raid on his own department. This represents a serious failure by the permanent head of the department to his Secretary of State.'

This implies that Sir John eventually got around to telling his master, but this is not so. Mr Cook actually learned of Sandline's involvement in a letter from

Sandline's solicitors, S.J. Berwin, on 24 April, but the Affair had been bruited abroad in the press long before that, not least by an article in *The Observer* in mid-March. One has to wonder what sort of world the Foreign Secretary is living in if he is really not aware of major issues in his own bailiwick which have already been featured in the national press. The report also describes a briefing given by Foreign Office officials to government ministers about Peter Penfold's talks with Sandline and Kabbah as 'grossly inaccurate'.

The report adds that in February 1998 Peter Penfold told the Foreign Office 'clearly and unequivocally' that Sandline had a contract to supply arms to Kabbah and drew attention, yet again, to the confusion over whether the UN embargo applied to Kabbah's forces as well as to the junta, although, it continued, repeated statements by British officials and ministers emphasised that the embargo was aimed at the junta rather than at both sides in the civil war. It also pointed out that the Foreign Office had never told Peter Penfold about the terms of the Order-in-Council, an omission which the report describes as 'inexcusable'.

Finally, the report called on the government to draw up a Green Paper on new controls over the operations of British-based private security companies or 'mercenaries', as well as strict controls over arms trafficking. As I have said before, we would welcome such controls and ask only to be consulted over the terms they might contain.

And so the sorry story of the Sandline Affair concludes. A great deal of time, money and energy has been consumed but very little has been achieved. The incompetent are still in office and the civil war in Sierra Leone continues, although as these words are being written a truce has been declared. To add insult to injury, the FCO have refused to refund the substantial legal costs Sandline incurred in proving the innocence of its personnel.

One point seemed to get overlooked in all the arguments over who knew what and who told whom. Neither committee raised the question of the referral of Sandline's activities to Customs and Excise, the first step in a process that could have put several British citizens in jail, including the High Commissioner. Those citizens are members of the electorate that politicians and civil servants are supposed to serve and protect, and their failure to do so was, at best, lamentable.

The Sandline Affair is over. Many errors and evasions were uncovered, yet the same people are still running the country, still smugly assured that whatever they do is the 'ethical' thing to do. Perhaps we should not be too quick to condemn the practices so common in many Third World governments. If the Sandline Affair is any yardstick and actions like these are allowed to pass without punishment or correction, the government of the United Kingdom is in no position to point a finger or hold its head too high.

We were fortunate in that the truth prevailed in the end, but I would not pretend that this wasn't a difficult time for Sandline. Luckily we had the support of an excellent team: Richard Slowe and his team of lawyers, and Sara Pearson and her PR team. We all worked very closely together to formulate our response to this absurd and awkward situation.

SEVENTEEN

INTO THE FUTURE

*'Those who are first on the battlefield and await the opponents are at
ease; those that are last on the battlefield and head into battle get
worn out. Therefore good warriors cause others to come to them.'*

SUN TZU

And so we come to the end of this story, with Papua New Guinea, Sierra Leone
and the Sandline Affair at last behind us. In this final chapter I intend to round
off all these events, sum up the lessons Sandline has learned in the first years of
its existence, take a look at the future and see where private military companies
are going. Some of this will be speculation but it is still worth putting down, if
only to provide a dividing line between the past and the future.

Attitudes to private military companies are certainly changing. During and
after the Sandline Affair, I was asked to talk about PMCs to a wide range of
institutions, ranging from the Oxford Union and the Social Market Foundation
to a host of universities – including Aberystwyth, with its chair of Conflict
Studies – and a great many politicians, at home and abroad. The word
'mercenary' appears less frequently; the term 'military consultant' is more widely
employed – and people can see the difference. In part this is due to an extensive
public-relations exercise that we have undertaken, orchestrated by Sara Pearson
and her team.

With increasing speed, the concept of what PMCs are and have to offer is
gaining recognition, a fact signalled, in a very British fashion, by an entry in the
'Peterborough' column of the *Daily Telegraph* on 19 May 1999:

A spoof script is now circulating in the MOD computer network:

'Thank you for calling the British Army. If your crisis is small and close
to the sea, press 1 for the Royal Marines. If your problem is distant and can
be solved by one or two low-risk bombing runs, press 'hash' for the RAF.
This service is not available after 1600hrs or at weekends. If your problem is
not urgent, please press 2 for the Allied Rapid Reaction Force. If you are in
real trouble, please press 3 and your problem will be rerouted to Sandline
International.'

When your company becomes part of a good joke, you know you are part of the established order.

This is welcome because, as already related, when we started Sandline we had an idea, nothing more. We believed that there were situations where fragile governments could require professional military assistance, had failed to get it from friendly governments and were therefore obliged to seek it from the private sector. It is fair to say that that idea has proved valid. We got our first enquiry in a matter of weeks and have been furiously busy ever since. During that time we needed to develop the idea into a concept and establish the Sandline ethos. We also learned a few hard lessons.

It is ironic that our two worst experiences have been provided by people we assumed to be friends and certainly people we were trying to help: General Singirok in PNG and certain elements in the British Foreign and Commonwealth Office. Perhaps the main lesson we learned from their conduct is not to trust anybody, and I cannot deny that the attitudes of some Foreign Office staff were both uncalled-for and unhelpful, both to us and to the people we were trying to help.

On the other hand, some people – Bob Lowe in PNG, Peter Penfold, the officers of Customs and Excise who investigated the Sandline Affair, and the law officers, the Attorney and Solicitor Generals – were never less than highly professional. Their conduct lends credit to the entire governmental structure. Nevertheless, it is a pity that these good people are let down by elected Parliamentarians and civil servants.

Some of this could be depressing, but there is the comforting fact that Sandline was trying to do the right thing in both PNG and Sierra Leone. We were trying to make a living, certainly, but to do so in an open, honest and ethical way, helping legitimate governments that needed and had asked for our assistance. We shall continue to follow that course in the future, and with the expansion of our services – and the not-unmixed blessing of the higher profile generated by the Sandline Affair – the future looks good.

The future also looks brighter for Sierra Leone. On 19 May 1999, a cease-fire was agreed between the Kabbah government and the rebels. This cease-fire was brokered by the President of Togo and Jesse Jackson. We can only hope that the cease-fire will hold and lead to a negotiated settlement. If peace can be permanently restored, a rich country like Sierra Leone could have a bright future – and the truce in Bougainville, declared in May 1999, may also lead to a settlement. Again, we hope so.

When we left PNG we had a problem: they owed us the second half of our fee, the not-inconsiderable sum of US$18 million. This amount had been agreed by contract and the failure to deliver on that contract and solve the Bougainville problem rests with General Singirok and his supporters, not with Sandline. As a result of Singirok's 'coup', Sir Julius Chan left office and Bill Skate took over. One of Mr Skate's first actions was to publicly state a refusal to honour the Sandline contract, and our response was to take Papua New Guinea to court. Over the last two years we have brought a number of actions against PNG, actions handled by our legal team from S.J. Berwin: Richard Slowe, Tessa Blackwood, Daniel Serota, Sir Eli Lauterpraet and Michael Klug, whose work was successfully orchestrated by Michael Grunberg.

We brought our case before international arbitration tribunals in Cairns, Australia, and in London, and brought supporting legal actions in Europe and elsewhere. In every case we won; the courts agreed that we had a legitimate contract and were entitled to our full fee. We duly recouped much of the outstanding debt, and in April 1999 the government of PNG offered to settle our outstanding claims out of court. Michael Grunberg and Richard Slowe met representatives of the PNG government in Singapore and the action has now been settled on amicable terms.

With this behind us, we can press on and consider two outstanding matters: the future of the world as we enter the twenty-first century, and the prospect for PMCs as a new element in the political/military mix. Whether these two aspects can come into mutually beneficial conjunction depends very much on whether we can alter the mind-set of our elected representatives and their minions in government departments, but the security problems of the world are not going to go away and will almost certainly increase.

The twentieth century has seen its fair share of wars. The first half of the century was marked by two horrific world wars, and by the growing use of advanced military technology culminating in the use of the atomic bomb at Hiroshima and Nagasaki. Whatever the arguments for and against the use of the atomic bomb to destroy those cities, their destruction presented the world with the undisputed fact that the game of war had changed. Mankind had at last managed to develop the means to destroy the planet. That harsh fact made us pause, brought about a change in political thinking and introduced relative stability in the second half of the century. There have been no world wars since 1945 and the existence of the two superpower blocs has tended to limit many other conflicts to their national or regional boundaries. Unfortunately, I think that scenario is going to change.

The collapse of the Soviet bloc and the reluctance of the USA, post-Vietnam, to fight wars other than with technology are just two causes for unease, but fundamental ones. Lacking the suppression of conflict by the super-powers, old enmities are emerging and new causes for conflict lack resolution. Unfortunately war is still the way that business gets done in the world. In spite of all the diplomacy, and all the handwringing which goes with it, the reality is that if you want to stop conflict, protect the innocent, feed the starving and do all the other laudable things that need to be done, you will still need military force.

So, what are nations or people going to fight about in the coming century? First of all, the traditional reasons for conflict are still with us: politics, land, tribalism, ethnic tensions, ideology, economics. These causes, often in combination, are playing a part in some of the wars that are going on at the moment. In the Horn of Africa, for example, the conflict between Eritrea and Ethiopia is partly tribal and partly territorial, but it is also about the Ethiopian demand for a port on the Red Sea. The war in the Sudan is partly religious, Christian south versus Muslim north, but is also for control of mineral resources. The same is true of the war in Angola. This has been going on for almost forty years and is partly political but mainly economic, a battle for control of oil fields and diamond mines. The involvement of many Central African states in the ongoing problems of the Democratic Republic of the Congo is powered by interest in the Congo's vast oil and mineral resources. The Balkan war, be it in Bosnia or Kosovo, is partly political, partly tribal and partly economic – and fuelled by the release of historic ethnic tensions following the collapse of the Yugoslav Republic. This is also the case in the escalating tensions in the North Caucasus. Even if there were no other causes for war, these issues would keep the soldiers busy for the foreseeable future.

There are, however, many new causes appearing on the scene, and not just in the Balkans or the Horn of Africa. The world is shrinking and many of the new problems have, or will have, a serious knock-on effect on the developed Western nations unless they are resolved or at least tackled in the not-too-distant future.

There will be growing conflicts for control of basic necessities like food and water. In the Middle East there is growing concern over who will control the waters of the Euphrates. Since Israel controls most of Jordan's water supplies, another potential cause for conflict arises there. As the world's population grows, pressure on natural resources like water inevitably grows with it. This is not a necessary problem; if properly controlled and managed, there is more than enough food and water for everyone – but if national or tribal conflicts erupt and these assets are fought over and destroyed, millions will die.

The problem of water supply is not academic. Scientists already calculate that some 7 per cent of the world's population does not have enough water for survival. Measure that percentage against a world population running into billions and it affects millions of people – and these scientists also estimate that by 2050 the percentage will have risen to a startling 70 per cent. Even if this figure is overestimated by 50 per cent, the prospects for conflict are clear.

Egypt, said Herodotus, had 'the gift of the Nile'. Without the waters of the Nile, Egypt will become a desert – and the population of Egypt increases at the rate of one million every nine months. That alone would be a problem, but far upstream in Ethiopia the Nile is being dammed and diverted for irrigation. The

Sudan and a number of other countries are also taking water away from the Nile as it flows north to the Delta; if this continues and the water levels fall, what will Egypt do?

Fresh water is a finite resource. The earth has a certain amount of it and no more. When the taps cease to run and lavatories to flush, when cholera returns to cities and disease spreads, when the productive land turns into desert and their people are dying from thirst, the nations will fight over water; they will have no choice.

Far better, then, to resolve these conflicts now, before they start, but that is not easy either, for the political will is not there. The UN already has a convention on the sharing of international water supplies, which is supposed to be ratified by the end of the century. Thirty-five nations have been invited to sign, but with six months to go only eleven have done so. Must we wait until the trouble starts before we take action?

The growth in population has another effect, quite apart from an increased consumption of vital commodities. The wretched of the earth are on the move. All over the world families are moving, out of the Third World and into the First World, in ever-increasing numbers, poor people seeking peace, a decent livelihood and a better future for their children and grandchildren than they have enjoyed themselves. The effects of this can be seen all around the fringes of the Western world, from the Texan border with Mexico to the southern shores of the European Mediterranean and the British port of Dover. In all these areas the problem of the 'economic migrant' is growing, and the local populations are becoming increasingly concerned.

That people seek a brighter future in richer lands is understandable and even commendable, but there are limits to the number of people the West can absorb without a rise in internal tensions. To stem this tide before it becomes a flood, the condition of these unfortunate people in their own lands must be improved – and the first step to that improvement is the stamping out of civil wars and tribal conflicts and the introduction of stable governments committed to efficiency and the abolition of corruption.

Religious disputes are also growing, notably with the rise of Islamic fundamentalism, not just in 'rogue states' but increasingly among the educated young in currently stable countries like Turkey and Egypt. One of the underlying causes for the rise of radical Islam is a growing resentment of the power and culture of the West. In future, Western governments must adopt a much lower profile in their dealings with these countries, if only to avoid antagonising the developing political class. This is an obvious area for PMC assistance.

Debt could create another area for dispute. The World Bank and the G7 banker nations are growing increasingly frustrated at the failure of Western aid and loans to make any significant impact on the economies of Third World nations. For their part, these nations are resentful that a growing proportion of their GNP has to be used to service a debt, often on money which circulated briefly in the local economy before being whisked away to numbered bank accounts in a blizzard of corruption stirred up by absconding leaders.

This potential conflict is not just between foreign banks and corrupt governments. Debt affects the people in the streets and the paddy fields; it breeds resentment and is economically wasteful. Unless some way can be found to direct these vast sums of aid money to the points where they are needed, the exercise is fruitless and the outcome tragic. Keeping an eye on where aid is spent and protecting work-in-progress could be a PMC function and part of the basic aid package.

Disease is another area that has to be addressed, notably spreading and devastating epidemics, slow-burning killers like AIDS and fast-burning ones like the Ebola virus. There are African nations – Zambia for one – where the state structures are literally falling away from the impact of these diseases, and as they crumble, the national ability to cope with crisis crumbles with them. They are, quite literally in many cases, being reduced to skeletons; they have armies which do not actually exist, for all the soldiers are sick or dying.

Such diseases have to be contained and eventually eradicated, otherwise they will spread and affect other nations – and anyway, the world cannot stand by and watch a whole nation be destroyed in this fashion. In the absence of national military resources to carry out nationwide tasks, PMCs could be employed for humanitarian work: a national vaccination programme, AIDS awareness training and so on. PMCs have the organisation and the command structures to take on such tasks; to think that PMCs can only provide military assistance is to take a narrow view.

These are major, long-term issues – long term in the sense that they have been around for a long time, remain unaddressed and will not go away. There are other issues, sparks around the powder keg, which retain the capacity to blow up into something much bigger. Terrorism is one factor which has been around for decades and has the potential to become worse, with the possibility of nuclear, biological and chemical terrorism.

The nuclear club is expanding. In spite of the Non-Proliferation Treaty, nations like Israel, Iraq, Iran, India and Pakistan have acquired nuclear devices or the means to produce them. Other nations, like Libya, are certainly trying to develop them and the possibility grows that one day they will be used, a process aided by the theft of nuclear components and fissionable material, including weapons-grade uranium, from plants in Russia and the West. Kilos of weapons-grade uranium go missing every year. Where is it going? If tactical nuclear devices – and this crucial material – get into the wrong hands, into the possession of some Balkan or Russian warlord or that of some fundamentalist zealot, they could be used for nuclear blackmail or a massive strike against a city centre. PMCs could be employed both to guard nuclear plants and shipments of nuclear material and to train national police forces in the resolution of incidents involving this kind of terrorism.

However, the threat posed by terrorism, piracy and other forms of international banditry does not only lie in the threat itself. The real danger comes from its denial of authority and from the way it exposes the weakness of democratic governments, notably in their inability to protect their electorate and all too often in their eagerness to compromise with terror in order to gain political credit and short-term advantage. The reluctance of governments to act swiftly and with the appropriate means will be a prime cause of future conflicts.

Many terrorist organisations, such as the IRA and ETA, have played the threat of terror so well that they are now edging closer and closer to the control of regional government, exploiting – and degrading – the democratic process while retaining their capacity for terrorist action. This is an insult to the electorate and, rather more to the point, an action which downgrades the electorate's belief in democracy as an effective tool for change.

The great mistake governments make in surveying the future is to take the narrow, short-term, parochial view. This is true about their attitudes to growing threats but equally true about their view of private military companies, admittedly a new element in the political/military mix but one which, as Sandline has demonstrated over the last few years, could have a useful and significant part to play in seeking solutions to some of these pressing problems.

In the coming century, it will not be enough to react. Governments will need to anticipate, to be pro-active, to have forces trained and ready to respond to situations before they occur, and especially situations which may never occur – because they have taken steps to prevent them. So far, as we can see every day, governments are always on the back foot, always ceding the initiative to the opposition, the bad guys, the tyrants, the terrorists, the dictators and the mob. This must change. PMCs could be employed to advise on how to change or to actually implement the changes, but wherever it comes from, change must come.

The previous chapters have shown what PMCs can do for legitimate governments. They can, in fact, provide a lot more assistance and facilities than those I have already described, but before I go on to talk about the development of the PMC structure, it might be reasonable to explore the reasons why the use of PMCs is not more widely appreciated by governments. This question is particularly relevant to military consultants like Sandline International which will only work for legitimate governments.

At the end of the twentieth century we are seeing a growing impotence among Western governments, brought about by the difficulties of collective decision-making concerning military intervention in sovereign states, coupled with a decreased capability in terms of funding and resources. A number of conflicts, recent and current, illustrate this. In Rwanda in 1994 inactivity led to thousands being murdered – as Kofi Annan said at this century's last UN General Assembly debate in September 1999, 'The Rwandan genocide would define for our generation the consequences of inaction in the face of mass murder.' At the same time, the war in Bosnia had been dragging on for years due to indecision and ineffectiveness on the part of the UN and Western sovereign states; it ultimately ended or was stabilised by the deployment of a combat-effective military force, IFOR.

In Kosovo, 'ethnic cleansing' – or genocide, as I prefer to call it – continued for months while the Western European nations and the US dithered. Ultimately, the war crimes became so blatant that further threat, bluster and inactivity was futile and inexcusable, but rather than stop the problem in the shortest possible time, it was decided that an air campaign was the answer. There were many sighs of relief in Washington and European capitals when, on 3 June 1999, Milosevic capitulated. The success of air power was trumpeted loudly soon afterwards. However, it was not the air campaign that made Milosevic crack – it was the fact that the US, urged on by the UK, had finally agreed to a ground operation. This, together with a Russian decision not to support Serbia any longer, was communicated to Milosevic and he gave in. As this book goes to print, a multinational ground force has deployed to East Timor, the outcome as yet unknown.

A somewhat larger question is why this situation – trying to fight a war by remote control – was ever allowed to develop. Part of the answer must surely lie with the experience, attitudes and failures of the current crop of Western political leaders. The first failure is due to a lack of experience, a reluctance to learn from history. A whole generation of government ministers is now taking over, most of them without the slightest experience of war or how it should be fought. In an era of growing conflict, they simply do not understand how to use the tools.

On bombing, history has two lessons to teach: first, that bombing unites the bombed, rather than dividing them, and second, that without a ground offensive to back it up, bombing does not work. Bombing did not work in London during the Blitz, in Germany during the Combined Bomber Offensive of 1943–45 or in Vietnam. The atomic bombing of Hiroshima and Nagasaki does not refute this point; the vital element there was the bomb, not the bombing – and no one has yet suggested dropping an atomic bomb on Belgrade.

This lack of a historical perspective is exacerbated by a fascination with technology and by the idea that new devices can achieve results without casualties among our own forces or enemy civilians. Western political leaders have gained access to a whole new train set – the current wealth of military technology – and, as ever, are so anxious to see its benefits that they are unable to see its limitations.

And the fundamental limitation is that combat resolution will not work without ground troops. To stop ethnic cleansing, famine and massive destruction, you have to put troops on the ground quickly and effectively – and the Western governments are very reluctant to do this.

Our experience over the last three years has provided various reasons for this lack of commitment. First, there is the current 'mind-set' among some Western governments and especially among some of their advisers and civil servants. This mind-set dictates that only governments can take action in political situations, and if they decide to take no action, God forbid that someone else should – especially someone from the private sector. That objection can be doubled or trebled if the private party can be dubbed a 'mercenary'.

To this can be added a number of practical reasons, not least the writing down of Western forces as part of the so-called 'peace dividend'. Since the end of the Cold War, the armies of the Western alliance have been reduced but the number of commitments has increased. This process has reached the point where the Western armies are now seriously overstretched – and not all Western nations are willing to help anyway. Some Western nations, even some members of NATO – Greece and Italy, for example – are unwilling to commit their forces at all, and other nations, such as Germany and the Scandinavian countries, are chronically reluctant to provide the military muscle necessary to achieve the agreed political end. It may be that NATO will eventually divide into the 'core' nations – Britain, France, Spain – who are willing to commit forces and those who are not so inclined, especially if the United States quite reasonably declines to carry the main burden for settling European disputes.

Finally, the commitment of ground troops means the possibility of casualties, and so the deadly circle is complete: risks are unacceptable, ground troops will not be committed, air power cannot do the job alone, nothing will be done. In such a situation of military and political impotence, why will governments not consider the use of private military companies?

I would not argue that PMCs can or should ever replace national forces. PMCs could not do that anyway. They lack the combat power for major intervention – but there is a military maxim that 'a company can do today what a brigade cannot accomplish tomorrow'. In that respect PMCs might be very useful. To put it in simple terms, PMCs could be regarded like the fire brigade. If there is a small conflagration in the kitchen, why not send in a PMC – the fire brigade – to get there early and put it out when it is just starting? They can deploy quickly, they work within the rules governing armed conflict and they have the experience and the personnel to deal with that small fire and put it out. Up to a point, they can even handle the situation as it develops; if the fire spreads to other rooms or shows the need for other equipment or techniques, PMCs can deal with it – up to a point.

With luck and good management, this sort of fast remedial action will deal successfully with a large number of tricky situations. There are other advantages. If the conflagration continues, and larger, national forces have to be used, there will be time to build them up, the situation will be better understood and the political framework to handle the new situation can be moved into place. In such situations, PMCs provide governments and the UN with the vital assets of time – time to think, time to plan, time to act – and no political fallout.

Even when national forces are involved there will still be a useful supporting role for PMCs, not least in relieving the national forces of time- and troop-absorbing routine tasks: guarding convoys and vital installations, repatriation of prisoners, caring for refugees, clearing rear areas. They could also handle the numerous post-conflict tasks, bridging the gap between the ending of the conflict and the re-establishment of peace and helping the Non-Government Organisations (NGOs) to restore normality. Other duties could include the protection of refugees from harassment, mine clearance, food distribution, supplying clean drinking water, repairs to bridges, roads and railways, the restoration of public utilities, handling the media, running ports and airfields – the list of potential tasks is endless.

There is a vast amount of First World military and professional experience out there which PMCs have the training and the experience to deploy and which governments should be eager to utilise. This work could be funded or commissioned by the UN, or the intervening governments, or even the national government of the country at war – but the PMC would fit into the local command structure and work to a predetermined plan. Since PMCs largely employ ex-military personnel, they fit easily into such a set-up and are capable of taking orders.

PMCs can also be used in situations where the direct involvement of foreign forces would be seen as a provocation. If given adequate funds and a clear UN mandate, Sandline International would be perfectly prepared to take on and run a city like Mogadishu in Somalia, a city plagued by faction-fighting between various local warlords. Direct Western intervention would not be welcome here, but a PMC, with no political baggage and a clear mandate, could handle the job. This being so, why are the UN and a number of governments still reluctant to employ PMCs?

The main reason, I suggest, is that many politicians are unable to detach their minds from the old-fashioned, worn-out 'mercenary' concept and feel that using PMCs would be politically unacceptable to their electorate and the media. There is no reason for this blinkered attitude – and politicians are not widely regarded as centres of moral rectitude anyway, least of all by voters. Besides, if governments were pro-active they could enlist the support of well-regulated PMCs and gain the credit for employing them, as they gain credit from employing the best architects, designers or advisers on any publicly funded project. There is no real reason, least of all in this day and age, for regarding PMCs in a different light. The time will come when PMCs will be needed; far better to start now and work out ways of using them effectively.

In addition, by employing PMCs at the early stages of some conflicts, governments would gain political advantages. Firstly, PMCs offer governments the possibility of stamping out the problem in the early stages without risk. Secondly, by using PMCs they could sample the water, put a toe in and see what the situation actually involved before committing national forces. If the water proved too hot, they could hurriedly withdraw; if the intervention worked, they could hog all the credit.

All that presupposes that governments have the wit to see the advantages of employing PMCs and are capable of realising how a modern PMC differs from the 'mercenary' image currently embedded in the official mind. PMCs can offer a wide range of facilities ranging far beyond the provision of military assistance in the traditional form, but these useful assets can only be deployed if governments can bring themselves to accept that they cannot do it all and that some matters are best left to other hands and more professional experience.

This is not to say that governments must surrender control – far from it. A good PMC will always work to a legitimate brief and will only ask for a clearly defined role and a clear mandate. PMCs want to work with governments. In spite of the vitriol spilt over the Sandline Affair, we would like a rapprochement with the Foreign and Commonwealth Office. To feud with them is counterproductive and childish and we have a lot to offer each other, often at difficult times.

And so the story to date concludes. In the words of the Grateful Dead, what a long, strange trip it has been, but I am absolutely convinced that the journey will continue. Clearly there is a role for private military companies on the international stage and Sandline will continue to flourish. Sandline has come a long way in its first three years, a lot has happened and we have been thrust rather unwillingly into the spotlight, but there is no going back. As a legitimate business we will continue to try and help countries resolve their conflicts and we will try and prevent loss of life by getting in there early and stopping matters getting out of hand. We intend to be a successful and profitable company and we shall go on attempting to show people that we are a force for good in a hard and difficult world.

Sometimes that part of the task seems an especially uphill struggle, particularly when you run into the shuttered minds of the kind of people who appear on select committees, quote the Machiavellian view of 'mercenaries' –

that they are 'disunited, ambitious and without discipline' – and are clearly confusing us with the typical politician.

There is clearly a job to do here in removing this ingrained conviction and showing people what PMCs can really do. I do not think this task will be easy; as General Sir Ivor Maxse said in 1934 when talking about army reform, 'The British dislike of new ideas is so tremendous that one has to fight a lot of people to get any new idea seriously considered.' If our experience since 1997 is anything to go by, things have not changed.

Being a soldier, particularly an unorthodox one, is a fascinating job. Inevitably, when running a company like Sandline International you receive a lot more knocks than you do praise. But the job brings you into contact with the best as well as the worst of people and only rarely into contact with those who are mediocre, gutless and afraid of risk and adventure. Besides all that, and curiously enough, it's fun, and I look forward to some more unorthodox soldiering in the years and decades ahead.

INDEX

Some sub-sections are ordered chronologically for ease of reference
Abbreviations: PMCs = private military companies
                PP = Peter Penfold
                SI = Sandline International
                TS = Tim Spicer